Cycles, Growth and the Great Recession

Cycles, Growth and the Great Recession is a collection of papers that assess the nature and role of the business cycle in contemporary economies. These assessments are made in the context of the financial market instability that distinguishes the Great Recession from previous post-war slowdowns. Theorists and applied scholars in the fields of economics and mathematical economics discuss various approaches to understanding cycles and growth, and present mathematical and applied macro models to show how uncertainty shapes cycles by affecting the economic agent choice. Also included is an empirical section that investigates how the Great Recession affected households' housing wealth, labour productivity and migration decisions.

This book aims to:

1 Propose a novel understanding of the business cycle by comparing the approaches of various scholars, starting from Hyman Minsky and Piero Ferri.
2 Show that uncertainty is a main feature of the business cycle that affects decision-making and economic behaviour in general.
3 Explain with mathematical models how the behaviour of economic agents can lead to cyclical paths for modern developed economies.
4 Augment theory with empirical analysis of some central issues related to the Great Recession.

This book comprises an original view of such widely discussed subjects as business cycles, uncertainty, economic growth and the Great Recession, constructed around theory, models and applications.

Annalisa Cristini is Professor of Economics, University of Bergamo, Italy.

Steven M. Fazzari is Bert A. and Jeanette L. Lynch Distinguished Professor, Washington University in St. Louis, USA.

Edward Greenberg is Professor Emeritus of Economics, Washington University in St. Louis, USA.

Riccardo Leoni is Professor of Economic Policy, University of Bergamo, Italy.

Routledge Critical Studies in Finance and Stability
Edited by Jan Toporowski, School of Oriental and African Studies, University of London, UK

The 2007–8 Banking Crash has induced a major and wide-ranging discussion on the subject of financial (in)stability and a need to revaluate theory and policy. The response of policy-makers to the crisis has been to refocus fiscal and monetary policy on financial stabilisation and reconstruction. However, this has been done with only vague ideas of bank recapitalisation and 'Keynesian' reflation aroused by the exigencies of the crisis, rather than the application of any systematic theory or theories of financial instability.

Routledge Critical Studies in Finance and Stability covers a range of issues in the area of finance including instability, systemic failure, financial macroeconomics in the vein of Hyman P. Minsky, Ben Bernanke and Mark Gertler, central bank operations, financial regulation, developing countries and financial crises, new portfolio theory and New International Monetary and Financial Architecture.

1 **Banking Systems in the Crisis**
The faces of liberal capitalism
Edited by Sue Konzelmann and Marc Fovargue-Davies

2 **Post-Keynesian Views of the Crisis and its Remedies**
Edited by Óscar Dejuán Asenjo, Eladio Febrero Paños and Jorge Uxo Gonzalez

3 **The Rise and Fall of Money Manager Capitalism**
Minsky's half century from World War Two to the Great Recession
Eric Tymoigne and L. Randall Wray

4 **Cycles, Growth and the Great Recession**
Economic reflections in times of uncertainty
Edited by Annalisa Cristini, Steven M. Fazzari, Edward Greenberg and Riccardo Leoni

Cycles, Growth, and the Great Recession

Economic reflections in times of uncertainty

Edited by Annalisa Cristini, Steven M. Fazzari, Edward Greenberg and Riccardo Leoni

Routledge
Taylor & Francis Group
LONDON AND NEW YORK

First published 2015
by Routledge
2 Park Square, Milton Park, Abingdon, Oxon OX14 4RN

and by Routledge
711 Third Avenue, New York, NY 10017

Routledge is an imprint of the Taylor & Francis Group, an informa business

British Library Cataloguing in Publication Data
A catalogue record for this book is available from the British Library

Library of Congress Cataloging in Publication Data
Cycles, growth and the Great Recession /edited by Annalisa Cristini, Steven M. Fazzari, Edward Greenberg and Riccardo Leoni.
pages cm. — (Routledge critical studies in finance and stability) Includes bibliographical references and index.
1. Business cycles. 2. Recessions. 3. Economic development. I. Cristini, Annalisa, 1961-
HB3711.C9175 2014
338.5′42—dc23
2014020009

ISBN: 978-0-415-74819-3 (hbk)
ISBN: 978-1-315-79663-5 (ebk)

Typeset in Times New Roman
by Swales & Willis Ltd, Exeter, Devon, UK

The editors and contributors dedicate this book to Piero Ferri, our friend, colleague, teacher, and collaborator.

Bergamo, Italy, 2014

Contents

Figures

Tables

Contributors

Riccardo Bellofiore, Professor of Economics, Department of Management, Economics, and Quantitative Methods, University of Bergamo, Italy

Marida Bertocchi, Professor of Mathematical Methods for Economics and Actuarial and Financial Sciences, Department of Management, Economics, and Quantitative Methods, University of Bergamo, Italy

Annalisa Cristini, Professor of Economics, Department of Management, Economics, and Quantitative Methods, University of Bergamo, Italy

Domenico Delli Gatti, Professor of Economics, Department of Economics and Finance, Università Cattolica del Sacro Cuore, Milan, Italy

Saul Desiderio, Associate Professor of Economics, Business School, Shantou University, Shantou, P. R. China

Steven M. Fazzari, Bert A. and Jeanette L. Lynch Distinguished Professor of Economics, Washington University in St. Louis, USA

Mauro Gallegati, Professor of Economics, Department of Economics and Social Sciences, Università Politecnica delle Marche, Ancona, Italy

Laura Gardini, Professor of Mathematics and Finance, Department of Economics, Politics and Society, University of Urbino "Carlo Bo," Italy

Giancarlo Graziola, Professor of Economics, Department of Management, Economics, and Quantitative Methods, University of Bergamo, Italy

Edward Greenberg, Professor Emeritus of Economics, Washington University in St. Louis, USA

Gian Italo Bischi, Professor of Mathematics, Department of Economics, Politics and Society, University of Urbino "Carlo Bo," Italy

Riccardo Leoni, Professor of Economics, Department of Management, Economics, and Quantitative Methods, University of Bergamo, Italy

Ahmad Naimzada, Assistant Professor of Mathematical Economics, Department of Economics, Management, and Statistics, University of Milano Bicocca, Italy

Andrea Salanti, Professor of Economics, Department of Management and Information Technology, University of Bergamo, Italy

Jan Toporowski, Professor of Economics and Finance, School of Oriental and African Studies, University of London, UK

Costanza Toricelli, Professor of Mathematical Methods for Economics and Actuarial and Financial Sciences, Department of Economics "Marco Biagi," Università di Modena e Reggio Emilia, Italy

Fabio Tramontana, Assistant Professor of Economics, Department of Economics and Management, University of Pavia, Italy

Anna Maria Variato, Associate Professor of Economics, Department of Management, Economics, and Quantitative Methods, University of Bergamo, Italy

Alessandro Vercelli, Professor of Economics, University of Siena, Italy

Introduction

This book presents a collection of papers that assesses the nature and role of the business cycle in contemporary economics, in view of the financial market instability that distinguishes the Great Recession from previous post-war slowdowns. The contributions of the theorists and applied scholars in the fields of economics and mathematical economics that are contained in the book consider various approaches to understanding cycles and growth, and present mathematical and applied macro models to show how uncertainty shapes the cycles by affecting the choices of economic agents. The book includes an empirical section that investigates how the Great Recession affected households' housing wealth, labour productivity, and migration decisions.

The volume's objectives can be categorized under four logically related headings:

1 Propose a novel understanding of the business cycle by comparing the approaches of various scholars, with particular emphasis on those of Hyman Minsky and Piero Ferri.
2 Show that uncertainty is a main feature of the business cycle, which affects decision making and economic behaviour in general.
3 Explain, with mathematical models, how the behaviour of economic agents can lead to cyclical paths for modern developed economies.
4 Augment the theoretical analysis with the empirical analysis of some central issues related to the Great Recession.

On the whole, the book puts forward an original view of such widely discussed subjects as business cycles, uncertainty, economic growth, and the Great Recession, constructed around theory, models, and applications.

Part I of the book explores modeling strategies, linking explicitly to the research of Minsky and Ferri. In Chapter 1, Riccardo Bellofiore summarizes Minsky's financial instability hypothesis (FIH), points out some of its weaknesses and some misinterpretations by other economists, and presents a version of the FIH that is consistent with the way in which financial capitalism has evolved. In the original formulation of the FIH, "after a period of 'tranquil' growth and robust finance, units' liability structures tend to shift towards fragility, so that the economic system becomes prone to financial crises." Bellofiore refines this idea by developing in more detail Minsky's concept of "money manager capitalism," an economy characterized by big corporations, large banks and financial institutions, and such new intermediaries as mutual and pension funds. These are dominated by money managers, whose concern is the appreciation of the investments of liability holders. In the US, a major crash was avoided after 1980 first by Reagan's large fiscal deficits and then by the rapid growth of consumer debt. In the more recent period, the activity of the money managers resulted in an overcapitalization of productive enterprises, culminating in the collapse of the subprime bubble and the emergence of the Great Recession. For the future, Bellofiore recalls and endorses Minsky's suggestions for the mitigation of the business cycle: "A larger, not a smaller, role for the State; a low, not a high, private investment policy; serious controls on how capital moves and investment is financed; a bias against giant financial institutions."

Anna Maria Variato continues the exploration of the link between the financial instability theory of Hyman Minsky and the dynamics of the Great Recession in Chapter 2. The motivating concept is the "Minsky Moment," the point at which an unstable financial boom peaks and is followed quickly by financial crisis and recession. Variato explores different definitions of the Minsky Moment concept in the recent writing of a range of authors, some who agree with this interpretation, others who largely reject it. She develops an original perspective on this issue, considering in detail whether the location of financial instability in the household sector of the recent US subprime mortgage crisis is consistent with the theory of Minsky that locates the source of financial instability in the firm sector. This chapter supports the broad relevance of Minsky's work, along with the development of his ideas in subsequent research, for understanding the dramatic macroeconomic events of recent years.

Next, in Chapter 3, Steven Fazzari and Edward Greenberg trace the development of the accelerator–multiplier model of the business cycle originally proposed by Samuelson, which was later modified by Hicks to include floors and ceilings for the purpose of containing the explosive behavior that could arise from the models, but was rarely observed empirically. Minsky re-interpreted floors and ceilings as representing new initial conditions. An important transformation of this concept occurs in joint work by Ferri and Minsky, in which the emphasis changes from specifying a second-order difference equation to postulating an unspecified nonlinear model that requires thwarting forces to prevent it from exhibiting explosive behavior. The new formulation relies on generic properties of nonlinear models, which is more general than the earlier specification. Ferri and Minsky argue that contemporary capitalist economies utilize complex financial arrangements that involve strong interconnections between banks, other financial institutions, and borrowers. These arrangements are subject to constant innovation, which, in some circumstances, may lead to excessive risk taking and a consequent recession. In connecting this modeling framework to the events of the Great Recession, Fazzari and Greenberg argue that simple and mechanical floor-and-ceiling models do not capture the complex dynamics demonstrated by this historically significant business cycle. But a broader and more nuanced interpretation of the insights gained from the floor and ceiling approach does help to understand the dynamics surrounding the Great Recession. The chapter emphasizes financial fragility, as opposed to resource constraints, as the proximate source of the ceiling that triggered the Great Recession. The authors discuss how varied components of autonomous demand (demand that does not depend directly on the state of the economy) help explain both what turned the recession and why the recovery has been so sluggish. In particular, prompt monetary and fiscal intervention in the US likely prevented a much greater impact on income and employment than actually occurred, but fiscal policy drag has slowed recovery.

In Chapter 4, Andrea Salanti takes a broader view and provides a vivid picture of macroeconomics as a practical social discipline, a feature that makes it much more interesting but also unavoidably more difficult and open to criticisms. Its social character challenges scholars to deal with problems as they arise, independently of how deep their knowledge of the issues is. Moreover, by their very nature, social problems tend to recur from time to time, but always arise in circumstances which make them look alike even though they are not the same.

Economists' reactions to this complexity have been quite different. Some scholars have pursued the route of keeping things simple, thus assuming that an acceptable picture of macroeconomics can be obtained by summing up atomistic microeconomic pieces. Although this view has been highly influential, Salanti puts forward the methodological weaknesses of such an approach, whether one wants to test it empirically or assess its intrinsic logic. He concludes that it is best to accept the unavoidable intricacy of macroeconomics and carry on with aggregate analysis. The approach based on regime switching, to which Ferri and co-authors have largely contributed, is consistent with this view and can reproduce the intrinsic adaptation of the system to changes in some of the fundamental relationships such that the system can survive instead of exploding. As long as changes in coefficients do not change the causality of the relations of interest, this is also the best way to test the robustness of a model.

Part II stresses uncertainty and information – themes that are frequently addressed in the research of Minsky and Ferri. In Chapter 5, Jan Toporowski characterizes business cycle theory as a way of dealing with economic complexity by allowing model parameters to change over time. He contrasts an analysis orientated towards the business cycle with the mainstream emphasis on an economy that would always be in equilibrium except for random shocks. In such an economy, there is a systematically recurring business cycle. Departures from equilibrium are a series of accidents, and then equilibrium is restored. Toporowski notes that this approach ignores the reality of a diversified economy in which shocks may engender different responses from the wide range of industries that characterize a modern economy. In such a setting, some industries may be expanding even while others are declining – a process akin to Schumpeter's "creative destruction." But the mainstream equilibrium view takes the position that the economy should grow relatively smoothly over time, as the quantity and quality of labor and capital grow. Toporowski traces the development of business cycle theory over time from Marshall's idea of different time periods to Keynes's emphasis on changes in the marginal efficiency of capital to Minsky's insight that investment determines the extent to which business income is sufficient to service debt obligations. His conclusion, "The integration of complex financial structures into business cycle analysis remains one of the great unsettled questions of modern financial economics," is one of the major themes of this volume.

Alessandro Vercelli's Chapter 6 completes Part II. Noting that Ferri and Minsky stressed the role of changing institutions in modern capitalist economies, he is concerned with two important institutional changes that occurred in the recent past: the securitization of mortgages and the emergence of the shadow banking system. These innovations, acting through different types of asymmetric information, played significant roles both in precipitating the Great Recession and in hampering the ability of the monetary authorities to respond to it. Vercelli argues that both the asymmetric information arising from mortgage securitization and the asymmetric information associated with the growth of the shadow banking system contributed to the bank panic of 2007–8 and that both types played complementary roles in contributing to the Great Recession. He concludes by noting that the two types of asymmetric information imply different policy choices by regulators.

Part III takes up formal mathematical modeling issues – an area to which Ferri has made many contributions. By its nature, this part has less to say about the Great Recession than the previous parts, but it explores areas and methods that may have future applications.

This part begins with Chapter 7 by Gian Italo Bischi and Ahmad Naimzada, which formally models a situation in which a fall in the propensity to invest occurs when capacity utilization increases. This may occur if stockholders are more concerned with short-term dividends than with the long-term growth of the firm. The model they set up is characterized as Kaleckian because it assumes different savings behavior for consumers and firms. Clearly, the influence of capacity utilization on investment is a central issue in the modeling of the business cycle. A feature of their model is that the propensity to invest depends on the previous capacity utilization as well as the current value, and the behavior of the system as a function of the weight placed on the previous value is a major concern of the chapter. The models imply a two-dimensional discrete dynamical system, and the authors employ a combination of analytical, geometrical, and numerical methods to analyze the system. All three methods are necessary because limiting the analysis to linear approximations around equilibrium points may be incomplete and misleading. Depending on the value of the weight, the system may exhibit stable or chaotic behavior.

The contribution of Domenico Delli Gatti, Mauro Gallegati, Saul Desiderio in Chapter 8 models labor market dynamics in a setting where agents interact in markets for labor, consumption goods, and credit, and where disequilibrium and lack of coordination can result from uncertainty. The uncertainty can arise within and between markets. The emphasis on uncertainty and credit resonates with the chapters of the first three parts of this volume, where these issues are often invoked in understanding the Great Recession. Their model incorporates realistic features of the labor market, involving search behavior on the part of employers and employees, whose decisions are boundedly rational in the face of limited information. The resulting complex system is studied by simulation methods and exhibits realistic business cycle dynamics. A major finding, which ties in with the emphasis in this volume of inadequate demand as a major cause of business cycles, is that unemployment is due to under-consumption.

Chapter 9, by Laura Tramontana and Fabio Gardini, continues the theme of bounded rationality by examining the process by which producers learn about their environment. This question is relevant to the Great Recession because the reaction of decision-makers to innovations in finance, for example, has been emphasized in the analysis of the Great Recession found earlier in this volume. In this model, the production decision is a random variable that depends on the previous decision and the experience of the producer after the previous decision. A demand function represents the demand side of the market, and the cost of production and price determine whether production is profitable. The model reduces to a one-dimensional piecewise linear map, whose dynamic behavior is studied in detail. By varying two key parameters of the model and employing advanced dynamic methods, the authors are able to characterize the cyclical properties of the model completely.

Part IV applies the lessons of the more theoretical sections of this volume and presents empirical studies that shed light on some of the relevant issues. In Chapter 10, Marida Bertocchi and Costanza Torricelli are concerned with credit risk, a central concept in Ferri's and Minsky's ideas about the origin and propagation of the business cycle. The authors note that risk builds up during the upward phase of the cycle and may be highest at the peak, in contrast to the more common view that risk increases as the economy moves into a slump. They consider a number of modeling approaches to measuring credit risk over the course of a business cycle and relate them to the various Basel consultative documents that have been recently issued for the purpose of bank regulation. The behavior of risk is clearly crucial to regulation: if risk rises during the upswing, then banks should be required to hold more capital in those periods, whereas the opposite would be true if risks fall during upswings. Because the reluctance of banks to lend during the downswing has been a notable feature of the Great Recession, the question of when to tighten capital requirements is an important consideration. Bertocchi and Torricelli conclude with a survey of recent attempts to model the relationship between different rating systems and the real economy in a general equilibrium setting.

In Chapter 11, Annalisa Cristini focuses on wealth from households' point of view and asks, in particular, whether there is any relationship between household consumption decisions and housing wealth and, if so, whether the Great Recession has affected it and how. The answers to both question are relevant to an important channel affecting aggregate demand and are a concern for economic policy. Housing wealth and consumption is a controversial issue in the literature and an interesting example of the complexity of macroeconomic relationships. Cristini presents evidence from a panel of European countries and confronts it with the results obtained on US data by Case et al. and, successively, by Calomiris et al., whose findings are indeed rather different from those of Case and co-authors. Cristini's main conclusion is that household consumption responds to housing wealth with an elasticity that ranges between 0.03 and 0.28, depending on the measure used, while stock market wealth is largely insignificant. Given the endogeneity of both wealth and income, instrumental variables (IV) estimation has also been used; however, instruments turn out to be too weak for estimates to be reliable. Cristini then suggests the use of Pesaran's common correlated effects model, which controls for global and local common factors. With this specification, too, results support a primary role of housing wealth in households' consumption, thus reinforcing the previous findings. Finally, Cristini finds that the Great Recession has strengthened the relation between housing wealth and consumption, and concludes by suggesting various possible explanations: the drop of collateral as housing equity collapsed, the banking sector's reaction to uncertainty in their own balance sheets, or future scenarios of declining growth. These factors provide a detailed empirical link to many issues raised in the earlier chapters of this book.

Giancarlo Graziola, in Chapter 12, takes up the issue of migration by reverting to the original dual economy model proposed by Lewis in 1954, which highlights the most important links at work. In particular, whereas the presence of a surplus workforce from the backward agricultural sector can explain, even in a simple one-sector model, the initial migrations that led many Italians to move to America, the UK, or Germany in the second half of the twentieth century, the introduction of a second sector and specifically of a modern industrial sector, is necessary in order to explain the internal migration that took place in Italy before World War I. By confronting the data, Graziola finds confirmation of the plausibility of using, in succession, a single-sector and a dual economy model to explain pre-war migrations. He proposes the interesting result that the causation between migration and per capita income growth changes between the two models. Whereas in the basic one-sector model, the increase in per capita income is endogenously determined by migration, the role played by the wage gap between the country of origin and the country of migration is well captured in the two-sector model, suggesting that in a dual economy income per capita becomes the driver of the decision to move. As Graziola concludes, "migration and growth in this period seem to have become the components of a circular causation process."

To complete this volume, Riccardo Leoni, in Chapter 13, develops an analysis of the interaction between organizational innovation (specifically, from Taylor–Fordism to Toyotism and then to World-Class Management) and technological innovations (from electromechanical to microprocessor-based technologies), arguing that these constitute the primary drivers of changes in productivity and efficiency, and consequently in the structure of costs and in the potential mark-ups of single firms. These innovations sometimes completely overturn the existing order and at other times simply reshape it. Complicating the picture of the foreseeable consequences is the complementary nature not only between the two factors *per se*, but also between bundles of technological devices and organizational practices (where both the ingredients and their intensity of adoptions matter). In such a context, relative price is not an applicable tool to assess how the two factors combine. Taken in isolation, the two factors are unable to entirely explain the consequences of internal structural breaks for firm economic activity, since the concausal links are lost from sight. A formalization of the possible combinations of technology and organization through the mathematical concepts of convexity and concavity for the study of optimality conditions requires us to assume hypotheses that are hardly plausible, such as the infinite divisibility of choices, the possibility that a choice may be exercised on a single variable, economies of scale and learning, and spurious combinations within bundles – all conditions that are incompatible with the concavity of the objective function. In addition, the distinction between technology and organization as artefacts and technology and organization in use, the role of the knowledge gap and problem-solving gap in daily operational activities, combined with the non-ergodic nature of the real context in which technological and organizational innovations take place, make it more realistic – according to Leoni's analysis – to assume that these changes occur along sequential stochastic processes; more precisely, discrete-time sequential stochastic processes. The foreseeable outcome is a set of "local" optimal positions of firms, each of which reflects a certain consistency of the various ingredients used. With the addition of historical time, these local positions change, giving rise to completely different topographic profiles. These fundamental structural changes in the organization and operation of firms create the initial conditions for broader economic cycles generated within the economic system, with all the consequences that Ferri and Minsky have extensively studied.

We are pleased to dedicate this volume to Piero Ferri, a teacher, colleague, and co-author for many of us and a friend to all of us. His writings on macroeconomic cycles and growth have been important contributions to the literature of economics, and the chapters contained in this volume show how many and varied ideas can help in understanding the fluctuations of developed economies in general, and, in particular, the dramatic events of the Great Recession and world financial crisis.

A central aspect of Piero Ferri's career is the way in which he builds connections with a wide variety of scholars. He pushed research forward in his broad network, making those around him more productive and leading to an outcome in which the whole is greater than the sum of its parts. As one of us put it, Piero "stirred the pot" of the research project to make sure that ideas kept bubbling up – an activity that he continues to this day and, we expect, for years to come.

The diverse contributions to this book represent (although they do not fully span) the scholarly perspectives created in Piero's published work and the network that he has developed over recent decades. This book is a celebration of that career and a prelude of what is yet to come. We conclude this introduction by thanking Piero Ferri for his many contributions to economics and for his friendship. We hope that the chapters in this volume may stimulate his thinking and result in further contributions from the remarkable research network of which Piero is the common denominator.

Part I

Understanding cycles and growth

1 Minsky as a critic of Keynesianism

Riccardo Bellofiore

I first met Hyman Minsky in the late 1970s. He was often in Italy, one of the reasons being his collaboration with Confindustria's Centro Studi (research centre). His first friendship and most important collaboration was with Piero Ferri in Bergamo. I began working in Bergamo in 1977 as *assegnista di ricerca*, a temporary research position, called there by Piero Ferri.

Thanks to Piero, I met Minsky on several occasions. He had published *John Maynard Keynes* in 1975, translated into Italian in 1981. Piero's collaboration with Minsky was mainly focused on the cyclical dimension of growth theory and the labour market. My interest was a bit different. My dissertation had been on Rosa Luxemburg, and I was trained in Marxian economics by Claudio Napoleoni. From there I studied Schumpeter and Keynes. Thus, my perspective was primarily (though not exclusively) on the monetary and financial dimensions of capitalist dynamics. Schumpeter was Minsky's first Ph.D. supervisor, and Minsky (in a comment made at a 1994 conference and collected in the Minsky Archive at Bard College) labelled the Austrian economist a conservative Marxist. It seems that he once said that his own theory was also contained in Marx. Indeed, Minsky's interpretation of Marx, Schumpeter and Keynes, and his own theoretical developments, were far away, not only from the traditional *vulgate*, but also from the usual post-Keynesian perspective. He very much preferred to be called a *financial Keynesian*.

For these reasons, I saw in Minsky the right place to look for a meaningful extension of the Marxian cycle of money capital and Keynes's monetary circuit theory in *Treatise on Money* – even more so because in the late 1970s and early 1980s I became involved in Graziani's Italian version of monetary circuitism.

This is one of the reasons why in 1999 – after Minsky's death in 1996, and with the help, essentially, of Jan Kregel and Randy Wray – I organised in Bergamo a conference honouring Minsky's economic legacy. With Piero Ferri we edited the proceedings in two volumes, and the Department of Economics was named after Hyman Minsky.

The night when they reread Minsky

When Minsky died, he was respected in a few circles within the heterodox community, but was mostly unknown outside. Something, however, was happening.

During the Russian crisis in 1998 (soon spreading in the USA, and hitting the long-term capital management (LTCM) hedge fund and the US financial system), Paul McCulley, then managing director of PIMCO, coined the phrase 'Minsky moment'. McCulley used the phrase again after the collapse of the dot.com economy in 2000–1. That bubble-driven expansion, centred on capital market inflation, was resurrected for a few years thanks to the subprime mortgage loan explosion and the ensuing US housing bubble, which was nothing but a new kind of the usual inflation in capital asset prices. This second round of bubble-driven capitalist growth, so typical of the new capitalism, was short-lived. After the deflating of housing prices which began in 2005, the speculative boom crashed in the summer of 2007, triggering the so-called Great Recession, which has now been better named the Lesser Depression by Brad De Long. The financial bloggers saw this coming, but only very few economists: the 'Minsky moment' terminology was resurrected by George Magnus of UBS in March 2007, and spread around with much more prominence and influence than before.

After the crisis erupted, Minsky's name eventually gained wider fame, not only in the *Financial Times* and *The Economist*, but also within the economics profession. Even Paul Krugman was interested. You can find a trace in three lectures Krugman gave at the London School of Economics (LSE), especially the last one ('The night they reread Minsky', 16 December 2010), though he very much complained at the time that Minsky was too fond of Kalecki's 'bizarre' price and distribution theory. Krugman, unlike Minsky, likes to annoy the neoclassical economists with his feet firmly grounded in traditional macroeconomics. Indeed, he received the Nobel prize.

At LSE Krugman said that there were people thinking about financial instability ahead of time, and that was why there were a tremendous number of references to Minsky. The problem was that Minsky was out of the mainstream in the 1970s and 1980s (Krugman's lectures were on the state of macroeconomics, so he defined mainstream economics as monetarism and new classical macroeconomics, and New Keynesianism). Unfortunately, Minsky was not easily 'readable'. The core of his vision – that over an extended period financial institutions, firms and people become more and more indebted, until they feel they have too much leverage, and then they all try to reduce their debt at the same time – was spectacularly right. The result is debt deflation, i.e. catastrophe: the Minsky moment, as in East Asia and Argentina, and then the subprime crisis leading to the Lehman Brothers collapse.

Krugman insisted that Minsky's lack of influence was due only partly to the drift of the profession; it was also due to Minsky's attitude, according to which everything done by other economists was basically wrong. I personally think this was indeed Minsky's typical attitude, but it must be added that most of the Italian collaborators and pupils of Minsky had a different attitude, and were building bridges linking Minsky to New Keynesian macroeconomics, especially Stiglitz. My sense is that Minsky encouraged these efforts: he just couldn't help but restate his own break with any kind of old or new mainstream. Krugman noted that in being an outsider Minsky's strategy was clearly different from Keynes's strategy of trying to be a complete insider, at least in the *General Theory*. And Krugman, as I said, is vocal in rejecting Minsky's sympathy for the criticism of marginal productivity theory of capital and incomes, and Minsky's adherence (after his 1975 book) to Kalecki's income and distribution theory, embedded in the macroeconomic profit equation. It was, Krugman comments, like talking Greek to most people: it was 'too heterodox'.

The year before, Krugman had written in his blog that there is actually a deep insight in Minsky, far ahead of anyone else, and related to the concept of financial fragility. But that insight takes up only part of Chapter 9 of *Stabilising an Unstable Economy* (Minsky, 1986; the main reference for Minsky in Krugman's lectures). For the rest you have what Krugman defines as Minsky's turgid writing on Kaleckian income distribution theory (which, he thinks, has nothing to do with the fundamental point), and more. The gravitation of Krugman towards what he defines a Keynes–Fisher–Minsky view of macroeconomics materialised in Eggertsson and Krugman (2012). It is, as the authors say, a new Keynesian-style model of debt-driven slumps, because of the assumption that some agents are debt constrained.

The canonical financial instability hypothesis

I think that Krugman is wrong, both in his praise and in his criticism of Minsky. Let us see why.[1]

Minsky's canonical model, as represented in Minsky (1975, 1986) put together three themes. First, there was a reading of Keynes's theory focusing on the role of financial markets, the endogeneity and non-neutrality of money, systematic uncertainty surrounding the decisions made by economic units (banks, firms and other financial intermediaries), and the integration of an investment theory of the business cycle with a financial theory of investment. The second theme was the Financial Instability Hypothesis (FIH), according to which, after a period of 'tranquil' growth and robust finance, units' liability structures tend to shift towards fragility, so that the economic system becomes prone to financial crises. The third element was an economic policy structure according to which discretionary economic policies can smooth cyclical instability, creating ceilings and floors and constraining the dynamic behaviour of the economy, thanks to the intervention of the central bank as a lender of last resort and the management of the government's budget deficits. On these bases, Minsky built a cyclical theory of capitalist economies marked by an alternation of speculative waves followed by a tendency towards debt deflation.

Modern capitalism is characterised by expensive and long-lived capital assets coupled with a highly articulated financial system. Real equilibrium is affected fundamentally by the value of monetary variables and by the historical path of the economy. It follows that any approach that does not put money and finance at the very foundation of the theoretical building is bound to be irrelevant. Minsky's vision is a 'Wall Street' paradigm where the role of banks and financial markets, together with the temporal irreversibility of the capitalist process, is considered from the start. Such a vision stresses the dynamics of cash flows. Decisions have to be validated by monetary returns in historical, and hence irreversible, time. Opposing mainstream economics, for which equilibrium can be broken only by policy errors, exogenous shocks or market imperfections, Minsky stresses the endogenous evolutionary course leading from stability to instability. The economic cycle, evolving from tranquil growth to speculative boom and ultra-speculative mania, and then falling into panics and financial crisis, is nothing but the necessary result of the monetary nature of capitalism, and of the connection between investment and finance.

Minsky, following Keynes, considers investment in fixed capital goods as the basic determinant of income and employment levels. The purchase of new capital goods has financial aspects, while the stock exchange is subject to cyclical speculative waves. Let us start from a generic economy characterised by a tranquil expansion and a robust financial system. Initially mindful of past crises, firms, banks and financial intermediaries behave in a risk-averse manner. Monetary interest rates are low and stable, and the supply of credit is potentially limitless. Borrowers are capable of settling, with their regular flow of money proceeds, both the money interest and the stipulated part of the principal. If everything goes as expected, there will be enough profits to validate the previous financial commitments. This is what Minsky called a hedge financial structure. The hedge-financing units are those units where the prospective income cash flows, arising from their own economic activity, are greater than cash payment contractual commitments on debt for every period. The expected present value of business is positive for all likely rates of interest, so that the debt volume tends to fall from one period to another. A hedge-financing unit faces an economic risk, yet it is safe in regard to the financial risk.

The presence of profit opportunity drives units to embark on new activities, further stimulating economic growth. Since business goes well for a while, and units' profits exceed the expected level, entrepreneurs, bankers and financiers becomes less risk-averse, involving a greater disposition to take on additional debt. The process cannot be stopped even by a possible reluctance of the central bank to raise the supply of money. Indeed, the financial operators invent new payment instruments (which are substituted for fiat money), as well as new ways to use old instruments. The interest rates remain unchanged, while units' indebtedness grows, together with speculative positions. Minsky labelled 'speculative-financing units' those where cash-flow earnings allow for the servicing of the interest on debt, but no longer suffice to cover, in every period, the part of the principal which must be given back. Thus, for these units, the refinancing of debt positions becomes necessary, for some periods at least. Speculative units, which multiply with the boom phase, must face not only economic risk but also financial risk due to a possible drop in their assets' value or to a sudden unexpected increase in the short-term interest rate fixed by the central bank. In either case, expected profits may turn into actual losses.

Speculative behaviour is positive, since it allows for higher long-term investment and growth. The problem is that it makes the whole economic system more fragile. The economic boom soon degenerates into a bubble where units prone to take ultra-speculative positions tend to prevail. An ultra-speculative or Ponzi financial structure occurs when interest payments alone exceed the cash flow earnings for a significant number of periods, so that units must either liquidate part of assets (selling positions) or raise new funds (refinancing). An ultra-speculative position is held if the unit expects some bonanza, either exceptional profits or capital gains due to asset price inflation. In such a context a small, unexpected rise in short-term interest rates, or a fall in asset prices, opens the door to a financial crisis. This may result in an economic recession coupled with debt deflation that – if not adequately opposed by an active counter-cyclical economic policy involving government deficit spending and injections of liquidity – may lead to a chronic depression. The situation is worsened by the fact that, during the euphoric phase, all units (bankers, entrepreneurs and speculators) have been reducing their money balances and liquidity. When the crisis erupts, the liquidity preference starts rising again. The economic crisis is therefore the natural outcome of the fragility of the financial structure. This fragility is the upshot of the normal working of the capitalist economy.

Tranquil growth and prosperity naturally bring about changes in cash-flow interconnections, necessarily and endogenously leading from solidity to fragility. The normal functioning of the economy may easily convert fragility into open financial crisis and finally into a credit crunch. Stabilisation is pursued by means of government budget deficits, backed by the central bank acting as a lender of last resort: big government and the big bank. It is here that Minsky refers to Kalecki's macroeconomic equations, where gross profits are positively related to the government deficit. An active anti-cyclical fiscal policy increases the gross money profits for firms, which support and validate the financial structure of units. The government pumps public debt securities into the financial market, which are secure and readily marketable assets, so that the public's preference for liquidity is reduced and the 'robustness' of units' balance sheets is increased. This kind of intervention, which establishes a lower limit for the value of assets, must be coupled with the monitoring and regulation of financial institutions and practices. On the monetary policy side, the central bank cannot prevent the increase in the volume of the payment instruments actually supplied by financial intermediaries in the upswing. It can regain control over the effective quantity of money, but only if it is ready to risk the outbreak of a financial crisis. When the combination of liability structures, financing charges and profit dynamics leads to a financial crisis, the central bank must intervene to refinance banks' activity and extra-bank financial practices to help avert a balance-sheet recession.

Questioning the Financial Instability Hypothesis

What are the problematic points in this theoretical perspective? One of them is theoretical; others are historical. Let us begin with the analytical difficulty. Minsky maintains that the leverage ratio – that is, the ratio of debt to owned capital – increases as the economy grows. Yet, there is no compelling reason why an increase in leverage should necessarily materialise. During the growth phase, total money profits made by all units increase together with debt. While units taken individually do borrow, the debt ratio for the whole economic system may not change. The individual firm will spend the borrowed money on the market, in order to purchase capital goods. The payments for investment orders made by the firms of the first sector are the monetary profits for the firms supplying the capital goods. That the global leverage may not necessarily increase is consistent with the core of Kalecki's analytical framework, endorsed by the same Minsky in the 1970s. In my view, however, this does not deny the 'tendency' to a higher leverage. It rather says it is frustrated ex post.

Other issues point to the historical changes in capitalism after the neoliberal counter-revolution. The canonical model insists on a leverage made mainly by private firms' indebtedness. This is not what was happening in Anglo-Saxon capitalism in the neoliberal era. The most spectacular instance is the USA's exit from the 2000–3 crisis. Non-financial businesses' balances not only turned out to be positive, but even in excess of the volume of the real investments they undertook. The industrial sector ended up providing capital to the financial markets. This relates to the fact that, already in the 1990s, the 'Goldilocks economy' boom in the USA could not be fully explained by the demand for capital goods. More than that, in the post-2003 recovery private investment remained almost flat. The driver of the boom, as I shall clarify shortly, was a new component of autonomous demand, the indebted consumption sustained by collateralised lending thanks to capital market inflation. This was a dynamic that could not have happened without a new monetary policy, with the central bank acting as lender of first resort to speculation.

Banks changed in relation to the way Minsky depicted them in the canonical model. In Minsky's analysis, banks' lending decisions are usually based on borrowers' credit history and on expectations about cash flows. Banking in Minsky looks backward rather than forward. As a consequence of a steady expansion, the borrowing experience becomes increasingly positive. Economic growth itself, rather than any euphoric attitude or any variation in evaluation criteria on the part of banks, validates riskier behaviours. Since the reforms of the 1980s and the 1990s, however, banking activity has been very different. Nowadays, banks seek to maximise their fees and commissions by issuing and managing assets in off-balance-sheet affiliate structures. In this context, bankers have no interest in credit evaluation, which is now made by rating agencies.

It appears, then, that the FIH in its traditional version is ill suited to explain the ascent and collapse of neoliberalism. But which kind of capitalism is really neoliberalism? The fragile growth experienced after the Volcker–Thatcher–Reagan counter-revolution rests on the precarious condition of millions of wage-earners, who are, at the same time, 'manic-depressive' savers, 'indebted' consumers and – last but not least - 'traumatised' workers. Workers are 'traumatised', or 'scared', because of the transformations in the labour process and in the so-called labour market after decades of restructuring, deregulation and globalisation. This social reality cancels wage-induced price inflation, and flattens the Phillips curve.

Savers, in turn, are subject to a bipolar syndrome. They are 'terrorised' by the uncertainties of the new capitalism, which the new finance seems to sedate. They are also 'terrorised' by the progressive dismantling of national retirement systems, which seems to be healed by the building up of pension fund capitalism. Households are also increasingly in debt to sustain their consumption, partly as a paradoxical side-effect of capital asset inflation going hand in hand with the rising insecurity of labour.

Capitalist long waves and Minsky's stages view of capitalism

This changed capitalist reality requires a new version of the FIH. We need to put together the insights of Marx on labour as well as those of Minsky on finance, in a longer-term perspective looking at the different stages through which capitalism evolves. In other words, we must build a kind of Schumpeterian non-mechanical view about long waves, integrating Minsky's financial Keynesianism together with Marx's focus on capitalist relations of production. The late Minsky himself provided crucial elements to understand this world. These elements do not appear very much in his 1986 book, but are scattered in many articles and papers he wrote after the early 1980s. They can be regrouped under the heading 'money manager capitalism', the new form of capitalism which was taking over after the crisis of the so-called Keynesian 'golden age'.

Let us see how the theoretical picture about Minsky may be altered if we try to read his contributions backwards – from the later writings, to the early books. The focus here must be on the long-term changes in capitalism – what Randy Wray (2013) calls Minsky's stages approach.

To introduce this problematic, let me recall Minsky's argument in his chapter on 'Money and crisis in Schumpeter and Keynes' (first presented in Minsky, 1983). Keynes and Schumpeter recognise that money is not an outside asset; it is introduced in the economy as finance. In the abstract, but illuminating, case of a closed economy without a government and without household debts, this finance not only allows capitalist production to begin, but also finances longer-term investment demand and ownership of capital assets. As Kalecki taught us, cash flows to non-financial businesses are determined by their investments, and these in turn depend on two-price system dynamics. A careful interpretation of Minsky's two-price system should relate the supply price of capital to the price of current production, and the demand price of capital assets to the demand for those assets which can be held through time – capital goods are therefore only one instance among capital assets. The money supply may affect the demand price of capital assets, but not directly the price level of current output. Since money is related back to banks through credit creation in calendar time, it must be asked whether debt commitments are actually met, and what happens if they are not.

For the early Minsky, the money supply was not horizontal at a given point in time, though the shifts in financing supply and demand led him to reach conclusions similar to the horizontalist perspective. For the later Minsky, the insistence that loans make deposits out of thin air, together with the stress on innovations within the finance sector, took his views even nearer to other circuitist and post-Keynesian theories of money. The liability structure of businesses matters. The greater the liabilities due to private indebtedness, the greater the possibility of a collapse in asset values 'if something happens', as he used to say. Schumpeterian innovation within finance nurtures the shift from stability to instability, from hedge finance to fragility, whereas a fall in cash inflows and/or a worsening in financing conditions may trigger a financial collapse. Sustaining profits through big government (especially if through military expenditure or non-targeted unproductive demand; and/or through a welfare system based on transfer money payments; and/or through an interventionist central bank) justifies its cost: the fall in asset prices is, however, contained. All of this notwithstanding, the financial structure evolves towards a different form of fragility, building upon the continuous rise in capital asset prices.

Countering the old and new forms of financial turbulence requires a different kind of policy intervention, irreducible to the usual form of Keynesianism. Before dealing with the economic policy side we have to take into account the specificities of the new stage that capitalism has entered in the last few decades.

Minsky focused on US capitalism. Commercial capitalism (since, more or less, the seventeenth century) is the first stage, progressively turning into industrial capitalism (more and more relevant in the second half of the eighteenth century and the first half of the nineteenth century). Merchant banks and commercial banks financed goods in transit, inventories and goods in process. Business owners based their acquisition of capital assets on self-financing in commercial capitalism, while industrial capitalism in the USA saw the emergence of wild cat financing. This is the capitalism depicted by classical political economy, witnessing the opposition between the banking school and the currency school. During the nineteenth century, however, a new form of capitalism emerged: finance capitalism. Long-term investments in heavy infrastructure (railroads, factories and fixed capital) may require the involvement of the state and/or adventurous financing. Marx somehow captures the transition from industrial to finance capitalism. The tendency of the rate of profit to fall because of a rising capital composition is part of the story leading to the Long Depression of the late nineteenth century – a great capitalist crisis which accelerated the formation of finance capitalism, and then stimulated countertendencies such as technical and organisational innovations leading to a higher rate of surplus value. In this financial capitalism stage, the financiers were mainly investment bankers and big corporations: the large shareholders dominated over firm managers.

In Europe, and especially in Germany, this era was the background for Hilferding's *Finanz-Kapital*. Finance capitalism collapsed in the 1929 Great Crash followed by the Great Depression, both for financial reasons (Fisher's debt deflation) and for real causes (Luxemburg–Kalecki's realisation crisis). The next stage was managerial capitalism as the product of the Second World War. Household and business debts were low, and external financing ultimately relied on big government. Managerial capitalism was characterised by high profits, high investments and massive ex ante fiscal deficits. Ex ante deficits may be self-correcting, as long as the government runs a 'good deficit' policy – that is, expenditures lead not only to an increase in GDP but also to a better quality of its composition. In this period, power shifted from large shareholders to corporate managers.

Money manager capitalism

The Marx–Schumpeter point is, once again, that finance capitalism was inherently driven to dissolve itself, because of its internal contradictions and because it cultivated in itself the seeds of the next stage, money manager capitalism (Minsky, 1996). If we move from the end of the Second World War to the 1960s, we witness a capitalism of big corporations, large banks and financial institutions – new intermediaries such as mutual and pension funds. The economic process is dominated by money managers, who have as a target the 'valorisation of capital' (whose meaning shifted to the appreciation of the investments of the holders of their liabilities, including households). In managerial capitalism, employers offered pension plans to workers, and financial institutions started to manage aggressively retirement funds and other assets owned by organisations and households. As Charles Whalen (1997) says, after 1982 institutional investors became the new masters of the economy. Funds bought equity from highly leveraged non-financial businesses. Minsky insists that it is these funds' behaviour that made business management highly sensitive to stock-market evaluations, and transformed US capitalism into a predatory social formation. Such alterations affected corporate governance, favouring the institution of a network productive system far not only from the vertically integrated large-scale factory but also from the usual small- and medium-size firm. The new configuration pushed forward a policy of downsizing and variable costs compression, which jeopardised employment conditions, so that the latter became discontinuous and precarious.

In this framework, the FIH can be redefined in a cyclical perspective far more instructive about the characteristics of the 'new' post-1979–80 capitalism.[2] Reagan's and Thatcher's monetarist U-turn rested on a decisive compression of the money supply determining an upsurge in money and real interest rates, which squeezed private investment and spread uncertainty. Together with the attack on trade unions, wages and social provision, this could have created the conditions for another 1930s-style Great Crash due to a lack of effective demand, were it not for unexpected and powerful, expansionary counter-tendencies. Indeed, as Minsky (and Sweezy) well knew, a Great Depression is unlikely to happen again (and stagnation is not for ever). The first counter-tendency took the form of Reagan's twin deficits: the fiscal deficit (which Krugman has termed 'Weaponised Keynesianism') supported internal demand, while the negative trade account provided external outlets for European and Asian neo-mercantilism. The second counter-tendency was Greenspan's 'privatized Keynesianism'. Since the mid-1970s, the 'class struggle from above' has produced the continuous traumatisation of workers I mentioned earlier in this chapter. The dominance of Minsky's money manager capitalism meant that the middle class's and workers' household savings were channelled into private institutional funds and asset markets, fuelling capital market inflation. Managers were co-opted through stock options and their assigned mission of maximising dividends and share values. Together with a destructive competition between global players in manufacturing and services breeding over-production, the ensuing corporate governance generated a process of centralisation without concentration. Mergers and acquisitions continued to centralise capital. However, this did not universally bring about a higher concentration of units of production. The result was a disappearance of a homogeneous working class and its replacement by the fragmentation and precariousness of a working class 'lost in space' (Bellofiore and Vertova, 2006). In this new world, the monetary circuit sequence changed dramatically. The injection of credit into the system now found its main point of entry in households' indebtedness rather than the financing of production (Seccareccia, 2010). The liquidity injected by banks and financial intermediaries into households' debt accounts was later transferred to firms through 'goods' or 'financial' markets, thus enabling, at the same time, both the finance of production and the realisation of (surplus) value.

Rather than the over-generic term 'financialisation', Minsky's money manager capitalism more accurately describes what I have elsewhere called a real subsumption of labour to finance. This financial configuration impacted directly on the process of production, generating longer working hours and extracting greater effort from workers, and forcing an increase in the labour supply provided by families (what one might label the Marxian side of the story about money manager capitalism). The rate at which money flowed from funds to financial markets enabled non-financial firms to issue shares more cheaply, the returns of which increasingly depended upon speculative gains. This process gave way to an 'overcapitalization' of productive enterprises (Toporowski, 2010b). Given the convenience of expanding financial relative to real investment, ownership titles were issued in excess of the needs for industrial and commercial financing. The money mopped up by those issues was invested in short-term financial activities, propelling a cumulative upward disequilibrium in asset prices without any self-adjustment mechanism. Markets became more liquid, and the supposed quality of collateral assets was thought to be regularly improving. This led to a perceived ex-post increase in the cushions of safety (Kregel, 2008). It is not strange that the increasing indebtedness emerged mostly from financial businesses and households rather than from the physical investment of non-financial firms. This may be somewhat inconsistent with Minsky's canonical model before 1986, but it is coherent with his later description of money manager capitalism.

Manic savers, mesmerised by the rise in the asset values of their holdings, turned into indebted consumers, with the associated collapse of the propensity to save: the higher (paper) value of their assets gave rise to a reduction in saving. Stock market manias, first, and housing bubbles, afterwards, fuelled the expansion of consumption on credit, with consumption becoming an 'autonomous' form of demand, sustaining profits. In the subprime frenzy the two-price model probably incorporated the price of housing into the demand price of capital assets. Wage deflation, capital asset inflation and the increasingly leveraged position of households and financial companies were complementary elements of a perverse mechanism where real growth was doped by toxic finance. Nonetheless, it is important to recognize that 'fictitious' capital had 'non-fictitious' fallouts, contrary to the usual Marxist narratives, and confirming Minskian insights.

This new configuration of capitalism was made possible by a new role of the central bank as lender of first resort (De Cecco, 1999) to support capital asset price inflation. The central bank managed the creation of liquidity with the objective of sustaining the continuous increase in asset values; it also assured the viability of the shadow banking system and financial intermediaries. Under Greenspan, quantitative monetarism receded, being replaced by a policy where money was made available in unlimited amounts at any interest rate established by the central bank. The money supply became flat, and was finally recognised as endogenous even within the mainstream. This was an eminently political management of effective demand, manipulating indebted consumption as the pillar of autonomous demand. The configuration has been labelled 'privatised Keynesianism'. Because of workers' traumatisation, it was possible to have a reduction in unemployment without an increase in wages, so that the so-called Phillips curve flattened out (Lavoie, 2006). However, the resulting full employment was not characterised by decent wages and stable jobs. It was, instead, a situation of full under-employment, with unemployment penetrating into the employed labour force through the spread of part-time and casual/informal occupations.

It was a dynamic configuration of capitalism capable of manufacturing consent and yielding hegemony. The middle classes, too, were sedated by escalating property values and found an illusory security from uncertainty (Toporowski, 2010b). However, households' indebtedness in no way corresponded to a state of economic and social welfare. The US 'overspending' consumer matched the US 'overworking' wage-earner. Growing debt had its ultimate *raison d'être* in the insufficiency of income to support consumption of non-manufactured goods and services. This caused an escalation in expenditures, generating rents for the financial sector.

The socialisation of investment and of the economy

This backwards way of looking at Minsky, through the prism of his stages approach to capitalism and his characterisation of the neoliberal era as money manager capitalism, gives further weight to his economic policy perspective, which was heretical in Keynesianism and post-Keynesianism in the 1970s as it is now. I am referring to his proposal of a socialisation of investment and a socialisation of employment, which is critical of the 1960s policy synthesis and of Keynes himself. Keynes's view was that capitalism is inherently flawed, and that it requires regulation, fiscal intervention, and the central bank as lender of last resort. It is true that big government capitalism is superior to free market capitalism, and this can be said also of the 'Keynesian' economic policies of the Kennedy and Johnson administrations. The problem, however, is that these policies led to a high profits–high investment economy which gained full employment through waste and military expenditures at the cost of social and ecological disasters.

These limits of standard Keynesianism derive not only from a limited understanding of Keynes, but also from contradictions in Keynes himself. Where Minsky is clearest about his vision in economic policy is in the last two chapters of *John Maynard Keynes*. Keynes in the 1930s was proposing a moderately conservative perspective. His vision was that investment must be such as to assure full employment, and taxation such as to assure a reasonable income distribution. He mixed together two very different views: on the one hand, the need for a socialisation of investment; on the other hand, the free allocation of resources by the market mechanism after reaching full employment. There is an apparent inconsistency here. The Keynesian way out of the crisis was faithful to this contradictory Keynes. Wartime policy made large government deficits respectable, pushing up firms' quasi-rents; investment was accompanied by an accommodating monetary policy; a large tax bite subsidised individual consumption and money transfer payments. All this turned into a claim on productive capacity. Full employment like this, Minsky said, was socialism for the rich. It led to a fruitless inflationary treadmill and a deterioration in the biological and social environment.

Not only was Minsky able to anticipate the (internal) dissolution of the Keynesian economic policy of the 1960s – and the ensuing stagflation. He was also able to put forward an alternative economic policy which is insightful today. 'Alternative' here means opposed both to austerity policies and to generic pump priming of effective demand (through government spending and tax reductions, with low interest rates). Investment was not socialised in the Golden Age, when we experienced a boom driven by military spending, while individual discretionary consumption developed into waste. Minsky thought we had to return to the 1933 questions, the New Deal questions: for whom should the game be fixed, and what kind of output should be produced? The answer to these difficulties was to be found in a more radical approach than Keynes: a socialisation of towering heights and leading sectors, with communal consumption; a larger, not a smaller, role for the state; a low, not a high, private investment policy; serious controls on how capital moves and investment is financed; a bias against giant financial institutions.

Now that a serious business cycle is back during the Lesser Depression, and now that Fisherian debt deflation is on-going, we should learn the lesson that interventionist capitalism is better than (pretend) free market capitalism. The key question remains, which kind of interventionism? Minsky's 1975 answer looks incredibly perceptive, and even more so after the crash of money manager capitalism as we knew it. Minsky's socialisation of investment is a socialisation in the use of productive capacity: it means taking command over the utilisation of resources, and its immediate result is social use value. It is complementary to a socialisation of banking and finance, and to a socialisation of employment, such that it gives way to an increase in potential output. This last point may be better understood in its import if we see how the Keynesian welfare reforms allegedly pointing beyond it are framed as an alternative to Minsky's preferred economic policy: a full employment policy led by the government as direct employer (he wrote more generally of extra-market, extra-private enterprise and employment schemes). He went as far as to define welfare as a conservative instrument to increase government deficits, so that profits are sustained in a slump (Minsky, 1981). His ultimate lesson is that we need structural reform, not only expansionary demand policies; a commitment to the design of a new type of capitalism among the possible varieties: a guided interventionist capitalism, or a decentralised socialism. The label, he added, is of little importance.

Notes

1 For this interpretation, see Bellofiore, Halevi and Passarella (2010).
2 This outlook on the crisis is developed further in Bellofiore (2013).

References

Bellofiore, R. (2013). Two or three things I know about her: Europe in the global crisis and heterodox economics, *Cambridge Journal of Economics*, 37, 497–512.

Bellofiore R. and G. Vertova (2006). Lost in space? The geographical and political dimension of uneven capitalist development. In G. Vertova, ed., *The Changing Economic Geography of Globalization*, London: Routledge, pp. 23–44.

Bellofiore, R., J. Halevi and M. Passarella (2010). Minsky in the 'new' capitalism: the new clothes of the Financial Instability Hypothesis. In D. Papadimitriou and R. Wray, eds., *The Elgar Companion to Hyman Minsky*, Cheltenham, UK, and Northampton, MA: Edward Elgar, pp. 84–99.

De Cecco, M. (1999). The lender of last resort, *Economic Notes*, n. 1.

Eggertsson, G. B. and P. Krugman (2012). Debt, deleveraging, and the liquidity trap: a Fisher–Minsky–Koo approach, *Quarterly Journal of Economics*, 127, 1469–1513.

Kregel, J. A. (2008). *Minsky's cushions of safety: Systemic risk and the crisis in the US subprime mortgage market*, Public Policy Brief, 93A, The Levy Economics Institute of Bard College.

Lavoie, M. (2006). Introduction to Post-Keynesian Economics, Palgrave Macmillan.

Minsky, H. P. (1975). *John Maynard Keynes*, New York: Columbia University Press.

Minsky, H. P. (1981). The Breakdown of the 1960s Policy Synthesis. Telos 50 (Winter-82): 49–58.

Minsky, H. P. (1983). Money and crisis in Schumpeter and Keynes, *Hyman P. Minsky Archive,* Paper 334, http://digitalcommons.bard.edu/hm_archive/334.

Minsky, H. P. (1986). *Stabilising an Unstable Economy*, New Haven: Yale University Press.

Minsky, H. P. (1996). Uncertainty and the institutional structure of capitalist economies, *Hyman P. Minsky Archive,* Paper 24, http://digitalcommons.bard.edu/hm_archive/24.

Seccareccia, M. (2010). *Financialization and the Transformation of Commercial Banking: Understanding the Recent Canadian Experience before and during the International Financial Crisis*, working paper.

Toporowski, J. (2010a). The wisdom of property and the politics of the middle class, *Monthly Review*, 62, 10–15.

Toporowski, J. (2010b). *Why the World Economy Needs a Financial Crash and Other Critical Essays on Finance and Financial Economics*, London: Anthem Press.

Whalen, C. J. (1997). Money-manager capitalism and the end of shared prosperity, *Journal of Economic Issues*, 31, 517–25.

Wray, L. R. (2013). Minsky's money manager capitalism. In B. Z. Cynamon, S. M. Fazzari and M. Setterfield, eds., *After the Great Recession: The Struggle for Economic Recovery and Growth*, New York: Cambridge University Press, pp. 61–85.

2 Can we say "Minsky moment" when households matter?

Anna Maria Variato

Have you seen Cassandra? I should say I met Prometheus instead. To the few men of vision I had the chance to meet, the ones who being great teachers inspired intellectual enhancement.

Times of financial turmoil, followed by periods of real economic contraction, are often taken as empirical evidence of the downswing of the Financial Instability Hypothesis (hereafter FIH) at work. Since the 1998 Russian crisis, they are even more often qualified as "Minsky moments."[1] It is a well-known fact that Hyman Minsky's ideas on endogenous financial instability have been more popular and appreciated long before and more extensively outside of academic circles: Minsky's standard language, metaphors and tools were more suited to the "men of finance and accounting" than to economists.[2] Whether the theoretical setup implied by Hyman Minsky is a suitable framework for evaluating recent economic dynamics, whether it is relevant, original, and/or complete, gives rise to more controversial questions. Furthermore, among those who are sympathetic to Minsky's view, too, there is no agreement: even there, the debate ranges from strictly empirical issues to methodological matters.

As a scholar of Minsky, on the appearance of US subprime crisis, I just thought: "The moment has come, at last. Nobody will cast doubt on the fact that this is the turning point, the beginning of the FIH downturn." Facts were giving a striking (posthumous) vindication of the long-neglected ideas of Hyman Minsky.[3] Surprisingly enough, during 2008, two of the most prominent expositors of the post-Keynesian school and experts on Hyman Minsky's work, Paul Davidson and Jan Kregel, published two papers denying that the subprime crisis could be qualified as a Minsky moment, indirectly questioning the validity of the FIH as a general/comprehensive framework for explaining macroeconomic cycles.

Sometime later, the emergence of further economic research and the occasion of this collection of papers in honor of Piero Ferri, to whom I gratefully recognize my intellectual debt, constitute a coincidental reason to revisit this somehow unsolved puzzle, allowing a more personal line of argumentation.

The question in the title of this contribution leads directly to other strictly related queries: what set of conditions qualifies as a Minsky moment? Does the expression "Minsky moment" itself identify instantaneous features, or does it capture just one instant of a dynamic process? Furthermore, is the subprime crisis a case theoretically embedded into the FIH? The first two questions address the definition of a Minsky moment, while the last one points to an evaluation of the theoretical amplitude of the FIH.

Hence the answer to the question posed in the title is not simply a matter of philological relevance. There are, in fact, more profound implications related to the method of science (more precisely, to the evolution of economic science), and to the conduct of economic policy: two issues apparently independent, but intimately connected for particular kinds of economist (such as Minsky).

Therefore, despite first appearances, this is not going to be a paper trying to answer an empirical question; rather, the subprime–household crisis is the "pretext" to more radical reflections on the meaning of (my own) being Minskian. It is the search for elements that, though possibly overlapping with other approaches, identify an original and distinctive core of assumptions, which, while selecting some fundamental pillars, enable us to understand (represent, predict, handle) economic reality with specific reference to the macroeconomic dimension and its dynamics.[4]

In accordance with this line of reasoning, this chapter develops in two sections. The first is devoted to a comparative review of the recent literature related to Minsky moments, highlighting what one can conceive as a sort of destructive aspect of the Minskian approach. The second, in contrast, represents an attempt at critical reconstruction, combining Minsky's original contribution, the existing literature, and my own interpretation to achieve the objective.

Minsky moment or not? A brief literature review

The following review, without any pretense to be exhaustive, surveys a number of papers published after 2007 that directly address the issue of Minsky moments, mostly considering the query in the title.[5]

This review of the literature is not philological but functional; it strives to highlight and collect themes to explain the building blocks that are emphasized in the next section. Hence, I will not give equal weight to the arguments in favor as opposed to critical ones, in order to avoid repeating concepts (as supporting claims constitute themselves probable building blocks of a Minskian perspective). At the end of each paragraph, where critical remarks are raised, a research question is posed that will be faced in the third section.

Before going into the detailed examination, a couple of considerations are worth stressing. First, as stated by Vercelli (2011), whether the subprime crisis of 2007 is a Minsky moment depends upon the definition of the Minsky moment itself. So, the observed disagreement with the proposition simply reflects a different (implicit or explicit) account of what a Minsky moment is supposed to be. Here I am not going to replicate considerations I basically subscribe to and that one can find well expounded in Vercelli's work. Nonetheless, and this is the second remark, the different notion of "moment" basically entails a different use of the concept of time. On one side, behind the negative answer to the question we have "historical time." Hence the observed reality is not a Minsky moment because the features of the system at a particular point of time are not homogeneous with the features directly described (or at least implied) by Minsky. On the other side, the positive answer is related to a notion of "logical time," where the moment is not a "moment" at all: it is not a fixed point in time, but it is the recognition of the existence of the beginning of a reversal process inside another process. In order to clarify this statement, it is helpful to use the metaphor of yin and yang, intertwined and interacting forces (giving rise to a never-ending circular/cyclical dynamic system). The "moments" are the two black and white spots in the picture. As a result, if we contrast two authors who are analyzing the same empirical facts, who end up one denying and the other supporting the interpretation of the US subprime crisis as a Minsky moment, it will not be surprising to find that the latter locates the "historical moment" earlier than the former.[6] A nice example of the particular view implied by those who take the "logical time" perspective is expressed by Tymoigne (2006, p. 38), who states: "The immediate cause of a crisis does not matter. The forces at work that led to the crisis started to operate a long time before the factor triggering the occurrence of the crisis."

The first and simplest selective comparative criterion for the review is to separate the authors who answer the question positively from the ones who answer in the negative.

It has been a Minsky moment: Wray (2009, 2011), Whalen (2008a, 2008b), Kregel (2010a, 2010b)

The most prominent paper in this review, expressing the idea that the subprime crisis is a Minsky moment, can be found in Wray (2009, 2011). Here the author describes the sequence of events involved in this specific episode, but then connects them to a broader evolutionary process which Minsky himself explained and somehow predicted. According to the author, all the relevant elements of analysis of subprime financial crisis were present at the core of FIH, before the emergence of the subprime crisis itself.

More specifically, Minsky was referring to stages of capitalism, which are related to the complex interactions between real and financial sides of the economy, but also to institutional settings (especially to policy behavior) and sociological considerations (conventions, expectations, social conflicts). All these aspects, interacting through time, have led to three stages in capitalistic development: each of the stages moves cyclically through expansions and contractions. The distinctive feature of the FIH is that the more sophisticated the financial arrangements in an economy become, the higher the potential speed of real growth, but also the higher the potential of a disruptive downturn. Such a likelihood becomes a fact when the speed of financial evolution turns out to be incoherent with the speed of change of real conditions. The crisis is usually stopped historically not by endogenous adjustments of markets, but instead through an institutional change involving policy action. As a result, the crisis marks the beginning of a new stage. After the introduction of "safety nets" intended to solve the previous crisis, a process of endogenizing the new rules by agents creates the basis for a new crisis which is "resistant" to the containing mechanisms learned by authorities, and by economic agents in general. Minsky could not forecast the exact timing of the crisis of the "money-manager capitalism" stage; nevertheless he understood very well that the path of the economy was moving towards this end-point well before 2007.

The recognition that the subprime crisis was a Minsky moment is also evident in Kregel (2010a) and Whalen (2008a). Both authors, relying on personal knowledge of Hyman Minsky, recall the past and imagine what the author would have said if he had been alive during 2007. They suggest that he would not have been surprised. Furthermore, Kregel sustains such a perspective using a reference to Minsky (1964) where, in his opinion, one can find the basic intuition and statements implying the evolution eventually leading to crisis like the one that triggered the Great Recession. The same implications, but from a more technical perspective, can be found in Kregel (2010b). This contribution is interesting in the sense that it shows a sort of change in position by the author, which could be due to the effect of agreement with the position expressed by Vercelli (2011).[7]

Not only has it been a Minsky moment, we may add . . . : Henry (2009), Reinert (2009), Barbera and Weise (2010), Galbraith and Sastre (2010)

As underlined at the beginning of the section, the authors falling in this set share the same view that the subprime crisis is evidence of a Minsky moment, and take the fact as a proof of a wider validity of the FIH. Hence the subprime crisis is conceived as a part of the more general process of financial instability, endogenously leading towards increasing fragility, and eventually to self-destruction. The cyclical behavior affecting the interaction between real and financial forces of the macroeconomic realm, basically explaining macro dynamics, is then used by the authors as an interpretative framework which can be applied either to other fields or to other aspects of economic theory. More specifically, Henry (2009) focuses on extending the application of FIH to the field of regional economics. Similar observations, in a more sophisticated approach focused on theoretical rather than empirical aspects, can be found in Dymski (2010), who builds a spatial model to show the interaction between patterns of regional economic growth rates and the likelihood of generating endogenous asset bubbles (as opposed to modeling the process through regional contagion). The author also examines the linkage of structural/institutional features and the interaction between real and financial wealth flows and policy arrangements (either types of capital flow or types of capital flow allowed by economic policy). The contribution is especially valuable as it draws attention to most[8] of the complex interactions involved in the dynamic process due to FIH (see, for the intuition, the picture presented on Dymski, 2010, p. 226), and it also emphasizes the critical role played by international economic linkages.

Barbera and Wiese (2010) suggest a model incorporating the FIH in the conduct of monetary policy. The authors construct a modified Taylor rule in an otherwise standard IS–LM model, showing that such a change better captures the past behavior of the economy and may even help to mitigate (though obviously not eliminate), through a self-containing policy mechanism, the perverse endogenous market effects of "financial excess."

In Galbraith and Sastre (2010) the approach is extended to the field of broader social science, in particular to the evolution of international relations involving the power of nations.

The final extension is the most pervasive one, and refers to the contribution of Reinert (2009). Here the Minsky moment event is not simply the culminating peak before the collapse of an unsustainable path of economic dynamics; it is more radically the signal of the definitive crisis of a theoretical paradigm that had become progressively more detached from reality and incapable of facing and solving the problems of the real world. Furthermore, not only can the FIH be considered a general framework to describe the endogenous cyclical nature of the economy (in ways that the author suggests are even wider than usually accepted), but it can be extended to explain the evolution of economic method and science as well. In other words, according to Reinert, economic science (in a process which is not exactly overlapping the evolution of other sciences) evolves through an endogenous unstable process, where the homologous of the pairing real/financial forces is empirical orientation and language (real) as opposed to abstraction and formalization (mathematical language): the "evil" is always the same, an instrument (finance or abstraction) which becomes "excessive" with respect to the limits posed by contingent reality.

The unifying consequence of all these different observations is that, Minsky moment or not, Minsky's thought is extremely fertile, in the sense it gives rise to paths of reflections that the author himself did not even imagine: a typical hallmark of the "makers" of the history of (economic) science.

It has been a Minsky moment, but . . .: Vercelli (2010, 2011), Erturk and Ozgur (2009, 2010), Toporowski (2005, 2010)[9]

The literature considered in this part of the chapter is sympathetic to Minsky. Nonetheless it points out some weaknesses and the need for refinements and qualifications. These authors do not underplay the general validity and relevance of FIH as an interpretative tool useful to the understanding of the recent crisis. In this spirit, one can read both Erturk and Ozgur (2009, 2010), and Toporowski (2010). The first two authors underline the importance of Minsky's contribution, emphasizing its unicity and hence urging a Minskian research agenda; Toporowski, taking the broader perspective also advanced in previous contributions (Toporowski, 2005) and considering Minsky one of the relevant exponents of endogenous financial instability theories, emphasizes his connections with other similar authors (in this case with Simons).

For the purposes of the present chapter, Vercelli (2011) deserves particular mention. The exercise presented in the paper is especially interesting as it is not simply a formal exercise, but has different merits. First, it is useful in clarifying the issue of Minsky moments, trying to delineate the criteria helping to build a unique definition; second, it makes an important distinction between "moments" and "processes," which is of critical importance when evaluating the validity of FIH, and in particular while assessing whether or not the subprime crisis belongs to the core of FIH; third, it builds a continuous time/type model where the endogenous path of the economy is generated as an effect of the interaction of two critical dimensions (namely solvency and liquidity), overcoming the criticism usually addressed to Minsky, pertaining to the lack of an explanation of the endogenous floor. So the model stresses that the FIH is complete and symmetric *per se*, as the specific relevance of the concepts of solvency and liquidity originates from Minsky himself, not from further interpretations. Fourth, taking the model as an intuitive basis for the understanding of macro dynamics, the author suggests some policy implications.

As I explain in the next section, I basically subscribe to most of the propositions and implications presented by the author. Nevertheless, while appreciating the model as a "descriptive" tool, I am quite skeptical about the transformation of the discrete varieties of Minskian units (namely hedge, speculative, and Ponzi) into a continuous range. This passage, in my view, is not simply a matter of analytical convenience, but implies setting aside a fundamental building block of the FIH. Furthermore, the loss of this block is relevant to the discussion leading to policy prescriptions.

It has not been a Minsky moment, nonetheless . . . : Davidson (2008), DeAntoni (2010), Behlul (2011), Kregel (2008), Bellofiore and Halevi (2011), Prychitko (2010)

Critique 1: The most recurrent critique one can find while reading the abovementioned contributions is that the subprime crisis cannot be qualified as a Minsky moment because it does not comprise the basic features usually associated with the typical Minskian downturn. At the risk of being quite schematic, the issues under scrutiny involve the fact that:

1 The subprime crisis was not triggered by over-indebted firms, but by households (or banks, or other financial institutions) (all the papers listed above).
2 It was not caused by a "ponzification" of the system (that is, a dynamic process where the structure of the system was transforming hedge units into speculative ones, and speculative units into Ponzi): households were not allowed to be Ponzi (ponzification of households was an effect, not a cause, of the development of the crisis) (Davidson and all the others except Kregel).
3 It was due to mispricing of risk (Kregel and Behlul).
4 It was not due to a boom in firms' productive investment; or, put another way, was not due to profit-seeking firms, but to other profit-seeking units (again households, banks, or other financial institutions) (all the papers listed above).

5 While implying speculative bubbles, it did not lead to wage and price inflation (Bellofiore and Halevi).

This critique also contains a twin argument that blames Minsky for overemphasizing the role of banks as compared to other financial institutions.

The criticism is quite open and sharp, as can be witnessed in the following quotation from Behlul (2011):

> . . . while Minsky does provide some useful insight into the financial crisis of 2008–9, the ability of his most prominent theory of financial instability – the financial instability hypothesis (FIH) – to explain the current crisis is absent. (p. 137)
>
> . . . I argue that in the decade leading up to the crisis, financial behavior at the firm level did not show a gradual and progressive deterioration toward instability – an essential requirement for a Minsky moment. (pp. 137–8)
>
> . . . Thus, the fragility of the macroeconomy in this case was not caused by the nonfarm, nonfinancial corporate sector. (p. 145)
>
> . . . The "moment," in a true Minskian sense, arrives after a cumulative process towards instability, the "moment" being a debt-deflation process. However, in order to arrive at that "moment," the economy should have first moved from hedge to speculative and finally to Ponzi financing. In the current crisis, the banking system was either speculative – or Ponzi – financing from the beginning (p. 151)

Or one may quote Davidson (2008):

> . . . over the course of any expansion, the economy moves from hedge to speculative to Ponzi finance. Minsky argued that this is a *necessary* precondition for an unstable financial system (Papadimitriou and Wray, 1999, p. 10, emphasis added)
>
> . . . Consequently, with no movement from hedge to speculative to Ponzi finance, the "necessary precondition" for a Minsky moment has not been met. Instead, the current financial market problem was set off by insolvency problems of large financial market underwriters who attempted to transform illiquid noncommercial mortgages into liquid assets via securitization. (p. 670)

Hence, a Minsky dynamics has, indeed, occurred but elsewhere and with a different set of modalities than those envisaged by the author. We must direct our attention to households and to financial intermediaries (Bellofiore and Halevi, 2011, pp. 26–7).

All these remarks capture serious points in the sense that they state correctly the facts as they historically occurred; nevertheless they miss the main point, from the theoretical point of view. If the question one wants to investigate is whether or not the subprime crisis was as Minsky described in his own work, through specific examples, the answer is no. But if the alternative question is: can the FIH be used to understand and/or predict processes of endogenous financial instability, and is the subprime crisis, even not explicitly referenced, an event coherent with this framework, the answer is yes. So the criticism, while being correct from the point of view of "history," is pointless from the point of view of theoretical relevance. Furthermore, using one of the most restrictive criteria to validate theories, which is the Lakatosian perspective (of theories preceding the facts), one could even conclude that FIH passes the test, being more powerful than implied by the critical observations quoted above.

Research question 1: These statements require a detailed answer, as they pose a unique question: is the FIH too much unbalanced towards firms' investment and towards the role of banks? In other words, does the FIH overlook the complex financial evolutions of modern monetary economies of production, and hence does it need emendation?

Critique 2: The other piece of more fundamental criticism emerging from the attempt to establish a connection between the subprime crisis and FIH is addressed to the supposedly asymmetric interpretation of cyclical dynamics and the implicit explanation of instability and growth characterizing the core of FIH. This second critique reveals that some of the authors have a more general scope than simply assessing whether or not the subprime crisis was an empirical example of the FIH. The points can be summarized as follows:

1 (embedded in the previous critique) The FIH is a dynamic process of transformation of units towards more fragile financial structures, but this process is neither necessary to the crisis nor implied by the process of growth *per se* (explicitly Davidson, implicitly all the other papers).
2 FIH does not explain the floor and how to come out of depression (the so-called "obsession" with upward instability) (De Antoni).
3 FIH does not explain how to reach a euphoric boom (it is sort of given; hence implicit theorizing) (De Antoni and Prychitko).
4 Inside FIH growth is conceived as a destabilizing phenomenon *per se* without explanation (De Antoni and Prychitko).
5 The cyclical process is too much related to psychological–sociological explanations (such as expectation disappointments and the disruption of conventional views) and detached from real considerations (hence a bias towards finance) (Prychitko).

One of the most representative passages is from De Antoni (2010, p. 18):

> If we consider the subprime crisis in itself, it is probably legitimate to interpret it as a "Minsky moment" followed by a "Minsky meltdown" (Roubini 2007a, 2007b; Whalen 2007; Wray 2007). Many features are in fact the same. Our problem, however, extends beyond the episode in itself: to what extent does the subprime turmoil fit with the "core" of Minsky's financial instability hypothesis? I refer to the hypotheses (i) that the fundamental instability of

capitalism is upward and (ii) that growth endogenously leads to financial fragility and consequently tends to be shaken by financial crises followed by debt deflations and deep depressions. The two theses are equally essential to Minsky's construction. As we will see, the recent experience seems to gainsay the latter and, perhaps, also the former.

Research question 2: Obviously, the question raised by these accounts pertains to the nature of cycles and growth, and their connection.

Critique 3: The third statement, common to all papers, is not an objection, but a particular interpretation of one of the unit types described by Minsky's taxonomy of agents. More specifically, all authors conceive Ponzi units as a limit case of speculative units, as if Ponzi units were not a category *per se*, but just a sub-set of speculative units (the most speculative ones). The assumption that Ponzi finance is nothing but a variant of speculative finance, for example, is explicitly stated by Prychitko (2010, p. 205).

Furthermore there is a negative attitude towards Ponzi units, the relative incidence of this kind of agent in the system being the cause of increasing fragility and hence the cause of more disruptive downturns (see Galbraith and Sastre, 2010, p. 268). Such a viewpoint is also due to the fact that Ponzi units are mostly connected to behavior that is at least extremely opportunistic, if not openly fraudulent. As a result, representative agents, the "good" ones, are not supposed to be Ponzi. Direct exposition of the idea that units are not supposed to be Ponzi can be found in Reinert (2009, p. 8). Indirect evidence of this position can be found in Papadimitriou and Wray (1999), who divide Minsky moments into two phases: 1) intentional: implying the transformation of units from hedge to speculative; 2) mostly unintentional: implying the transformation from speculative to Ponzi. Without a negative connotation of Ponzi units, the distinction of the two phases of the Minsky moment would not require an explicit reference to the "will" of agents. In other words, if being speculative is not a fault, as being Ponzi is not a fault, there is no need to distinguish between being speculative or Ponzi as a matter of choice, and as a consequence of an exogenous change of financial conditions.

Research question 3: Are Ponzi units really just a particular kind of speculative unit? More generally, what is the role of heterogeneity and diversity inside the FIH?

Was it a Minsky moment? So what: Prychitko (2010)

The last question examined in the section is the one raised by Prychitko (2010), who acknowledges that the subprime crisis was a Minsky moment, but blames either Minsky, or more generally all post-Keynesians, for not mentioning the Austrian school as an alternative (even more powerful) theoretical framework capable of explaining the events of the last few years.

Whether the Austrian is a better framework than Minskian or other post-Keynesian approaches for addressing the issue of financial instability is a question beyond the purposes of the present chapter. Nonetheless, the Austrian perspective of the author affects the second point of criticism, which entails the role of policy authorities in generating/dampening the instability of the system. According to Prychitko, while suggesting the presence of "big players" (lender of last resort, big government, employer of last resort) to foster the expansion of the economy after a collapse, Minsky overlooks two dangers: first, public authorities can be as faulty as the market when operating in a fundamentally uncertain environment, so there is no guarantee that public intervention will be more effective than the market in reaching any collective goal; second, it may well be the case that the public authority itself will undertake the wrong policy, hence generating the preconditions eventually leading to higher fragility, increased instability, and then a more harmful crisis. According to Prychitko, to have a *financial crisis* such as the subprime-induced one (or such as the Great Depression), one always needs to have a *faulty monetary authority*: the market alone cannot generate a devastating financial crisis without a previous massive injection of liquidity that does not take into account the limits posed by the real side of the economy.

Research question 4: What is the appropriate role for big (public) players in the economy?

Choosing the pillars: towards a Minskian paradigm?

While approaching this section, I take the methodological standpoint expressed by Erturk and Ozgur (2009): answering the question of whether or not the subprime crisis is a Minsky moment is not relevant *per se*, but refers to the possibility that the attribute "Minskyan refers to an evolving literature that emanates but transcends his work" (p. 3). What matters, therefore, is the identification of a Minskian approach, which "is needed more than ever to . . . learn anew the lesson that capital markets sooner or later self-destruct when left to their own devices. That however calls for a vibrant evolving research agenda with a focus on what is happening in the real world" (p. 9).

Up to this point in the chapter, one question clearly emerging is the attribution of the turning point of the cycle. The previous section showed that, in a sense, this attribution is a matter of convention, as it happens either in other fields or in economics itself. As we know with historical events that had enormous impact on human beings, so too economic phenomena such as what we now know as the Great Contraction do not come about as the effect of singularities, but instead as a complex result of the interaction of different (not necessarily many) forces, giving rise to dynamic processes.[10]

Hence, while not denying that "moments" are relevant (as they locate turning points), in what follows the attention to "processes" will be privileged, so one has to see whether there are levers connected to the subprime crisis that are fundamental to FIH.

Looking for pillars of an endogenous explanation of financial instability, one may say that Great Contraction requires: 1) the existence of a conflict between the micro and macro dimensions; putting it differently, it requires an intrinsic contradiction inside the workings of the economy (the fallacy of composition); 2) money that is not neutral with respect to real variables (real and financial sides of the economy are not independent);[11] 3) instability as a result of the interaction between the structure of the economy (fundamentals) and market self-adjustments (incoherence, lack of coordination), including the possibility that an economic policy authority may exacerbate (ameliorate) the conditions of the system while introducing wrong/misplaced/misunderstood (correct/on-time/correctly perceived) policies.[12]

The conventional interpretation of FIH recognizes that the core of the theory embeds these three conditions.[13] Hence FIH encompasses the subprime crisis. These features, on the other hand, do not qualify Minsky as an original author. They are essential to a theory of financial disturbance (Toporowski, 2005), but they do not give rise to the same kind of evolutionary process (think, for example, of the different interpretations and implications of post-Keynesian theory as opposed to Austrian theory). Hence, one must find something else which is peculiar to Minsky, in order to develop a "Minskian" paradigm.

In the remaining part of the section, I will face the questions raised in the previous section in order to highlight such distinguishing aspects.

Answering research question 1: too much investment and/or too many banks?

> The main reason why our economy behaves in different ways at different times is that financial practices and the structure of financial commitments change . . . The behavior and particularly the stability of the economy change as the relation of payment commitments to the funds available for payments changes and the complexity of financial arrangements evolves . . . The evolution from financial robustness to financial fragility did not take place in a vacuum. The sources of the change can be traced to profit opportunities open to financial innovators within a given set of institutions and rules; a drive to innovate financing practices by profit-seeking households, business and bankers; and legislative and administrative interventions by governments and central bankers. (Minsky, 1986a, p. 197)[14]

This direct quote from Minsky makes explicit at least four important points: 1) cycles are somehow unique manifestations; 2) the endogenous nature of instability is mainly related to financial causes (hence no neutrality, no dichotomy); 3) the tendency towards fragility is due to the rational behavior of profit-seeking agents (fallacy of composition, incoherence, destabilizing forces); 4) the financial structure of the economy changes in a complex way.[15]

> To analyze how financial commitments affect the economy it is necessary to look at economic units in terms of cash flows. The cash-flow approach looks at all units – be they households, corporations, state and municipal governments, or even national governments – as if they were banks. (Minsky, 1986a, p. 198)[16]

This second quote can be considered the distinctive mark of the Minskian microfoundation of macroeconomics. It is the picture of his own "most" representative agent.

> Capitalism may very well work best when capital assets are cheap and simple. Instability may very well be exacerbated as production becomes more capital intensive and as the relative costs and gestation periods in investment goods increase, for in such a capitalist economy financing arrangements are likely to appear in which debtors pay debts not with cash derived from income production but with cash obtained by issuing debt. We have to investigate the implications of debt and external financing of the financial structures we all know exist, for the stability of the economy. (p. 200)

These three direct quotes from Minsky, in my view, answer all the criticisms raised in the previous section. More specifically, they show that the reference to firms' investment (which is not stressed in these quotes, but is clearly evident in Minsky's writings) is not a weakness but the result of a specific choice, made for different reasons. The first one relates to the fact that investment is the most unstable component of aggregate demand and hence the most likely driver of aggregate fluctuations. Second, investment directly connects and locates Minsky into the Keynesian tradition through the exposition of the theory of two prices. The emphasis on the theory of two prices can be viewed as the easiest way both to confront the mainstream neoclassical position, assuming independence between the real and financial sides of the economy,[17] and to contrast with the IS–LM reduction of Keynes which led to the neoclassical synthesis. Third, this is a way to state that the explanation of the FIH requires integrated real and financial sides of the economy. A financial theory of instability does not imply that the real side of the economy is obscured (almost absent) while affecting dynamics. It is not financial innovation or financial sector growth per se that is the vehicle towards instability; it is the lack of coordination of the pace of change of finance with respect to the pace of change of the real economy.[18]

Does FIH require only the instability of firms' investment? As the general prototype of agent suggested by Minsky is a financial unit, not a productive unit, the answer is likely to be negative again. Minsky refers to units "as banks." If one attempts to generalize the concept of "bank" to each individual in the economic system, one also discovers that the only possible generalization is related to "financial intermediation": that is, the fact that each individual may be the channel of exchange between "flows of money/liquidity today" against "money/liquidity in the future." Nevertheless, such an exchange cannot be established without the presence of capital assets which are simultaneously the means and the end of the transfer process of liquidity through time. In other words, financial intermediation is not a distinctive feature of a "bank" in a strict sense: any individual who does not live in a never-ending present, but has to face inter-temporal decisions, needs to face the problem of synchronizing liquidity flows and hence is compelled to behave "like a bank."

Answering research question 2: on the dynamic interaction between cycles and growth

The issue of cycles is of vital importance in Minsky's writings. The contribution by Fazzari and Greenberg in this book (Chapter 3) stresses the relevance of the issue, as do most of the joint works by Ferri and Minsky (1992), and Ferri himself (2010, 2011).[19] Here I am going to focus on the most critical aspect, which is the interaction between cycles and growth.

First, it has to be underlined that the FIH, from the theoretical point of view, implies a symmetric structure for cycles. Accordingly, just as there exists the possibility of a euphoric boom, Minsky quotes the opposite case of a pessimistic slump. He does not greatly emphasize this case, as economic policy authorities since the Great Depression have learned how to deal with the problem. The so-called "upward obsession," then, is not an obsession at all. It is simply a claim for attention to the fact that authorities have not yet understood how dangerous it can be to overlook the upward destabilizing force of finance.

If cycles and growth were independent, as is usually understood in standard economic theorizing, one would not worry too much about upward instability (or downward instability either). The consequences of the crisis, though massive and undesirable from the point of view of efficiency, equity, distribution, and social justice, would be temporary.

But Minsky does not subscribe to this point of view; his idea of the interaction between cycles and growth is that both processes are intertwined. Hence the disruptive fallout of a euphoric boom is especially worrisome, as it contains the seed of the worst potential negative effect on the potential long-run path of the economy, which will be experienced ex-post as evidence of a downturn in the overall cyclical dynamics.

If one accepts the assumption that cycles and growth are not independent, one also has to accept the consequence that the thrust towards instability is due to the growth process.

Here the argument points to the fact that the criticism does not take into proper account the connection between FIH and the Kaleckian theory of increasing risk. In various places, Minsky states that the objective of all units is profit seeking (not growth). In general, each unit may obtain profit by exploiting the interaction of two levers: operational and financial. The first lever makes profits out of the "core activity" of the business; the second makes profits out of a joint interaction between external favorable conditions of financial markets, internal operational leverage, and internal financial leverage. The thrust towards instability is an endogenous consequence of growth, due to the fact that, in order to seek profits in a competitive environment, a firm which is comparatively less productive with respect to the core business will face competition by increasing leverage, hence increasing the return on "equity" and possibly bettering the results of its competitor. As changing financial structure during a positive phase of the cycle is much easier than changing the "core productivity," it is consequential that firms, especially in the short run, pursue profit-seeking through financial leverage instead of operational leverage. In the aggregate, this means increasing leverage and, accordingly, increasing fragility (Minsky, 1964, p. 177; 1986a, p. 213).

If one recognizes the Kaleckian part of Minsky's FIH, one also sees that business cycles are generated not only by the disappointment of expectations or other psychological facts relating to the issue of fundamental uncertainty. In fact, the behavior may be produced by the different timing of the evolution of the forces behind real dynamics and the forces behind financial dynamics. If finance has a destabilizing nature, the real side of the economy, without any change in expectations, may very well trigger a downturn (just moving at a pace which is inconsistent with financial developments and/or liquidity injection into the system). As a result, the real part of the FIH is not missing, even though one may think about refining it.[20]

Answering research question 4: on the meaning of Ponzi units, or the role of heterogeneity/diversity

First of all, I will quote from Minsky (1986a), where one can see that he did not consider Ponzi units as just a mere subset of speculative units. And the fact that Ponzi units are distinctive units from the financial point of view is explicitly stated in the last passage of the quotation.

> A Ponzi-financing unit is similar to a speculative financing unit in that, for some near-term periods, the cash payment commitments exceed the expected cash receipts on account of owned assets . . . Ponzi units capitalize interest into their liability structure. (p. 207)

The issue of Ponzi units is particularly relevant as it stresses the role of "diversity," which may be understood as "relevant heterogeneity," in economic theorizing (see Reinert, 2009). Up to what point does one need to push heterogeneity to explain and fully understand complex economic dynamic processes? On this point and on the nature of Ponzi units, my perspective is quite different from the one emerging in Vercelli (2011).

My first remark is that the term "Ponzi" is quite unfortunate; like "speculation," it evokes a negative moral connotation, which is difficult to eradicate even among educated economists. If the moral evaluation is set aside, the negative evaluation of Ponzi units (as well as speculation) nevertheless remains with respect to the emergence of fragility and instability, as they are the most dangerous consequences of units' behavior.

Nevertheless, a Ponzi unit does not need to be "a bad" unit; indeed, it is quite the opposite. The Ponzi nature which Minsky attaches to agents is only related to financial conditions, not to other individually relevant features. Typical examples of Ponzi units (or actions implying that at least some individual actions follow a Ponzi scheme) are a high-technology firm, a chemical researcher, and so on, but also a brilliant student coming from a poor family, a government financing education, and a bank financing the building of a highway. All these examples are connected by the common feature that none of the people is bad in principle, but all have to face decisions that imply, for quite a long period of time, that outflows of liquidity exceeds inflows, and the ability to pay back the debt associated with the present liquidity unbalance is so far away in the future that such agents have to capitalize interest into their liability structure.

Must one think that these kinds of units (or situations) must be kept under control, as this is beneficial to the stability of the system? It is true that a higher proportion of Ponzi units increases the fragility of the system, but the converse is also true: that a system without Ponzi units (like the ones just mentioned) is going to lose important growth opportunities.

So the very existence of Ponzi units creates a trade-off between stability and growth on the dynamic path of the economy. Without an explicit acknowledgment of the particular positive nature of Ponzi units, this trade-off would be lost. This would imply not only the loss of an interpretative piece of the FIH, but also probable wrong economic policies (like a generalized restriction on capital requirements in bad times, which is good for speculative units, but not for Ponzi).

The other perplexity raised by Vercelli (2011) is due to the transformation of the discrete Minskian triad into a continuous interval of types. Here the remark is merely methodological. The change allows us to take into account an extremely high degree of heterogeneity, and it is also a convenient technical smoothing tool (this transformation is essential to have the kind of endogenous interaction illustrated in the paper). On the other hand, the economic implication of this infinite variety is the same as the representative agent representation: individuals do not matter.

In my view, instead, one of the core points of Minskian analysis is that individuals do matter, with their own individual features. Some features may be collapsed into broader types, but they do not need to be many (in no way must they be infinite), and the interaction of even a small number of features is sufficient to generate complex dynamics. Here I argue that the interactions of just three kinds of unit, having three different kinds of cash flow, is an adequate basis for the dynamic setup of the FIH.

Answering research question 4: on the role of big players – are policy errors more relevant than policy actions?

Here I present a short remark on the role of policy actors. Answering Prychitko's (2009) criticism, I think that Minsky did not mention the Austrian school in order to emphasize the difference of his position on this specific point. Minsky was surely aware of the possibility of having faulty authorities. Furthermore, a good deal of his research is an explicit account of his dissatisfaction with the decisions made by policy authorities (Minsky, 2013). So the trust placed in big players is not naive faith. But being Keynesian, he was pragmatically oriented: even aware of the limits of policy action, he would always prefer to take the risk of intervention rather than leave the market to its own cures.[21]

Conclusion

When I started to work on this chapter, my first concern was to answer the objection I have continuously faced while presenting my contributions with Ferri that connect the subprime crisis and Minsky.[22] My intuitive answer to the recurrent objection that the crisis did not involve firms, but households and/or financial intermediaries, was that the theory of two prices (namely the setup based upon the notion of borrower's and lender's risk) can be quite easily extended (obviously with the appropriate changes in the definition of the two relevant prices) to depict the behavior of households, banks, other financial intermediaries, and government. In my view, even if not explicitly developed, the FIH already embeds the potential behavior of all relevant agents. Personally, during these recent years, I did not practically pursue the development of the intuition, because I thought that such a "simple" exercise would not have received any attention. As I turned to writing this chapter, however, the exercise proved to be more demanding than expected; but more important (at least to me), it became less urgent with respect to the other matters I decided to deal with in the chapter. In a sense, I preferred to serve the vision instead of being slave to the detail.

Although the literature examined in the chapter has adopted different attitudes towards the question posed in the title, the arguments presented in the critical analysis reveal that part of this contrast may be reconciled, leading to fruitful enhancements. At certain points, it also shows that part of the contrast relates to an excessively reductionist interpretation of Minsky's work, rather than to the limitations of the FIH itself.

The development of a dynamic discrete time/type model incorporating a limited number of varieties of agents (such as the Minskian triad of hedge, speculative, and Ponzi) that integrate the issues raised by Vercelli (2011) is a suggestion for future research, and it is conceived as a tool capable of taking into consideration the profound difference existing between heterogeneity and complexity.[23]

The issue of the Minsky moment appears related not simply to the FIH, but to the search for a new paradigm which does not just encompass a false dichotomy already acknowledged and, at last, widely accepted: the independence between the real and financial sides of the economy. It also calls for the overcoming of other resistant dichotomy myths of conventional theorizing: that is, the separation between cycles and growth, giving rise to an illusory idea that there exists a stable equilibrium path that the economy may follow independent of cyclical vicissitudes; and the separation between efficiency and equity, giving rise to the illusion that policy authorities can first take care of allocation, and then solve the problems of social justice, or they can first face financial exuberance and then address the issues of high unemployment or poverty. Such themes are part of the original full research program pursued by Minsky in his own life, but which still cry out for a complete recognition.

My last consideration borrows Reinert's (2009) argument, on the parallelism between economic dynamics and the evolution of economic science (and method). The attention to diversity, which, applied to economic units, implies that Ponzi units are neither evil nor anomalies, but a distinctive useful analytical category, also evokes the parallel need that even inside the body of economic science one may allow the existence of different kinds of "species." In economic science, the obvious counterparts to Ponzi units are the "men of vision" – those who extend our horizons, having the courage to venture in the darkness, over the boundaries set by conventional thinking and established knowledge.[24]

Notes

1 For a historical account of the first appearance of the term and its use, see among others, Vercelli (2011) and Bellofiore and Halevi (2011, pp. 23–4).
2 See Dymski and Pollin (1992) for an account and explanation.
3 See as examples Yellen (2009) and Lahart (2007).
4 The exercise is similar in scope to the one pursued by Assenza, Delli Gatti, and Gallegati (2010), but the arguments and the implications are fairly different.
5 The issue of the relevance and interpretation of FIH is obviously not simply related to the recent subprime crisis; furthermore, many authors addressed the issue well before 2007. To mention a few examples, from different schools of thought: Arestis, Bellofiore, Davidson, Dimsky, Fazzari, Ferri, Glickman, Kregel, Papadimitriou, Toporowski, Wray, Whalen . . . I don't mean to deny the value of any of these contributions; they simply do not fall into the specific question selected for consideration in this chapter.
6 For example, if you compare Bellofiore and Halevi (2011) and Wray (2009), you see that in Bellofiore and Halevi, the "moment" which is not considered a true Minsky moment is the subprime crisis of 2007; while the "moment" for Wray, which *is* a Minsky moment, is a process that started basically 10 years before, which he calls the "crisis of money manager-capitalism."
7 This paper was first published in 2009 as a working paper of the Levy Economics Institute.
8 Other relevant complexities are underlined by Vercelli (2011), an issue that will be examined later in the chapter.
9 I put Toporowski in this set, and not in the next, as my personal impression is that his attitude towards the Minskian perspective is critical, but overall "favorable," in the sense that his own view of economic dynamics is somehow closer to Minsky (the connection is probably the common Kaleckian influence). The same kind of reasoning is applied (with opposite consequences) for Bellofiore and Halevi (where a common Schumpeter influence does not overcome a Marxist influence specific to these authors).
10 See Minsky (1989a, 1989b, 1991).
11 See Minsky (1964, p. 175).
12 See Minsky (1980, 1982, 1984).
13 These conditions are differently stated, but basically the same in Variato (2001); see also Bellofiore and Ferri (2001).
14 See also Minsky (1977, 1986a, 1995).
15 See also Vercelli (2011) and Minsky (1991, 1995).
16 The same point also stated in Minsky (1964).
17 The theory of two prices implies a violation of the Modigliani and Miller theorem.
18 See Nasica (2010).
19 See also Minsky (1991, 1995) and Minsky and Vaughan (1990).
20 See Cimoli, Dosi, and Stiglitz (2009).
21 See Minsky (1971, 1989b, 1994) and Minsky and Whalen (1997).
22 I am referring to Ferri and Variato (2010a, 2010b), and to the objection that the subprime crisis was not coherent with the core of the FIH.

23 Ferri and Variato (2010a, 2010b) can be viewed as attempt in this direction.
24 By the way, at the moment, most of the men of vision, as Ponzi units, have disappeared. If both the parable of the FIH and Reinert's argument are right, we have to cheer, as this is the signal that an "upward swing" in economic science is imminent.

References

Assenza, T., D. Delli Gatti, and M. Gallegati (2010). Financial instability and agents' heterogeneity: a post Minskian research agenda. In D. B. Papadimitriou and L. R. Wray, eds., *The Elgar Companion to Hyman Minsky*, Cheltenham, UK, and Northampton, MA: Edward Elgar, pp. 182–205.

Barbera, R. J. and C. L. Weise (2010). It's the right moment to embrace the Minsky model. In D. B. Papadimitriou and L. R. Wray, eds., *The Elgar Companion to Hyman Minsky*, Cheltenham, UK, and Northampton, MA: Edward Elgar, pp. 134–52.

Behlul, T. (2011). Was it really a Minsky moment? *Journal of Post Keynesian Economics*, 34, 137–57.

Bellofiore, R. and P. Ferri (2001). Introduction: "things fall apart, the centre cannot hold." In R. Bellofiore and P. Ferri, eds., *Financial Keynesianism and Market Instability*, Vol. I of *The Economic Legacy of Hyman Minsky*, Cheltenham, UK, and Northampton, MA: Edward Elgar, pp. 1–30.

Bellofiore, R. and J. Halevi (2011). A Minsky moment? The subprime crisis and the "new" capitalism. In C. Gnos and L.-P. Rochon, eds., *Money and Macroeconomic Policy: A Post-Keynesian Approach*, Cheltenham, UK, and Northampton, MA: Edward Elgar, pp. 13–32.

Cimoli, M., G. Dosi, and J. Stiglitz (2009). The past and future of policies for industrial development. In M. Cimoli, G. Dosi, and J. Stiglitz, eds., *Industrial Policies and Development: The Political Economy of Capabilities Accumulation*, Oxford: Oxford University Press, pp. 1–18.

Davidson, P. (2008). Is the current financial distress caused by the subprime mortgage crisis a Minsky moment? or is it the result of attempting to securitize illiquid noncommercial mortgage loans? *Journal of Post Keynesian Economics*, 30, 669–76.

De Antoni, E. (2010). Minsky, Keynes, and financial instability: the recent subprime crisis, *International Journal of Political Economy*, 39, 10–25.

Dymski, G. (2010). A spatial approach to asset bubbles and Minsky crises. In D. B. Papadimitriou and L. R. Wray, eds., *The Elgar Companion to Hyman Minsky*. Cheltenham, UK, and Northampton, MA: Edward Elgar, pp. 222–45.

Dymski, G. and R. Pollin (1992). Hyman Minsky as hedgehog: the power of the Wall Street Paradigm in financial conditions and macroeconomic performance. In S. Fazzari and D. Papadimitriou, eds., *Essays in Honor of Hyman P. Minsky*, Armonk, NY/London: Sharpe.

Erturk, K. and G. Ozgur (2009). What is Minsky all about, anyway? *Real-World Economics Review*, 50, 3–15.

Erturk, K. and G. Ozgur (2010). A Minsky moment, or not? In G. Fontana, J. McCombie, and M. Sawyer, eds., *Macroeconomics, Finance and Money: Essays in Honour of Philip Arestis*, New York: St. Martin's Press/Palgrave Macmillan, pp. 209–23.

Ferri, P. (2010). Growth cycles and the Financial Instability Hypothesis (FIH). In D. B. Papadimitriou and L. R. Wray, eds., *The Elgar Companion to Hyman Minsky*, Cheltenham, UK, and Northampton, MA: Edward Elgar, pp. 206–21.

Ferri, P. (2011). *Macroeconomics of Growth Cycles and Financial Instability*, Cheltenham, UK, and Northampton, MA: Edward Elgar.

Ferri, P. and H. P. Minsky (1992). Market processes and thwarting systems. *Structural Change and Economic Dynamics*, 3, 79–91.

Ferri, P. and A. M. Variato (2010a). Financial fragility, the Minskian triad, and economic dynamics, *International Journal of Political Economy*, 39, 70–82.

Ferri, P. and A. M. Variato (2010b). Growth cycles, the Financial Instability Hypothesis and evolutionary expectations, *Economic Research*, 16, 297–310.Galbraith, J. K. and D. M. Sastre (2010). The generalized "Minsky moment." In D. B. Papadimitriou and L. R. Wray, eds., *The Elgar Companion to Hyman Minsky*, Cheltenham, UK, and Northampton, MA: Edward Elgar, pp. 263–75.

Henry, L. (2009). One huge "Minsky moment": lessons from the financial crisis, *Social and Economic Studies*, 58, 77–89.

Kregel, J. (2008). Minsky's cushions of safety: systemic risk and the crisis in the US sub-prime mortgage market, *Levy Economics Institute Public Policy Briefs*, no. 93, Annandale-on-Hudson, NY.

Kregel, J. (2010a). What would Minsky have thought of the mortgage crisis? In D. B. Papadimitriou and L. R. Wray, eds., *The Elgar Companion to Hyman Minsky*, Cheltenham, UK, and Northampton, MA: Edward Elgar, pp. 31–46.

Kregel, J. (2010b). Is this the Minsky moment for reform of financial regulation? *Levy Economics Institute Working Papers*, no. 586, Annandale-on-Hudson, NY.

Lahart, J. (2007). "In time of tumult, obscure economist gains currency – Mr. Minsky long argued markets were crisis prone; his 'moment' has arrived," *Wall Street Journal*, August 18.

Minsky, H. P. (1964). Longer waves in financial relations: financial factors in the more severe depressions, *American Economic Review*, 54, 324–35.

Minsky, H. P. (1977). Banking and a fragile financial environment, *Journal of Portfolio Management*, 3, 16–22.

Minsky, H. P. (1980). Money, financial markets, and the coherence of a market economy, *Journal of Post Keynesian Economics*, 3, 21–31.

Minsky, H. P. (1982). *Can It Happen Again? Essays on Instability and Finance*, New York: M. E. Sharpe.

Minsky, H. P. (1986a). *Stabilizing an Unstable Economy*, New Haven and London: Yale University Press.

Minsky, H. P. (1986b). The evolution of financial institutions and the performance of the economy, *Journal of Economic Issues*, 20, 345–53.

Minsky, H. P. (1989a). Financial crises and the evolution of capitalism: the crash of '87 – what does it mean? In M. Gottdiener and N. Komninos, eds., *Capitalist Development and Crisis Theory: Accumulation, Regulation and Spatial Restructuring*, New York: St. Martin's Press, pp. 391–403.

Minsky, H. P. (1989b). The macroeconomic safety net: does it need to be improved? In H. P. Gray, ed., *The Modern International Environment*, Greenwich, CT, and London: JAI, pp. 17–27.

Minsky, H. P. (1991). Financial crises: systemic or idiosyncratic, *Levy Economics Institute Working Papers*, no. 51, Annandale-on-Hudson, NY.

Minsky, H. P. (1995). Financial factors in the economics of capitalism, *Journal of Financial Services Research*, 9, 197–208.

Minsky, H. P. (2013). *Ending Poverty: Jobs not Welfare*, Annandale on-Hudson, NY: Levy Economics Institute of Bard College.

Minsky, H. P. and M. D. Vaughan (1990). Debt and business cycles, *Business Economics*, 25, 23–8.

Minsky, H. P. and C. J. Whalen (1997). Economic insecurity and the institutional prerequisites for successful capitalism, *Journal of Post Keynesian Economics*, 19, 155–70.

Nasica, E. (2010). Rational and innovative behaviors at the core of financial crises: banking in Minsky's theory, in D. B. Papadimitriou and L. R. Wray, eds., *The Elgar Companion to Hyman Minsky*, Cheltenham, UK, and Northampton, MA: Edward Elgar, pp. 100–15.

Papadimitriou, D. B. and L. R. Wray (1999). Minsky's analysis of financial capitalism, *Levy Economics Institute Working Papers*, no. 275, Annandale-on-Hudson, NY.

Papadimitriou, D. B. and L. R. Wray, eds. 2010. *The Elgar Companion to Hyman Minsky*, Cheltenham, UK, and Northampton, MA: Edward Elgar.

Prychitko, D. L. (2010). Competing explanations of the Minsky moment: the financial instability hypothesis in light of Austrian theory, *Review of Austrian Economics*, 23, 199–221.

Reinert, E. (2009). The terrible simplifiers: common origins of financial crises and persistent poverty in economic theory and the new "1848 moment," *United Nations DESA Working Papers*, no. 88, Annandale-on-Hudson, NY.

Toporowski, J. (2005). *Theories of Financial Disturbance*, Cheltenham, UK, and Northampton, MA: Edward Elgar.

Toporowski, J. (2010). Henry Simons and the other Minsky moment, *Studi e Note di Economia*, 15, 363–8.

Tymoigne, E. (2006). The Mynskian system, part I: properties of the Minskian analysis and how to theorize and model a monetary production economy, *Levy Economics Institute Working Papers*, no. 452, Annandale-on-Hudson, NY.

Variato, A. M. (2001). Hyman Minsky: what kind of (post-)Keynesian? In R. Bellofiore and P. Ferri, eds., *Financial Keynesianism and Market Instability*, Vol. I of *The Economic Legacy of Hyman Minsky*, Cheltenham, UK, and Northampton, MA: Edward Elgar, pp. 75–105.

Vercelli, A. (2010). Minsky moments, Russell chickens and grey swans: the methodological puzzles of financial instability analysis. In D. Tavasci and J. Toporowski, eds., *Minsky, Crisis and Development*, New York: St. Martin's Press, Palgrave Macmillan, pp. 15–31.

Vercelli, A. (2011). A perspective on Minsky moments: revisiting the core of the financial instability hypothesis, *Review of Political Economy*, 23, 49–67.

Whalen, C. (2008a). Understanding the credit crunch as a Minsky moment, *Challenge*, 51, 91–109.

Whalen, C. (2008b). A Minsky moment: reflections on Hyman P. Minsky (1919–1996), *Journal of Economic Issues*, 42, 249–53.

Wray, L. R. (2009). The rise and fall of money manager capitalism: a Minskian approach, *Cambridge Journal of Economics*, 33, 807–28.

Wray, L. R. (2011). Minsky's money manager capitalism and the global financial crisis, *International Journal of Political Economy*, 40, 5–20.

Yellen, J. L. (2009). A Minsky meltdown: lessons for central bankers, 18th Annual Hyman P. Minsky Conference on the State of the US and World Economies, Levy Economics Institute, Annandale-on-Hudson, NY.

3 Are macroeconomic models with ceilings and floors useful in understanding the Great Recession?

Steven M. Fazzari and Edward Greenberg

At a time when most mainstream economic theory modeled macroeconomic growth as following a stable equilibrium path, several decades of research by Piero Ferri, first begun with the late Hyman Minsky and then continued with a number of other co-authors, has explored the role of dynamic instability in explaining the performance of developed economies over the "medium run" – time periods of several years to roughly a decade. Many economists reject instability as unrealistic because real-world developed economies do not seem to exhibit explosive dynamics. But instability can be constrained by "thwarting mechanisms" that limit empirically unrealistic dynamics. This approach derives originally from the research in the 1950s of John Hicks and Hyman Minsky. Both Hicks and Minsky explained how economic structures create floors and ceilings that contain unstable macroeconomic dynamics

For much of Ferri's career, the study of fundamental macroeconomic instability may have seemed out of step with empirical reality. In the US, the primary laboratory for testing macroeconomic ideas, as well as in other developed countries, economic volatility seemed to decline from the mid-1980s onwards in what became known as the "Great Moderation." While Ferri and his co-authors explored instability, mainstream macroeconomics occupied itself with construction of the "new consensus" models that emphasized equilibrium-seeking behavior of market economies where the only policy challenge was to design monetary policy to enhance the inherent stabilizing forces.

The timeline of macroeconomic history has changed dramatically in the past few years. The Great Recession, beginning in the US in late 2007, and the associated global financial crisis that reached its most dramatic moments after the failure of the venerable Wall Street firm Lehmann Brothers in September, 2008, is the most significant macroeconomic event of the post-war period. US payroll employment, which had usually declined by between 1 and 2 percentage points in prior post-war recessions, plummeted by more than 6 percent in 2008 and 2009. This disruption spread quickly around the globe. Despite mainstream forecasts that a strong bounce-back would soon follow such a deep decline, the recovery has been painfully slow, with US employment still below its pre-recession peak more than 6 years after the recession began. Although the output losses and unemployment in this event are dwarfed by the disaster of the 1930s, its persistence makes it seem more like a "contained depression" than the garden-variety recession.[1]

This chapter considers how the many contributions of Piero Ferri's research on macroeconomic instability can guide our understanding of the historical events associated with the Great Recession. In the next section, we trace the sources of fundamental macroeconomic instability through multiplier–accelerator models, Minsky's early models of financial instability, and the development of these ideas in the work of Ferri and his co-authors. This section also summarizes the "thwarting mechanisms" developed in the work of Ferri and Minsky, which contain the fundamental instability of short-run dynamics. These mechanisms begin from the idea of macroeconomic "floors and ceilings," pioneered by Ferri's dissertation supervisor at Oxford, Sir John Hicks. While the ceiling, in particular, could arise from physical resource constraints, the ideas evolved to consider institutional and behavioral sources that could contain instability. Ferri's work with Minsky linked containment mechanisms to the world of finance, consistent with Minsky's lifelong focus on the interaction between finance and macroeconomics.

In the third section, we apply the theoretical contributions of Ferri and his co-authors to consider the effectiveness of this class of models for understanding the dramatic history of the Great Recession and the associated financial crisis. Although all theoretical perspectives abstract from many details and cannot track historical events perfectly, we nonetheless conclude that Ferri's body of work provides useful insights for understanding both the macroeconomics that created the conditions for the Great Recession and the stagnant aftermath that has followed. We conclude by comparing different kinds of macroeconomic model and how they conform to recent history.

Sources of macroeconomic instability and containment

Before turning to the contributions of Ferri and co-authors, it is useful to place them in the context of their predecessors. Shortly after Keynes's *General Theory* recognized macroeconomics as an area that should be studied in its own right, two important developments occurred: the empirical work of Tinbergen (1939) and the theoretical work of Harrod (1948) and Samuelson (1939a, 1939b). All three took demand-led dynamics as their basic context and examined interrelationships between income and investment as the key to understanding fluctuations. Much of the development of macroeconomics from then until the early 1970s can be considered as refinements of these ideas. Indeed, the influence of the ideas continues to the present: as examples, the large-scale empirical macro models of Ray Fair and Macroeconomic Advisers are Tinbergen-type models embodying the improvements in computer power and econometrics that have taken place over the years, and mathematically sophisticated models that focus on income and investment continue to be studied, for example, in Part IV of this volume. Theoretical modeling is the main subject of this section, although empirical models are briefly mentioned below. Of particular interest in the history of these models is their increasing emphasis on the financial sector. This theme is elaborated in the discussion that follows.

Hicks

For our purposes, the primary antecedent of Ferri's work comes from Hicks through Minsky. Hicks, in *A Contribution to the Theory of the Trade Cycle* (1950), acknowledges Harrod, for emphasizing a growing economy and for noticing that reasonable coefficient values predict a more unstable economy than we witness, and acknowledges Samuelson, for his formalization. Hicks's primary goal is to explain why the wild swings in income that can appear for certain parameter values in Samuelson's model are not usually observed. He argues that physical and/or monetary constraints prevent the economy from exploding in the upward direction and that the asymmetry between induced investment and disinvestment can act as a floor. It is important to note the role of formal modeling in Hicks's approach. Rather than analyzing in detail only the implications of the formal model, he uses it as a framework on which to add his understanding of how economies develop. We next look more closely at Hicks's work.

In Chapter VIII, "The cycle in outline," Hicks assumes that the ceiling is determined by a scarcity of employable resources, although he initially makes a weaker assumption, ascribed to Keynes, that at some point output becomes "inelastic in response to an increase in effective demand." This may occur if bottlenecks arise in some sectors before the system runs into absolute resource constraints. He is particularly interested in the possibility that resources for producing real investment may reach a ceiling before consumption expenditures peak, and the resulting decline in investment expenditures will ultimately lead to a decline in consumption and income. Hicks also considers the possibility that the cycle turns around without bumping into the ceiling, which can occur if coefficient values imply complex roots that are small enough to prevent large departures from the steady state.

But what happens if the economy bumps into the ceiling of full employment? In Chapter X, Hicks reminds us of Keynes's view: "when an uncontrolled economy reaches a position of full employment . . . , it will break into a boundless inflation of wages and prices, unless the inflation is counteracted by monetary policy." Even without explicit monetary policy intervention, according to Keynes, a sufficient rise in interest rates might prevent the boom from running away. The emphasis on monetary factors is later developed in Minsky's work, further generalized to financial factors more broadly. Hicks is concerned that monetary policy may not operate at exactly the right level. He allows that "the operative ceiling may be a monetary ceiling; the real ceiling, on which we have relied for the explanation of the downswing, looks like being relatively ineffective." He thinks lags in price and wage adjustments may mitigate the effect of monetary factors and goes on to consider the likely movement of prices of consumptions goods relative to investment goods. This is an example of Hicks adding his own interpretation of economic events to the formal model, which does not model prices explicitly.

As another example of thinking outside the box of the formal model, he emphasizes the role of the financial system in creating a serious depression. On p. 160, Hicks sketches out a scenario after the real economy hits the ceiling:

> Output then begins to fall, and effective demand to fall; sales become difficult and fixed costs oppressive; the rate of bankruptcy rises; all these things are inevitable even in the absence of monetary strain, but they breed conditions in which there is bound to be a sharp rise in liquidity preference. This rise in liquidity preference is itself the monetary reaction, or what, in common speech, is called the crisis. Thus even a real downturn is almost certain to be accompanied by monetary crisis; and the monetary deflation is an additional contractionary force, of which pure accelerator theory has taken no account, and which must tend to aggravate the depression.

In the same vein, Hicks distinguishes (pp. 162–3) between the over-extension of trade credit compared to banking credit, arguing that collapse of trade credit causes limited harm if the reserves of the banking system are adequate. In the presence of a sound banking system, central banks can mitigate the crisis. "Really catastrophic depression is most unlikely to occur as a result of the simple operation of the real accelerator mechanism; it is likely to occur when there is profound monetary instability – when the rot in the monetary system goes very deep." These ideas, of course, become central in the work of Minsky and Ferri. In a footnote (p. 163), the Great Depression of 1930–4 is blamed on a weak monetary system that can be traced to the dislocations occurring from World War I, particularly the weakness of the Bank of England and of the Reichsbank.

To contain the economy on the downside, Hicks postulates (in Chapter VIII) a floor due to the presence of autonomous investment that grows at the equilibrium rate of growth. He briefly considers the possibility of active monetary and fiscal policy, and concludes (p. 168) with the thought that a policy "of monetary reform to re-establish monetary security, combined with a moderate use of public investment and fiscal controls, designed to quieten, but hardly to eliminate the real cycle" is the "alternative alone which holds out Hope."

Thus, from Hicks we obtain the prediction that real dynamics of the multiplier–accelerator process can cause macroeconomic instability. But he does not predict an exploding system. Rather, he envisions an economy that cycles between ceilings and floors that arise from de-centralized real aspects of the economy (such as resource constraints and autonomous investment), monetary/financial relations, as well as fiscal policy intervention.

Minsky

In two important papers that appeared in the late 1950s, Minsky elaborates Hicks's ceilings and floors approach. These papers represent an early stage in Minsky's intellectual development, although they point to his later emphasis on the importance of the financial system in the modern economy – an idea which is developed further by Ferri.

Minsky (1957) is very explicit about the effects of money supply and velocity, but monetary variables are not directly specified in the model. Instead, he talks about their effect on the coefficient of the accelerator relationship, which, in turn, affects nominal income, implying that price levels may change. Because of the need to finance investment expenditures, which may come from equity or debt, Minsky argues that the value of the accelerator coefficient depends on the interest rate and the structure of firms' balance sheets, the latter because of the financial risk associated with high debt/equity ratios or low cash holdings. Although risk and interest rates are not directly part of the model, it is interesting to note that these considerations are important because of their influence on the accelerator coefficient. In his later contributions, these considerations become central. We have noted above that Hicks also emphasizes the importance of the financial markets on the effects of ceilings and floors.

Minsky (1957, p. 867) proceeds by examining the effect of money in the sense of quantity (*M*) and velocity (*V*) in four stylized cases: *M* and *V* constant, only *V* changes, only *M* changes, *M* and *V* change. In the first case, the interest rate changes immediately to equate saving and investment, which prevents the occurrence of an accelerator–multiplier cycle. In the second case, he concludes that a ceiling in velocity, which is related to liquidity preference, creates a ceiling on income:

> Ignoring any effects that the interest-rate and balance-sheet changes accompanying velocity increases have upon the accelerator coefficient, a monetary system with a constant quantity of money may impose a ceiling to money income. This ceiling is not determined by full employment or by the capacity of the investment goods industries; it is determined by the limited ability of changes in velocity to finance investment. Symmetrically if a minimum velocity exists, a floor to money income exists. However the floor is not entirely symmetrical with the ceiling, and in this paper the lower turning point is essentially unexplained.

Minsky (1957, p. 875) identifies situations in which an explosive situation may develop:

> Therefore, at least two monetary situations allow full scope to an explosive accelerator process: the Keynesian liquidity trap and an infinitely elastic money supply. It is perhaps no accident that the emphasis upon "real" floors and ceilings as causes of the nonlinearity of the accelerator coefficient occurred at a time when the high volume of government bonds outstanding and their support by central banks made the money supply in fact infinitely elastic. An era of tight money on the other hand naturally leads to an examination of the monetary prerequisites for the operation of the accelerator phenomena.

Finally, Minsky introduces the idea that hitting a ceiling or floor may be interpreted as changing the initial conditions of the solution to the Samuelson-type second-order difference equation that is employed. This device is exploited intensively in Minsky (1959), which relies much more than the 1957 paper on formal mathematical analysis.

In an apparent return to the original Hicksian formulation, Minsky (1959, p. 134) assumes that the primary determinants of the ceiling and floor are physical: "there exists an exogenously determined ceiling to income which depends upon population growth and technological change, and which does not depend upon the existing capital stock." And "there exists a maximum possible amount of net disinvestment, which depends upon the capital stock and a technologically determined depreciation rate. The consumption function is a determinant of aggregate demand, whereas the ceiling and floor to income are determinants of aggregate supply." But Minsky relaxes the reliance on physical constraints by allowing the constant in the consumption function α_0, to depend on past incomes, where the consumption function is a linear relationship between current and lagged consumption. This dependence is justified on two grounds: a Duesenberry-type ratchet effect in consumption and a Tobin–Pigou type of asset consumption relation. In contrast to later developments in his thinking, changes in the relative prices of income and wealth are considered to be exogenous factors. In Minsky's (1959, p. 134) words:

> As the accelerator–multiplier apparatus is here interpreted, it is simpler to consider changes in the relative prices of income and wealth as exogenous factors which influence the generation of aggregate demand by affecting α_0. Therefore, in the formal model, α_0 will be assumed to depend upon the previous peak income. In interpreting events, any development which raises (lowers) the ratio of consuming units' wealth to income will tend to increase (decrease) α_0. In more concrete terms, a large increase in the ratio of monetary assets to income (such as took place during World War II) will tend to raise α_0, whereas a large fall in the market price of assets relative to income (such as took place in the fall of 1929) will tend to lower α_0. It will be shown that by feeding financial and money market developments into the formal model through the ratchet in the consumption function, booms and depressions of varying amplitude and length can be generated.

By 1960, therefore, ceiling–floor models had been incorporated into the original Samuelson version of the accelerator–multiplier model by Hicks and Minsky. Although physical constraints were possible reasons for such constraints, both Hicks and Minsky emphasized the importance of monetary and more general financial factors in the generation of cycles. Both thought of these factors as exogenously changing coefficients in the formal model, foreshadowing Minsky's and Ferri's later attempts to endogenize these factors.

Ferri and Minsky

In this section, we discuss three papers by Ferri and Minsky (1984, 1989, 1992) that put financial and monetary considerations front and center and that relegate formal models to supporting roles.

Ferri and Minsky (1984) are concerned with determination of employment and prices in a period characterized by stagflation. It introduces a second-order difference equation, but it is not of the accelerator–multiplier variety. Instead, the model deals with the dynamics of wages and prices, and how aggregate relations determine the set of possible values of price and employment. Behind this model is a vision of the economy in which firms require validation that an investment will pay off. Such validation comes from market power that generates profit flows, and the market power is used to control the mark-up on unit labor costs. Wages are determined by bargaining between firms and labor unions. The price and employment outcomes generated by the model are limited by ceilings and floors that arise from the actions of big government and the central bank through their fiscal and policy actions. In this formulation, we again see an emphasis on the financial side of the economy. In addition, we see the seed of the idea that complex market economies are inherently prone to explosive behavior, which must be controlled by institutional arrangements and policy interventions.

Ferri and Minsky (1989) is an agenda for how post-Keynesians should respond to the loss of faith in the IS–LM synthesis as an appropriate theory for the understanding of capitalist economies and, therefore, for the formulation of economic policy. Of particular concern in the IS–LM formulation is a simplistic view of money markets. They define the problems that confront political economy as being twofold: 1) understanding the dynamics of a capitalist economy in which financial, product, and labor markets are both complex and evolving, and from which explosive growth and implosive dynamics are likely to be observed; and 2) the development of policies to thwart such dynamics and sustain growth in employment and income and stable prices.

In their view, the IS–LM synthesis has been replaced by the new Keynesian economics, rather than by post-Keynesian principles. The former has been successful as a critique of IS–LM, but is not considered a good basis for research going forward. Much of the article is concerned with fleshing out these ideas. We concentrate on only a few of their points.

One important idea has to do with long-term investment decisions that are financed partly by debts. This property of a capitalist economy introduces interactions between bankers and business people, where bets "are placed every day on the basis of imperfect, private and therefore asymmetric information, i.e. in conditions of uncertainty." These considerations were swept under the rug both in the IS–LM synthesis and in new Keynesian thinking. Ferri and Minsky regard these characteristics of modern capitalist economies as central to the way in which they behave. Serious economic repercussions arise if expected profits are insufficient to cover the debt incurred to finance investment, and the retrenchment that follows worsens profit expectations. Downward wages and wage flexibility make matters worse because deflation further reduces profits and discourages investment. Many aspects of these dynamics are reflected in asset prices, which are highly dependent on expectations and the perceived need for liquidity. In a remarkably prescient thought, they say (Ferri and Minsky, 1989, pp. 133–4):

> Liquidity preference is in the first instance a theory of asset prices and of how present effective demand is linked to present expectations of what the future

> will bring, but is ultimately an explanation of why instability is a natural characteristic of financially sophisticated economies. This is so because financial intermediaries are vulnerable to being in a position where they need to make position by selling out positions.

We shall see below how this feature of capitalist economies is crucial to understanding the Great Recession.

Although the bulk of their paper eschews equations and formalism, there is a brief mention of dynamic processes modeled in terms of initial conditions and roots of polynomial equations. The possibility that such systems may generate chaotic or other undesirable states leads to interventions and constraints – the ceilings and floors that we have been discussing. But, unlike in the earlier papers, there is no attempt to build such a model, because of their belief that change is inevitable as an economy proceeds through time. Institutional changes will take place, making economic processes irreversible. The ways in which governments intervene in a given situation change, depending on the political process. Agents change their behavior as they adapt to constraints imposed by authorities.

Ferri and Minsky (1992) now view the ceiling-and-floor version of the accelerator–multiplier model as a simple prototype model. Rather than specify a model in detail, they argue in this paper that a realistic model of a modern economy – characterized by inter-temporal linkages and the endogenous determination of expectations – will be a complex, time-dependent system that can generate unstable behavior, which rarely becomes explosive. Their reading of economic history in the period before 1992 suggests that explosive behavior was not often observed, because of the presence of "thwarting" mechanisms, which are institutions and interventions that interrupt the endogenous process of the economy and set new initial conditions to offset the economy's natural tendency to display extreme behavior. Thus, the original accelerator–multiplier theory, augmented by ceilings and floors and reinterpreted as changes in initial conditions, has evolved into an unspecified but highly nonlinear system, which, on the evidence of history, will spin out of control in the absence of interventions of various sorts. In their words (Ferri and Minsky, 1992, p. 84), "The piece-wise linear model of business cycles based upon ceilings and floors can be construed as a metaphor for the interplay between market valuations and outcomes, on the one hand, and the impact of the thwarting forces, on the other."

The models that are implied by these considerations are far more complex than any that have been proposed. Rather than start from a utility-maximizing consumer, Ferri and Minsky (1989, p. 79) argue that "in capitalist economies the core decision makers are profit seeking businessmen and bankers." At any given time, the decisions of firms, banks, consumers, and other decision-makers reflect many institutional, historical, and economic facts, including the capital assets and financial commitments they have previously made. In addition, financial and other markets are constantly evolving in ways that are largely unpredictable. The idea that institutional and historical factors cannot be neglected is at variance with mainstream models that neglect such factors in favor of an abstract, institution-free setting. As we discuss later, these factors loomed large in the period leading to the Great Recession.

Ferri and Minsky provide three examples of thwarting forces: labor market institutions, uses of market power, and central bank mechanisms. With respect to the first of these, they refer to research by Piore and Sabel (1985), who argue that, in the US after World War II, a consensus developed that wages should increase to reflect productivity gains and inflation. This increase in wages allowed consumption expenditures to grow, which resulted in a tranquil economy. Monetary policy during this period accommodated the consensus. The system broke down in 1968–9 as a result of wage increases in excess of the consensus, and the accommodative monetary policy led to inflation.

Market power, the second example of a thwarting force, encourages investment in long-lived assets because it gives firms a reason to believe that they will have the funds to pay their creditors. As a result, they are willing to undertake the investment, which adds to aggregate demand. An alternative mechanism – sufficiently high aggregate demand –would have the same effect, but financial markets see market power as a more convincing guarantor of the ability to pay than the possibility that actions will be taken to assure sufficient aggregate demand. Ferri and Minsky note that this market power became less of a factor with the growth in international trade and the erosion of market power. Moreover, in other circumstances, market power may be conducive to inflation.

The third example of a thwarting mechanism is central bank intervention as the lender of last resort. Ferri and Minsky provide a number of examples in the US and in other countries. Little more need be said about this mechanism in view of the prominent role of the US central bank in the Great Recession, as will be discussed in the next section.

Economic institutions can change rapidly and in unpredictable ways: for example, the proliferation of such new instruments as collateralized debt obligations and credit default swaps. These changes are a challenge to central bankers and fiscal policy authorities, who have the task of designing and implementing some of the thwarting forces. Moreover, agents will not necessarily accept constraints designed to limit their behavior. Instead, they will adapt their behavior to avoid restrictions, thereby undermining the thwarting forces and setting the stage for an unstable economic path. In addition and paradoxically, a tranquil period of economic growth can encourage excessive risk taking, which in turn can lead to great instability. The Great Recession provides examples of all of these, as we discuss below.

We conclude this section with some reflections on the role of economic models in understanding economic events and in guiding policy decisions. We have seen in this section the evolution of economic models from the simple accelerator–multiplier model of Samuelson, the ceiling-and-floor version of Hicks, and Minsky's reinterpretation of the latter. Both Hicks and Minsky do not stop at exploring the formal properties of the model; instead, they consider aspects of the real world, in addition to the models, that enhance their usefulness.

One way to interpret the work of Ferri and Minsky is that formal modeling is futile in view of the constantly changing nature of economic institutions.

Interventions that help in one setting will aggravate bad situations in other settings. Decision-makers will constantly take steps to maintain their profitability and will always be one step (or more) ahead of the authorities, which must react under constraints of their own – for example, insufficient information and an uncooperative legislature. Although empirical macro models may provide useful information in the short term, they cannot be expected to perform well over longer horizons unless they are continually tweaked to reflect some of the more obvious changes. The period leading up to the Great Recession was a period of rapid institutional changes, which were not readily incorporated into such models. And theoretical models, with their paucity of institutional detail, were even more unable to cope.

A modeling possibility that we have not discussed is the inclusion of random disturbances in both empirical and theoretical models. These allow outcomes that are different from those predicted by the model; in the case of additive disturbances, the predictions can be regarded as expected values of random variables. Whether such disturbances can adequately capture the changes in the economy that we have been discussing is not clear. On the one hand, since the changes are not easily predicted, thinking of them as random may be reasonable. On the other hand, they are not really random. An astute observer of the economy may notice them (as many warned of the housing bubble and other dangers that foreshadowed the Great Recession), and their effects are long lasting and may lead to structural changes in the model. Random disturbances add a note of realism to deterministic models, but do not readily capture long-term structural changes.

Despite these difficulties, Ferri has continued his study of dynamic models using the newest sophisticated mathematical techniques, perhaps in the hope that these can better capture the complicated nature of the real world. Some of this work, co-authored by us and others, is discussed in the next section.

The Ferri–Hicks–Minsky tradition and the Great Recession

What insights does the theoretical work of Ferri and his co-authors provide for the dynamics that led up to the economic collapse and financial crisis of 2008 and 2009? As described in the second section, the theory focuses on demand dynamics as the engine of macroeconomic growth and fluctuations, which implies that we should look for the source of instability in demand, and the most obvious demand problem associated with the recession is the collapse of the US housing market. Not only did residential construction plummet, but personal consumption expenditures fell more than in any economic crisis of the post-war period.

Sources of instability in the "Consumer Age"

If the engine of economic instability in recent years came from household demand, we must immediately face an issue in explaining the critical dynamics of the Great Recession with the framework of Ferri et al. This is because the source of demand instability in various strands of the theory comes primarily from *business* spending on capital goods to be used in the production process. The source of complex dynamics in the foundational accelerator model is business investment. Minsky, in particular, focuses almost exclusively on financial instability arising from business borrowing for capital investment. He views consumption as largely passive: magnifying fluctuations that arise initially from investment. In our co-authored work with Ferri (Fazzari, Ferri, and Greenberg, 2008, 2010), the focus of analysis and source of cyclical fluctuations is, again, business investment and its dependence on cash flow. On the surface, the models seem to be looking in the wrong place to match the Great Recession history.

A deeper look, however, changes this perspective. First, in many cases, residential construction is a business investment. Construction of rental properties follows much the same logic as industrial capital investment, driven by the expectation of future cash flows from customers. Much of single-family home construction is "on spec," motivated by the chance to sell the new unit at a profit even though there is no identified buyer at the time of construction. Second, the instability in residential construction was undeniably *financial*, consistent with the Ferri–Minsky analysis.

The basic accelerator model of business investment posits that net investment spending is determined by the change in expected output, with expectations usually proxied by an extrapolation of past output. For business investment, the foundation for such a specification is rather obvious. If production depends on the stock of capital, then net investment, which is the change in the stock of capital, is determined by the anticipated change in output, perhaps with an adjustment that accounts for any gap between current and desired capacity utilization.[2]

A similar specification for residential capital is reasonable, but its foundation is somewhat less intuitive. The most obvious analogy arises from the link between population and housing demand. People must live some place. The demand for new dwellings, residential investment, depends in part on the number of new households formed. Fluctuations in household formation probably depends to some extent on the state of the business cycle, as the desire of children to leave the parental home, marry, or purchase a home depends on job opportunities. Our view, however, is that this linkage is not the primary motivation for new housing demand, and it was not the primary reason for either the dramatic rise in US residential construction prior to the Great Recession or the historic collapse in 2008 and 2009. To the extent that residential construction has accelerator-like properties, it seems more likely that the level of residential construction is related to the *level*, rather than the change, in output. The level of output determines the level of household income. As incomes rise, more households can afford to upgrade their residence, raising the demand for newly construction housing as well as renovation and remodeling.[3] Although the specification of residential investment as a function of the level of output differs to some extent from the business investment accelerator, the practical implications for model stability are likely to be similar, especially if expectations induce lags of output into the model. The change in output and its lags cause lags in the level of output to appear in a reduced-form business investment function. The expected coefficient pattern may be somewhat different from a model based on a residential investment function that depends structurally on lags in the level of output. But the driving variables will be the same. We conclude that unstable dynamics from accelerator effects in the business investment models of Samuelson, Hicks, Minsky, and Ferri may also be relevant to residential investment, possibly helping to explain the huge residential boom that preceded the US Great Recession.

We believe, however, that the accelerator effect is not the most important source of instability in Ferri's research to explain the Great Recession and its aftermath. The link is much clearer, in our judgment, to *financial instability*. This discussion precedes Minsky and Ferri, with ideas coming from Keynes and Hicks, as discussed above. But Minsky, more than any other author, focuses on financial instability, which becomes a central theme in the work of Ferri and his co-authors. As discussed in the previous section, instability goes beyond basic quantity dynamics. The exposition of the "Minsky Cycle" usually begins after a financial crisis with relatively high levels of risk aversion among lenders and relatively strong balance sheets among potential borrowers. In this environment, decisions to extend credit are more likely to be successful. Validation of new lending, as discussed in Ferri and Minsky (1989), encourages more aggressive practices, greater lending, and more demand stimulus. Lending and spending evolve into a self-reinforcing boom that pulls output and employment up with it, but the boom is accompanied by rising financial fragility that ultimately leads to a financial crisis and recession.

While Minsky and Ferri analyze this dynamic process largely in the context of business investment, it explains the dynamics of the US housing market very well in the decades leading up to the Great Recession and the events that ultimately triggered the financial crisis. A variety of technological, institutional, and policy changes increased the credit flow to US households, especially mortgage lending. Innovations in both information technology and the ability to share electronic information made possible the individual credit score. This standardized measure improved household access to credit. It also facilitated securitization of household loans because they could now be viewed as a generic commodity rather than the outcome of a personal relationship between borrower and lender. Deregulation greatly widened access to credit cards. Tax reform initiated in 1986 eliminated deductions for household interest expenses *except* those secured by home equity. This change, perhaps unintentionally, spawned the quick emergence of home equity lines of credit, so that households could take out what were effectively second mortgages to easily finance *non-housing* expenditure. These credit lines had low costs because of both their tax benefits and the value of the collateral in the house. As a result, US homeowners could borrow very cheaply just by writing a check (and later, by a few clicks on their banks' websites). The result was a substantial upward movement in households' debt–income ratios beginning in the middle 1980s, relative to a quite stable ratio that prevailed for the previous two decades (see Cynamon, Fazzari, and Setterfield, 2013).

The effect of these structural changes, which directly increased lending to households, was complemented by a powerful indirect effect. In the effort to fight the inflation of the 1970s, the US Federal Reserve raised interest rates in the early 1980s. The nominal interest rate on 30-year fixed-rate mortgages peaked near 16 percent. The deep recession of 1980–2 broke the back of inflation and raised unemployment to the highest rates since the 1930s. Energy prices also fell and disinflation began. The result was a two-decade decline in nominal interest rates. The combination of falling interest rates, looser credit standards, and lower transactions costs in the mortgage industry initiated multiple waves of mortgage debt refinancing. With lower rates and less restrictive terms, it was easy for homeowners to increase their borrowing, and many households engaged in a regular habit of refinancing their mortgages. Of course, this practice accelerated the rise in debt ratios.

These effects were powerful engines of consumer demand and led to significant Keynesian stimulus. From 1980 through 2007, real personal consumption expenditures rose at an annual rate of 3.4 percent while all other components of demand expanded at 2.5 percent. This increase in consumer expenditures and the historic increase in household debt led Cynamon and Fazzari (2008) to label the period from the middle 1980s to the eve of the Great Recession the "Consumer Age." The US experienced strong growth relative to other developed countries, and recessions were relatively mild in what came to be known as the Great Moderation. This good macroeconomic environment, resulting in large part from household lending, validated the more aggressive financial practices and encouraged lenders and borrowers to push financial fragility even further (for example, in the rapid growth of subprime lending). These practices not only stimulated aggregate demand, but also led to a rapid boom in housing prices. The rise in collateral value further validated the household finance boom and created even more equity that could be tapped with aggressive borrowing.

This history fits very well the basic Minsky model of financial instability, even though it emerged in the household rather than the business sector. Validation justified past practices and encouraged lenders and borrowers to push the envelope of "prudence" even further. Financial fragility, however, was rising to unprecedented levels in the household sector. To paraphrase Minsky's famous description, "stability," in the form of low unemployment and relatively strong growth, was "destabilizing," as represented by the increasingly fragile financial structure. The themes emphasized by Ferri and his co-authors were playing out in the US economy.

One might ask whether the "thwarting mechanisms" discussed by Ferri and Minsky (1992) were operating during this period that set the stage for the Great Recession. Our answer is largely no, but for reasons that are consistent with the broad Minsky perspective. The most obvious containing mechanism would have been tighter financial regulation. One can imagine restrictions on what, in retrospect, seem clearly to have been Ponzi-like loans that required households to refinance at "teaser" interest rates to dodge the upward reset of debt service. Regulation was also lax, in retrospect, on the supply side of credit. There was virtually no oversight of rampant securitization and the issue of credit default swap insurance on securitized mortgage debt with no requirement for accountability or reserves. The entire "shadow banking" system seemed to operate without meaningful regulation. Perhaps the authorities *could have* reined in these excesses. But, as Minsky teaches, financial institutions innovate around regulation to pursue the high profits available in the upward swing of the financial cycle. Also, the system seemed to deliver good outcomes, despite rising financial fragility, year after year. Housing prices sky-rocketed, suggesting that the loans were based on sound collateral. Lenders were caught up in the heady profits of the boom, and they used their substantial political power to weaken the institutional restrictions that emerged from the 1930s crisis. These, they argued, were no longer needed in the brave new world of sophisticated financial models and financial risk management.

The Ferri–Minsky perspective warned that this process would not end well. Indeed, the financially driven boom came to an abrupt and dramatic end with the Great Recession and global financial crisis. The sources of this instability are clearly linked to the perspectives developed by Ferri as he learned from the master of this way of thinking, Hyman Minsky. But what economic mechanism finally did contain the boom and initiate the Great Recession? Can the end of the Consumer Age be usefully linked to some kind of ceiling, as the models discussed earlier proposed? We consider these questions next.

Triggers of the Great Recession and "ceiling" models

The most obvious source of a ceiling that would limit the upward financial instability of the Consumer Age is a resource constraint. Following Ferri's recent paper with us (Fazzari et al., 2013), the most relevant place to look is the labor market. Was the US pushing up against labor constraints that stopped the growth arising from the financial instability of the Consumer Age, described in the previous subsection? The unemployment rate prior to the beginning of the Great Recession was rather low relative to the previous three decades, hovering around 4.5 percent in late 2006 and the first half of 2007, possibly suggesting the presence of a tight labor market. Other indicators, however, do not support the view that the economy was bumping up against a labor constraint. The employment–population ratio, while up somewhat by 2007 from the low point that followed the bursting of the technology bubble and the 2001 recession, was still well below the peak it reached in the late 1990s (when there *was* some evidence of a tight labor market). Wage growth was relatively slow. The economy did not seem to be bumping up against labor constraints.

Indeed, what turned the business cycle from expansion to collapse is fairly obvious, especially with the benefit of hindsight. The Great Recession began with a housing crisis linked to the rising financial fragility of the household sector that we discussed previously. This is the classic Minsky source of a ceiling. The housing boom was self-reinforcing as more loans stimulated high demand, rising incomes, and soaring home prices. But the engine of this process was increasing financial fragility, which could not continue indefinitely. A process that becomes continuously more fragile must break at some point.

Although the official beginning of the recession was December 2007, the breaking point should probably be dated somewhat earlier. Asset prices may be the best indicator of when the cycle turns. The Case–Shiller home price index peaked in April 2006, and declined only slightly until it began to plummet in May 2007. How did this dynamic generate a financial ceiling on the housing–consumption boom of the previous years? One indicator of the rising financial fragility was the extent to which mortgage loans were based on asset values rather than on cash flows.[4] As long as home prices were rising, households could refinance and take more equity out of the home. But a moment's reflection suggests that this is the mortgage-loan equivalent of Minsky's version of Ponzi finance: lending that is validated only as long as asset prices rise. When the growth in home prices stalled, the participants in this risky practice needed to sell their houses to meet mortgage obligations. This strategy can work for isolated homeowners who receive random negative shocks. But if a large number of homeowners are simultaneously forced to sell, as occurred in 2007, the implications for home prices are disastrous. The recession followed soon after, and the default problem spilled over to Wall Street, ultimately leading to the failure of Bear Stearns, Fannie and Freddie, Lehman Brothers, AIG, and many others. In the language of Ferri and Minsky, homeowners and the intermediaries that provided housing finance were forced to "make position by selling out positions."

The proximate ceiling in this episode was financial, not physical. While this event broadly conforms to the "thwarting mechanism" perspective from Ferri–Minsky, it is less clearly linked to the resource ceiling in Ferri's recent paper with us (Fazzari et al., 2013), which interpretation suggests that we extend our model to incorporate financial effects and an explicit treatment of housing. Before we leave this topic, however, we note that resource constraints could play an indirect role in determining *when* rising financial fragility would impose a ceiling on upward financial instability. An important trigger of the housing crisis in the US was a rise in the interest rate on adjustable rate mortgages, which were a feature of many of the risky loans made in the years prior to the Great Recession. After hovering at historic lows, to that point, of near 4 percent, with occasional dips below 3.5 percent, this rate rose sharply in early 2005. The most obvious reason for this increase was the decision by the Federal Reserve in mid-2004 that the economy was recovering fast enough from the aftermath of the bursting technology bubble to begin raising the federal funds rate from historic lows to a more "neutral" level. Higher interest rates interrupted the refinancing cycle necessary to sustain the financing of much of the mortgage market, triggering first the slowdown in home prices and then the crisis itself, as discussed previously. Why did the Fed raise interest rates in this precarious situation? The answer is clear: it feared that inflation would arise because of the low and falling unemployment rate. Thus, the policy response related to a fear (possibly unjustified) that the economy would soon hit a resource constraint in the labor market.[5]

This discussion supports the view that resource constraints, or at least perceptions by policy-makers that the economy was approaching resource constraints, were relevant for the ceiling that turned the boom in housing and consumption expenditure into the Great Recession. But the mechanisms through which a resource ceiling operates were more nuanced than the capacity constraint modeled in Fazzari et al. (2013) and other related research. An elaboration of this mechanism in formal models is a useful direction for future research.

Great recession to slow recovery: what provided the floor?

The NBER business cycle dating committee declared that the US downturn that would become the Great Recession began in December 2007. Employment began to decline in March of 2008. The NBER trough occurred in June 2009, with employment beginning to grow slowly in March of 2010. From that point through early 2014, US output and employment have grown; there has been no "double dip." But the recovery has been slow, especially in the labor market, regularly under-performing mainstream forecasts for a quicker bounce-back. To complete our study of how the theoretical research of Ferri, his co-authors, and his predecessors can illuminate the forces that drove the Great Recession cyclical dynamics, we need to consider what turned the economy around. What provided the "floor," and why has the recovery been so disappointing?

The models surveyed in the second section identify a variety of economic structures that could contain downward instability. One category of mechanisms can be classified as components of autonomous demand, when that term is given a broad definition. "Autonomous" certainly does not mean constant, nor does it imply strictly exogenous. The most useful definition of autonomous demand in this context is spending that evolves independently of the current state of the economy.[6] The models propose autonomous investment and consumption as possible sources for the floor, and government spending is a particularly salient source of autonomous demand. Of course, since we cannot observe autonomous demand directly, evaluating the role played by autonomous spending in a particular historical cycle requires some detective work.

Let us begin with the possibility that autonomous investment was an important source of the demand floor that turned things around in 2009 and 2010. A quick look at the data suggests that business investment followed the cycle turning point. The trough in quarterly real GDP occurred in the second quarter of 2009, and growth was almost flat between the first and second quarters. Real non-residential business fixed investment did not hit its cyclical trough until the fourth quarter of 2009. Investment was a follower, not a leader, in the dynamics that contained the Great Recession. But this naive timing story does not eliminate the possibility that autonomous investment played a role in setting a floor for demand. Again, the problem is that autonomous demand components are not directly observable. There is no doubt that business fixed investment has a strong induced cyclical component, but there may be underlying autonomous elements as well.

An interesting idea for further research is to consider the empirical relevance of the idea from Hicks, Minsky, and Ferri that pent-up demand for capital replacement eventually turns investment around to provide a floor under collapsing demand dynamics. This theoretical proposal suggests that investment need not simply decompose into autonomous and output-induced components. The pent-up demand for investment could depend on the recent history of both output and investment in more complicated ways. A drop in output typically causes a much larger proportional drop in business investment, which certainly occurred in the Great Recession. But, as existing capital depreciates and new technologies emerge when investment spending is depressed, pressure builds up on firms to invest more *even if output is not yet growing.*

It is also interesting and perhaps somewhat surprising to look for signs of autonomous demand in the dynamics of residential construction in the Great Recession. It is entirely clear that the collapse in residential construction was a huge part of the demand crash that triggered the recession. Real residential investment fell by an astounding 57 percent, with the decline clearly leading the recession (the peak was in late 2005). And home construction remains depressed into 2014. It may not seem, therefore that this is a place to look for the significant floor effects that turned the recession into recovery. But in exploring these ideas, we find that the concept of autonomous demand is rather nuanced. Indeed, residential investment collapsed to a far greater degree than typical cyclical dynamics would predict. Therefore, the residential construction crisis implies a large reduction in that part of the floor to aggregate demand that had contained cyclical dynamics prior to the Great Recession.

Despite the home-building disaster, the collapse in construction leveled off rather abruptly. From the first quarter of 2006 to the first quarter of 2009, the decline was sharp and almost linear. In the second quarter of 2009 (slightly before the trough in GDP), residential construction leveled off; it was roughly flat through 2011, and then began a modest recovery. The data suggest that home building hit a floor of its own, and this floor, low though it was by recent historical standards, contributed to autonomous demand that contained the cyclical dynamics of the broader economy. This interpretation is in line with the results of Fazzari et al. (2013). Autonomous demand provides a *dynamic* floor to the economy that changes with other economic conditions. The economy transits between the floor and the ceiling, but that range can widen or shrink as conditions evolve. In this case, it is clear that the floor declined significantly, which helps to explain the stagnant recovery of the economy.

Furthermore, in the model of Fazzari et al. (2013) it is possible that a turning point at the top of the cycle occurs below the level of output at which the resource constraint binds. In this case, the steady-state path becomes dynamically stable, and the economy converges to a growth rate determined by the growth of autonomous demand. The stagnant recovery from the Great Recession may be an example of this kind of dynamic. Much lower, but stable and slowly growing, residential construction could shift the economy into a regime with a stagnant but stable medium-term growth path.

A more obvious source of autonomous demand, and one emphasized in the Ferri and Minsky papers reviewed in the previous section, is government spending. (We focus on government consumption and investment expenditures, which directly create demand, not transfers, which may indirectly induce demand but are also cyclically sensitive.) The figures are quite interesting in the context of understanding possible demand floors for the Great Recession. Again, the lesson from Fazzari et al. (2013) is that both the size of autonomous demand and its growth rate are important for understanding cyclical dynamics. Government spending is large, constituting almost 20 percent of GDP on the eve of the Great Recession in 2007, and justifying the "big government" characterization found in the Ferri–Minsky research. Real government expenditure grew at an annual rate of 1.3 percent from the first quarter of 2004 (after much of the effect of the early 2000s recession had been resolved) to the fourth quarter of 2007. From the beginning of the recession through the early quarters of the recovery (the fourth quarter of 2007 through 2010, fourth quarter), the growth rate of government expenditure rose slightly to a 1.4 percent annualized growth rate. This period included the ramp-up of the American Reinvestment and Recovery Act (ARRA, the "stimulus" bill associated with the early Obama administration). Thus, it seems that government spending did help maintain demand as it continued to expand when the economy collapsed.

The story changes after 2010, however. The spending from ARRA peaks, and policy "pivots to austerity." Total real government spending declines at an annual rate of 2.3 percent from the fourth quarter of 2010 through the most recent data available at this writing, the fourth quarter of 2013. This directional shift was not primarily a cyclical response (again, the cyclically sensitive transfer payments are not included in the measure of government spending we analyze here); it was largely autonomous. Thus, this important component of autonomous spending shifted from a modest positive growth rate to a strongly negative rate *when demand was weak*. Interpreted in the context of our approach to the Ferri modeling tradition, this is close to a "smoking gun" for understanding why the recovery has been so sluggish. While it seems clear that "big government" spending was a central mechanism to "thwart" the Great Recession collapse, as proposed in the work of Ferri and Minsky, the timing of the turn to fiscal austerity was most unfortunate and inconsistent with the policy structure Ferri has developed throughout his career.

Monetary policy and the lender of last resort

The work of Ferri, particularly his co-authored papers with Minsky, emphasizes the importance of monetary policy, particularly lender-of-last-resort intervention, as a critical "thwarting mechanism" that contains downside instability. It is more difficult to interpret this kind of intervention as providing a demand "floor," as discussed by Fazzari et al. (2013), which does not include monetary or financial aspects. But it no doubt played a central role in containing the downward collapse of the Great Recession.

The US Federal Reserve, often in coordinated action with the US Treasury, provided a sequence of targeted bailouts to quell the cascade of financial collapse. These began even before the recession with actions designed to bolster the mortgage-backed securities market. The Fed played a central role in the bailout of Bear Stearns in March 2008, and the coordinated action of the Fed and the Treasury made good on what market participants believed to be an implicit guarantee to backstop Fannie Mae and Freddie Mac, major players in the secondary mortgage market, in August 2008. The decision *not* to bail out Lehmann Brothers in September triggered the worst months of the recession, and what followed was an unprecedented sequence of government financial actions to shore up the banking system and even the US auto industry.

We believe that the recession would have been disastrously worse, and it would have been much more difficult to ultimately arrive at a demand floor, without this kind of intervention. In a sense, a functional financial system provides the means to allow autonomous components of demand to exist. Had the payment system, which allows solvent businesses to finance working capital, collapsed completely, the expenditures that function as private autonomous demand in quantity-driven models would probably have fallen much further than they did.

Conclusion: macroeconomic models and recent history

A central message of this chapter, drawing to a large degree on the research of Piero Ferri, is that modern market economies can be inherently unstable. Instability can arise from multiplier–accelerator quantity dynamics, financial instability as emphasized in the work of Hyman Minsky, or a combination of both. This message conflicts with the implications of most mainstream models, in which endogenous mechanisms generate convergence to stable growth paths, or in which equilibrium paths that emerge from dynamic models are simply assumed to describe reality without any attention to the behavior of the system when it is pushed off the equilibrium path.

One rationale for the mainstream research focus on stable models is that real-world developed economies did not explode or implode in the post-war decades. It may seem, superficially, that this empirical fact renders unstable models unacceptable for interpreting this history. Such a conclusion creates intellectual tension because it does not directly criticize the logic, or even the empirical relevance, of the detailed structural elements of unstable models. For example, there is no careful refutation of the Minsky Financial Instability Hypothesis in mainstream macroeconomics that would justify assuming that the most useful model for analyzing historical growth and fluctuations has stable dynamics. Rather, the largely implicit rejection of unstable models in mainstream macroeconomics comes from the observation that, in some global sense, the dynamic paths of modern economies do not seem unstable, so something must be wrong with models that make unstable predictions (even though we are not told *what* is wrong).

The addition of ceilings and floors or, more generally, "thwarting mechanisms" to unstable models helps to resolve the intellectual tension. The local dynamics of a model may well be unstable, but other mechanisms contain the explosive/implosive dynamics so that the overall dynamic path predicted from the model may appear stable, as is broadly consistent with the history of recent decades.

The macroeconomic cycle that culminated in the Great Recession is an excellent case study with which to test the relevance of both instability and containing mechanisms. The run-up to the crisis illustrates the kind of financial instability identified in much of the research surveyed in this chapter. The recession itself was the most unstable and frightening macroeconomic dynamic since the early 1930s. This path conforms much better to the predictions of unstable models explored by Ferri, Minsky, and others than to the equilibrium-seeking models popular in mainstream macroeconomics. Nonetheless, these dynamics were contained. The upward financial instability in the US housing market turned around in 2006 and 2007. This turn triggered the scary collapse of the Great Recession, but the downturn too was contained. Our analysis in this chapter explores the particular mechanisms responsible for containment in this historical context.

To answer the question posed in our title: yes, macroeconomic models with ceilings and floors *are useful* in understanding the Great Recession and the economic processes that spawned the crisis and turned the business cycle. This success adds to the credibility of models in this tradition, particularly the ideas developed in the research of Piero Ferri.

Notes

1 The label "contained depression" was, to our knowledge, coined by David Levy. Paul Krugman has called the macroeconomic disruption of recent years the "Lesser Depression."

2 In Fazzari et al. (2013) this kind of investment function is discussed in more detail.

3 A large share of US residential construction consists of home improvement spending rather than the construction of complete new homes.

4 In conversations during the 1980s, Minsky strongly warned against such practices. His framework for prudent banking starts with the rule that expected cash flows must be adequate to service debt; collateral is only valuable as a back-up if cash flows fall short of projected values. It is clear that many mortgage loans in the years prior to the Great Recession could never be serviced to full term based on the cash-flow incomes of the borrowers. This is especially true of borrowers who relied on temporary "teaser" interest rates to qualify for loans. They had to refinance or sell the house before the interest rate reset upward to avoid default. See the discussion in Andrews (2009).

5 Ferri and Minsky (1989) identify problems from inflation fighting in the context of the monetary policies that caused the financial instability and recession of the early 1980s.

6 The word "current" in this definition is of some importance. It would be unrealistic to argue that any component of spending with macroeconomic significance was *permanently* independent of the state of the economy. Long swings in economic growth are likely to feed back over decade-plus horizons on spending that might be usefully considered autonomous over the medium term. A definition of autonomous spending as adjusting very little over annual horizons is less analytically precise than the definition given in the text, but it would make the concept more empirically relevant.

References

Andrews, Edmund L. (2009). My personal credit crisis, *New York Times*, May 14, magazine section.

Cynamon, B. Z. and S. M. Fazzari (2008). Household debt in the Consumer Age – source of growth and risk of collapse, *Capitalism and Society*, 3, 1–30.

Cynamon, B. Z., S. M. Fazzari, and M. Setterfield (2013). Understanding the Great Recession. In B. Z. Cynamon, S. M. Fazzari, and M. Setterfield, eds., *After the Great*

Recession: The Struggle for Economic Recovery and Growth, New York: Cambridge University Press, pp. 3–30.

Fazzari, S. M., P. Ferri, and E. Greenberg (2008). Cash flow, investment, and Keynes–Minsky cycles, *Journal of Economic Behavior and Organization*, 65, 555–72.

Fazzari, S. M., P. Ferri, and E. Greenberg (2010). Investment and the Taylor Rule in a dynamic Keynesian model, *Journal of Economic Dynamics and Control*, 34, 2010–22.

Fazzari, S. M., P. Ferri, E. Greenberg, and A. Variato (2013). Aggregate demand, instability, and growth, *Review of Keynesian Economics*, 1, 1–21.

Ferri, P. and H. P. Minsky (1984). Prices, employment, and profits, *Journal of Post Keynesian Economics*, 6, 489–99.

Ferri, P. and H. P. Minsky (1989). The breakdown of the IS–LM synthesis: implications for post-Keynesian economic theory, *Review of Political Economy*, 1, 123–43.

Ferri, P. and H. P. Minsky (1992). Market processes and thwarting systems, *Structural Change and Economic Dynamics*, 3, 79–91.

Harrod, R. F. (1948). *Towards a Dynamic Economics: Some Recent Developments of Economic Theory and their Application to Policy*, London: Macmillan.

Hicks, J. R. (1950). *A Contribution to the Theory of the Trade Cycle*, Oxford: Clarendon Press.

Minsky, H. P. (1957). Monetary systems and accelerator models, *American Economic Review*, 47, 860–83.

Minsky, H. P. (1959). A linear model of cyclical growth, *Review of Economics and Statistics*, 41, 133–45.

Piore, M. and J. Sabel (1985). *The Industrial Divide*, Cambridge, MA: MIT Press.

Samuelson, P. A. (1939a). Interactions between the multiplier analysis and the principle of acceleration, *Review of Economics and Statistics*, 21, 75–8.

Samuelson, P. A. (1939b). A synthesis of the principle of acceleration and the multiplier, *Journal of Political Economy*, 47, 786–97.

Tinbergen, J. (1939). *Business Cycles in the United States of America, 1919–1932*, Vol. 2 of *Statistical Testing of Business-Cycle Theories*, Geneva: League of Nations.

4 The theory of business cycles from a methodological perspective

Andrea Salanti

> [E]ach cycle being a historical individual and in part conditioned by circumstances for which there is no exact analogue in other cycles, we have always to deal with – and even to construct *ad hoc* theories for – facts the relevance of which varies according to the level of abstraction on which we wish to move: a cycle theory may still aim at being general or fairly general, and yet contain elements that are nonessential from the stand point of a pure model. (Schumpeter, 1954, p. 748)

The passage I have chosen as an epigraph might be regarded as a reminiscence of the nowadays almost completely forgotten *Methodenstreit*, the lost battle of the German historical school against early marginalism. Actually, however, the question of the possibility of attaining general patterns/theories/laws in economics (and, more generally, within the realm of the so-called social sciences) was raised well before. Indeed, it can be traced back at least to the following passage by David Hume, which exhibits one of the first explicit statements of the possibility of a "scientific" approach to what we currently identify as social sciences:

> But it is at least worthwhile to try if the science of man will not admit of the same accuracy, which several parts of natural philosophy are found susceptible of. There seems to be all the reason in the world to imagine that it may be carried to the greatest degree of exactness. If, in examining several phenomena, we find that they resolve themselves into one common principle, and can trace this principle into another, we shall at last arrive at those few simple principles on which all the rest depend. (Hume, 1938 [1740], p. 5)

The consequences of the advocated change of perspective can hardly be overestimated.[1] We can realize how far reaching they may have been by comparing the following two passages by Richard Cantillon and Adam Smith.

> [T]he price or intrinsic value of a thing is the measure of the quantity of land and of labour entering into its production, having regard to the fertility or produce of the land and to the quality of the labour. But it often happens that many things which have actually this intrinsic value are not sold in the market according to that value: that will depend on the *humours and fancies* of men and on their consumption. (Cantillon, 2001 [1755], p. 16, italics added)

Apart from the curious absence of the quantity of capital as a concurrent factor in determining the price of a good, the modern reader may be somewhat baffled by the reference to the "humours and fancies of men" as an explanation of the frequently observed deviations of market prices from the corresponding intrinsic values. Just two decades later, however, we may find an entirely different attitude toward the same question:

> In order to investigate the principles which regulate the exchangeable value of commodities, I shall endeavour to show, [. . .] First, what is the real measure of this exchangeable value; or, wherein consists the real price of all commodities. Secondly, what are the different parts of which this real price is composed or made up. And, lastly, what are the different circumstances which sometimes raise some or all of these different parts of price above, and sometimes sink them below their natural or ordinary rate; or, *what are the causes which sometimes hinder the market price* [. . .] *from coinciding exactly with what may be called their natural price.* (Smith, 1976 [1776], Book 1, Chapter IV, italics added)

Even if Cantillon and Smith compete – among others – for the title of founding father of modern economics, there can be no doubt that on the issue of market versus natural prices Smith's approach is far more rigorous and intended at discovering general patterns. As we now know, Smith's offered solutions to the problems at hand may have been quite rough and unsatisfactory, but at least after him nobody could any longer refer to "humours and fancies of men" as a serious explanation of the deviations of market prices from their natural counterparts. His problem setting looks much more definite and suitable for investigation than Cantillon's previous account. Indeed, it established the agenda for decades of subsequent analyses of value and distribution by classical economists.

However, the search for "those few simple principles on which all the rest depend" raised a number of methodological problems, whose discussion characterized for several decades the first wave of methodological reflections in economics by authors such as John Elliott Cairnes (1857), William Nassau Senior (1836), John Stuart Mill (1844) and John Neville Keynes (1890). Before identifying the appropriate method for economics (then referred to as political economy), these authors had to accomplish the task of attaining a definition of the object of the new discipline. In order to do this they proceeded to isolate an aspect of human behavior and in this way they succeeded in establishing recognizable disciplinary boundaries. In doing so, however, they had to pay a price: as a result, economics emerged as a truly "separate" discipline, but also somehow "inexact."[2]

Macroeconomics

The explicit recognition of the need to isolate a particular aspect of human behavior from all the other activities that characterize it was a risky, albeit courageous, methodological choice, subject as it might have been (and, indeed, actually was) to highly varied criticisms: from those directed at the realism of the (fundamental) assumptions, to the moral strictures towards a discipline which seemed to have elected the utilitarian calculus as the ultimate principle governing human action. Instrumental to such a methodological decision was the portrayal of the economic agent as a sort of *homo oeconomicus*.[3] Apart from old-fashioned critiques, even if we adopt the present view of "economic man" as implying nothing else than the adoption of the principle of rationality, we remain with the problem of justifying the disciplinary boundaries of the various sub-disciplines within economics.

One of the main cases in point is undoubtedly that of macroeconomics, which has always represented a sort of methodological paradox within economics. If only because of the problem of aggregation, macro theories and models look less rigorous and theoretically justified than their counterparts in microeconomics. In addition, due to its having to deal with "analysis applied to facts" (Hicks, 1979, p. ix) in the shape of either "commonsense perception" and "everyday experience" (Solow, 1998, pp. 1–3) or "empirical modelling" (Granger, 1999), it should be more easily approachable by means of conceptual tools, traditionally connected with the empiricist tradition, suited to develop a causal analysis of the economic system considered as a whole, analogous to the causal analysis of physical systems.[4]

In any case, the agenda for macroeconomics, more than that for microeconomics, is dictated by circumstances coming from outside the discipline. Macroeconomics has to provide diagnoses and remedies for problems such as unemployment, inflation, productivity slowdowns and financial crises, whether or not these are the issues that the discipline, at a certain stage of its development, is best equipped to deal with. For this reason, for instance, in the Introduction to a widely adopted advanced textbook on macroeconomics we meet statements like the following: "Working macroeconomists, like doctors treating cancer, cannot wait for all the answers to analyse events and help policy. They have to take guesses and rely on a battery of models that cannot be derived from first principles but have repeatedly proved useful" (Blanchard and Fisher, 1989, p. xii).

In this respect macroeconomics appears to be more like social science as seen by Thomas Kuhn: "The latter [social scientists] often tend, as the former [natural scientists] almost never do, to defend their choice of a research problem – e.g., the effects of racial discrimination *or the causes of the business cycle* – chiefly in terms of the social importance of achieving a solution" (1970, p. 164, italics added). Indeed, while natural scientists may often choose their research subjects according to their own judgment about the feasibility of the research activity involved, social scientists are often obliged to deal with problems (whether or not they are sufficiently equipped to do so) whose importance depends on practical reasons at the individual or social level. Given this situation, it would be really surprising if the results achieved in the social sciences were as impressive as those achieved by the natural sciences (whose achievements, in spite of the possibility of taking advantage of the laboratory, are much less impressive than usual when natural scientists are required to solve problems because of their practical or social urgency), and the task for the former becomes even more difficult when faced with the formidable questions that scholars interested in political economy are unwilling to leave out of the domain of their discipline.[5]

The theory of business cycles

As Jan Toporowski's contribution to this volume (Chapter 5) forcefully testifies, within macroeconomics the issue of business cycles is surely one that: 1) is in urgent need of further research devoted to select – among all the available ones – the effectively operating mechanisms and the corresponding countercyclical policies, and 2) offers the discouraging spectacle of a messy collection of different explanations, including the most exoteric examples of what brilliant scholars may figure out, working at the two extremes of the trade-off between "rigor and relevance" or, in slightly different terms, "truth versus precision" in economics.[6]

Two glaring examples will suffice to illustrate the previous (seemingly too bold) claim. The first one is taken from Royal Swedish Academy of Sciences (2005, p. 202, italics added), containing the official motivations for the award of the Nobel memorial prize in economics 2004 to Finn Kydland and Edward Prescott. Apropos of their work on models of real business cycles (RBC), it is said:

> Research by the laureates also transformed the theory of business cycles by integrating it with the theory of economic growth. Whereas earlier research had emphasized macroeconomic shocks on the demand side of the economy, Kydland and Prescott demonstrated that shocks on the supply side may have far-reaching effects. In their business-cycle model, *realistic* fluctuations in the rate of technological development brought about a covariation between GDP, consumption, investments and hours worked close to that observed in actual data. [. . .] The laureates laid the groundwork for more robust models by regarding business cycles as the collective *outcome of countless forward-looking decisions made by individual households and firms regarding consumption, investments, labor supply*, etc. Kydland and Prescott's methods have been widely adopted in modern macro-economics.[7]

Although unifying growth and business cycle theory might have a particular appeal, the particular solution offered by RBC literature is not without problems. Indeed, somewhat ironically, we may find arguments for rejecting a supply-side explanation of business cycles as early as in the Introduction to Irving Fisher (1932, p. 5) in a section headed "The mystery of depression":

> For in times of depression, is the soil less fertile? Not at all. Does it lack rain? Not at all. Are the mines exhausted? No, they can perhaps pour out even more than the old volume of ore, if anyone will buy. Are the factories, then, lamed in some way – down at the heel? No; machinery and invention may be at the very peak. But perhaps the men have suddenly become unable or unwilling to work. The idea is belied by the spectacle of hordes of workmen, besieging every available employment office.

At the other end of the spectrum we may find George Akerlof and Robert Schiller (two more Nobel prize winners in, respectively, 2001 and 2013) trying to convince the reader of the possibility of explaining, among other things, why economies fall into depression (and why there are people who cannot find a job) without any formula whatsoever, but only in terms of the influence of various kinds of "animal spirits."[8]

Both these approaches, to be frank, seem to have been crafted with the intent of justifying all the recent derogatory and scornful opinions publicly put forward about economists' competence and integrity. Luckily enough, however, a more serviceable attitude is available and well documented in recent and not so recent economic literature. In order to appreciate the possibilities that an intermediate attitude might offer, we have to reconsider the connection between micro and macroeconomics.

The presently prevalent belief is that macroeconomic theories should be derived from microeconomic foundations which, in their turn, ought to be based on the assumption of individual rationality. A major problem, however, is that the conditions under which it is possible to aggregate from micro to macro are almost never satisfied. In this respect two possible responses can be given. One is to disregard aggregation problems, using devices such as the representative agent, maintaining that if this turns out to be illegitimate, this will show up when the resulting macro models are confronted with macro evidence. This strategy, however, is always open to the criticism of simply begging the relevant questions in more than one respect. In any case, even apart from doubts about aggregation conditions, the representative agent fiction prevents macroeconomics from exploiting all the richness of modern microeconomic theory.

Another response is that aggregation problems undermine the search for microfoundations and, if only for that reason, economists should instead search for regularities at the macro level. But such regularities can never be established by induction, however much data is available, because the processes whereby data are collected and aggregated mean they can never be free of theory, so it becomes almost unavoidable having to resort to arguments based upon the adequacy of the theory in explaining some "stylized" facts. Nowadays this might admittedly appear as a defensive abandonment of more ambitious undertakings, but it should be remembered that this was precisely the strategy followed by an array of Nobel prize winners of previous generations. Think of, for instance, two prominent scholars such as John Hicks and Paul Samuelson. They were surely well acquainted with microeconomics,[9] but did not disdain – when coping with macroeconomic issues – to deal with aggregate variables without even attempting to provide any kind of microfoundations.[10]

Concluding remarks

Let me conclude with some words of appreciation for Piero Ferri's contributions to the theory of business cycles, as we may find them mainly in Ferri and Greenberg (1989, 1992) and in Ferri (2011). This is due not so much due to the occasion of this volume, as to the fact that the previous methodological remarks go precisely in the direction that we may easily identify in Ferri's writings on the subject. In Ferri (2011, p. 41), for instance, we may find the following assertion:

> Macro equations are not easily reducible to behavioral equations because they also depend on interactions and they may imply nonlinear structural equations that transform aggregation into a complex process. This is the reason why a strict microfoundation of macroeconomics is only one possibility that cannot be imposed as a precondition for its validity.

Indeed, in order to mimic the cyclical behavior of the system, in his various contributions on this subject Ferri consistently investigated the properties of various models in which the nonlinear behavior of the relevant variables is obtained by introducing a regime-switch discontinuity in different sub-models. Analytically this approach requires: 1) the identification of a threshold marking the boundary between two different regimes; 2) the specification of the equations affected when the threshold is reached, and 3) the study of the (cyclical) dynamics of such a system (see Ferri 2011, pp. 8, 121).

So, in Ferri and Greenberg (1989) we find a regime switching in a model otherwise belonging to the Keynesian tradition, introduced in order to avoid an explosive behavior of the system and obtained by assuming a change in the parameters of the autoregressive sub-model for prices and wages triggered by a "threshold level" of employment. Such a discontinuity could be due to a change either in government policy rules, or in the behavior of agents whose decisions about prices and wages might be influenced by another variable (for example, the rate of unemployment or the rate of inflation). In either case the explanation of this regime switching must be found in institutional and/or social constraints rather than in the physical constraints typical of the old "ceilings and floors" approach to the theory of trade cycle.[11]

In Ferri (2011) a similar analytical framework is applied to a sequence of models characterized by a different regime switching concerning inflation and monetary policy rules, labor productivity and income distribution, investment and (Markovian) expectations with different kinds of threshold (alternatively set in terms of a given rate of unemployment, a given rate of growth, or a stochastic financial solvency condition). The growing complexity of these models prevents them from providing analytical solutions and induces us to make use of simulations.

All of this (namely, the absence of microfoundations and dynamics obtained through simulation) is admittedly somewhat at odds with the current style of mainstream macroeconomics. There is no need, however, to be exceedingly worried about this. After all, it still remains to be demonstrated that a belief in the intertemporal substitutability of leisure time and in exogenously determined fluctuations of productivity is more reasonable[12] than trying to reproduce the (cyclical, usually not explosive) observed behavior of our economies by means of aggregate equations subject to some kind of regime switching. Rather, what in my opinion remains to be settled is the question of how robust such analyses may turn out to be. The practice of deriving known results from slightly different assumptions may be understood as an examination of the robustness of modeling results with respect to particular modeling assumptions.[13] The idea is that by comparing results obtained with different arrays of particular assumptions, we should obtain "robust" results, in the sense that they do not depend on the details of the particular (and often unrealistic) assumptions employed.

However, when different sets of assumptions entail different causal mechanisms, the virtue of robustness so defined becomes far less obvious: it is, indeed, not so clear how we could identify progress of our knowledge with the proliferation of models featuring *different* causal mechanisms. The abundance of models of this kind might be interpreted as evidence of our inability to detect the best representation of the situation we want to investigate and/or of the true mechanism at work.

Notes

1 Even a century later, for instance, Hume's point is forcefully reiterated by none other than John Stuart Mill: "There is nothing chimerical in the hope that general laws, sufficient to enable us to answer these various questions for any country or time with the individual circumstances of which we are well acquainted, do really admit of being ascertained; and that the other branches of human knowledge, which this undertaking presupposes, are so far advanced that the time is ripe for its commencement. Such is the object of the Social Science" (Mill, 1856, p. 456).
2 For a modern restatement of the Millian methodological perspective, the authoritative reference is Hausman (1992). In this respect, from a Marshallian standpoint, see also Sutton (2000).
3 The corresponding English expression ("economic man") was probably firstly adopted by Ingram (1888) with reference to the Millian methodological perspective, while the Latin version is due to Pareto (1892), who then used it in several other places.
4 In this respect the quest for microfoundations of macroeconomics would appear to go in the opposite direction. For a balanced methodological assessment of the reductionist program in economics, see Hoover (2014).
5 For more detailed considerations of the particular methodological issues concerning macroeconomics, let me refer to Backhouse (1995, 1997) and to the Introduction to Backhouse and Salanti (2000, Vol. 1, 1–19).
6 These two accounts of the difficult choice between formalist and empirical science criteria when dealing with specific subjects are due to, respectively, Gordon (1976) and Mayer (1993).
7 A more balanced (even if equally sympathetic) assessment of the line of research on RBC can be found in Rebelo (2005).
8 See Akerlof and Schiller (2009, Chapters 6 and 9).
9 Obvious references in this regard are Hicks (1939) and Samuelson (1947).
10 Cf., for example, Hicks (1937, 1950) and Samuelson (1939).
11 Apart from this (important) difference, Ferri's approach may be regarded as a reappraisal of that style of theorizing which characterized business cycle theory as developed in the 1950s and 1960s by authors like John Hicks, Nicholas Kaldor, and Richard Goodwin (to name but a few and not to speak of the seminal contributions by Michal Kalecki in the 1930s), and subsequently ended by being unduly neglected.
12 In addition, the poor (to say the least) results of policies inspired by such a kind of model are no help in this respect.
13 See, for instance, Kuorikoski, Lehtinen, and Marchionni (2010).

References

Akerlof, G. A. and R. J. Shiller (2009). *Animal Spirits: How Human Psychology Drives the Economy and Why It Matters for Global Capitalism*, Princeton, NJ: Princeton University Press.

Backhouse, R. E. (1995). *Interpreting Macroeconomics: Explorations in the History of Macroeconomic Thought*, London: Routledge.

Backhouse, R. E. (1997). *Truth and Progress in Economic Knowledge*, Cheltenham, UK: Edward Elgar.

Backhouse, R. E. and A. Salanti, eds. (2000). *Macroeconomics and the Real World* (two volumes), New York: Oxford University Press.

Blanchard, O. J. and S. Fisher (1989). *Lectures on Macroeconomics*, Cambridge, MA, and London: MIT Press.

Cairnes, J. E. (1857). *The Character and Logical Method of Political Economy*. London: Longman.

Cantillon, R. (2001) [1755]. *Essai sur la nature du commerce en général*, edited with an English translation (and other material) by Henry Higgs in 1931. Now with a new introduction by Anthony Brewer, New Brunswick, NJ: Transaction Publishers.

Ferri, P. (2011). *The Macroeconomics of Growth Cycles and Financial Instability*, Cheltenham, UK: Edward Elgar.

Ferri, P. and E. Greenberg (1989). *The Labor Market and Business Cycle Theories*, Berlin, Heidelberg, and New York: Springer-Verlag.

Ferri, P. and E. Greenberg (1992). *Wages, Regime Switching, and Cycles*, Berlin, Heidelberg, and New York: Springer-Verlag.

Fisher, Irving (1932). *Booms and Depressions: Some First Principles*, New York: Adelphi.

Gordon, R. A. (1976). Rigor and relevance in a changing institutional setting, *American Economic Review*, 66 (1), 1–14.

Granger, C. W. J. (1999). *Empirical Modeling in Economics: Specification and Evaluation*, Cambridge and New York: Cambridge University Press.

Hausman, D. M. (1992). *The Inexact and Separate Science of Economics*, Cambridge: Cambridge University Press.

Hicks, J. R. (1937). Mr Keynes and the "classics": a suggested interpretation, *Econometrica*, 5, 147–59.

Hicks, J. R. (1939). *Value and Capital*, Oxford: Clarendon Press. [2nd ed. 1946].

Hicks, J. R. (1950). *A Contribution to the Theory of the Trade Cycle*, Oxford: Oxford University Press.

Hicks, J. R. (1979). *Causality in Economics*, Oxford: Basil Blackwell.

Hoover, K. D. (2014). Reductionism in economics: causality and intentionality in the microfoundations of macroeconomics, *The Center for the History of Political Economy Working Paper Series*, no. 2014-03. Available at SSRN: http://ssrn.com/abstract=2398476.

Hume, D. (1938). *An Abstract of a Treatise of Human Nature, 1740: A Pamphlet Hitherto Unknown by David Hume*, Cambridge: Cambridge University Press.

Ingram, J. K. (1888). *History of Political Economy*, Edinburgh: Adam & Charles Black.

Keynes, J. N. (1890). *The Scope and Method of Political Economy*, London: Macmillan.

Kuhn, T. (1970). *The Structure of Scientific Revolutions*, 2nd ed., Chicago and London: University of Chicago Press.

Kuorikoski, J., A. Lehtinen and C. Marchionni (2010). Economic modelling as robustness analysis, *British Journal for the Philosophy of Science*, 61 (3), 541–67. Mayer, T. (1993). *Truth versus Precision in Economics*. Aldershot, UK: Edward Elgar.

Mill, J. S. (1844). On the definition of political economy; and on the method of investigation proper to it, *Essays on Some Unsettled Questions of Political Economy*, London: J. W. Parker & Sons, pp. 120–64.

Mill, J. S. (1856). On the logic of the moral sciences. In *System of Logic, Ratiocinative and Inductive*, 4th ed., London: J. W. Parker & Sons, Vol. II, Book VI, pp. 403–531.

Pareto, V. (1892). Considerazioni sui principi fondamentali dell'economia politica pura, *Giornale degli Economisti*, Vol. IV, Serie 2ª, pp. 389–420 (now in *Écrits d'économie politique pure*, ed. by Giovanni Busino, Ginevra-Parigi: Librairie Droz, 1982, pp. 59–90).

Rebelo, S. (2005). Real business cycle models: past, present and future, *Scandinavian Journal of Economics*, 107 (2), 217–38.

Royal Swedish Academy of Sciences (2005). Press release: The Nobel Memorial Prize in economics 2004, *Scandinavian Journal of Economics*, 107 (2), 201–2.

Samuelson, P. A. (1939). Interactions between the multiplier analysis and the principle of acceleration, *Review of Economics and Statistics*, 21 (2), 75–8.

Samuelson, P. A. (1947). *Foundations of Economic Analysis*, Cambridge, MA: Harvard University Press.

Schumpeter, J. A. (1954). *History of Economic Analysis*, London: Allen & Unwin.

Senior, N. W. (1836). *An Outline of the Science of Political Economy*, London: W. Clowes & Sons.

Smith, A. (1976) [1776]. *An Inquiry into the Nature and Causes of the Wealth of Nations*, two volumes, edited by R. H. Campbell and A. S. Skinner, Oxford: Clarendon Press.

Solow, R. M. (1998). *Monopolistic Competition and Macroeconomic Theory*, Cambridge: Cambridge University Press.

Sutton, J. (2000). *Marshall's Tendencies: What Can Economists Know?*, Cambridge, MA: MIT Press.

Part II

Uncertainty and information in business cycle models

5 The business cycle as a method of analysis

Jan Toporowski

I would like to begin this chapter by paying a warm tribute to the work of Piero Ferri, whose book *The Macroeconomics of Growth Cycles and Financial Instability* represents the best of an analytical approach derived from his teacher, J. R. Hicks (Ferri, 2011). This Hicksian approach was an influential trend in the breakthrough that occurred in the middle of the twentieth century from narrative accounts of business cycles (e.g. Robertson, 1915; Harrod, 1936; Lavington, 1922; and even Tugan-Baranovsky, 1894) to analytical accounts of business cycles stressing recurrent movements in economic variables and the relationships between them, epitomised in the work of Samuelson and Hicks (Samuelson, 1939; Hicks, 1950).

In between were economists such as Kalecki and Schumpeter, and latterly Minsky, who sought to identify the systematic, recurrent changes that may be observed in economic activity, and to model them in cyclical form (Kalecki, 1933; Schumpeter, 1939; Minsky, 1975).

Towards the end of the twentieth century, the discussion became confused by the emergence of the 'equilibrium' business cycle, which in turn becomes the foundation of Dynamic Stochastic General Equilibrium (DSGE) models (Kydland and Prescott, 1982). The latter are something of a misnomer, as far as business cycles are concerned, because they deny the possibility of systematic, recurrent changes in economic activity. Instead, these models argue that changes in economic activity are due to stochastic 'shocks' to an economic system that is essentially in general equilibrium: any serial correlation in differences of variables over time is due to the adjustment of a previous general equilibrium, to a 'shock'. One consequence of this is that business cycles may be simulated. But actual cycles are only of historic interest because it is in the nature of stochastic events that 'shocks' cannot be predicted. This reinforces the hostility to counter-cyclical economic policy, and the quietist political philosophy, that characterise the proponents of such models.

In the section that follows it is argued that business cycle theory is a way of dealing with complexity in the economy by allowing model parameters to change over time. This is followed by some reflections on the approach to economic dynamics of Marshall and Keynes. The chapter concludes by arguing that Minsky is more correctly viewed as belonging to the business cycle approach of Kalecki and Schumpeter, rather than that of Keynes.

The business cycle versus general equilibrium

Business cycle theory presents an intellectual, political and practical challenge to the preoccupation with general equilibrium that has characterised the mainstream approach to economic theory since the end of the nineteenth century. In equal measure it reveals the most obvious features of what is wrong with capitalism – instability, unemployment and poverty; promises practical business people insight into the prospects that await their business; and, by reason of its complexity, provides the greatest intellectual challenge to the honest and objective economic researcher.

The business cycle – that is, successive periods of economic growth and prosperity, followed by periods of economic contraction and rising unemployment – is a phenomenon of industrial and post-industrial capitalism. Before the industrial revolution, periods of prosperity and economic distress had natural or political causes: disease or natural disasters, good or bad harvests, civil disorders or the extension of markets by means of empires, such as the Roman Empire, that could protect trade and construct useful infrastructure such as roads and irrigation. From the nineteenth century onwards, however, a new type of fluctuation in business activity emerged that was unrelated to natural or political factors. By the twentieth century the notion put forward by Jevons that business cycles are caused by sunspots was considered to be an amusing eccentricity.

Nevertheless, the business cycle has remained a matter of controversy. Part of its enigma arises because it is not obvious whether it is real, like the output of a gold mine that may observed, weighed and valued, or whether it is a mental construct (like language, geometry, causality, probability or time) that we use to apprehend reality, rather than being objectively a part of that reality. The business cycle certainly has much in common with other synthetic concepts, such as 'globalisation' and 'financialisation', which economists use to organise linked economic processes. But use of the term does not really reveal the mechanics that cause such systematically recurring changes in economic activity.

Until the twentieth century, business cycle theory was an approach largely confined to continental European economic discussions. Most English-speaking economists, under the influence of Mill and the neo-classical revolution in the later part of the nineteenth century, believed in equilibrium in markets that were only temporarily disequilibrated by changes in the money supply (Laidler, 1991) or changes in technology. The study of the business cycle as it developed in continental Europe, by authors such as Wicksell (among the neo-classical writers) and Tugan-Baranovsky (among the Marxists), was a challenge to the prevailing orthodoxy in economic theory, built around the idea of equilibrium between demand and supply in markets, or the general equilibrium put forward by Walras and Pareto. Viewed from the starting point of equilibrium, changes in the underlying conditions of production and distribution, conditions such as individual preferences, technology, and the fiscal and monetary policy of the state, only give rise to a new equilibrium. By implication, in such an analysis, economic dynamics – that is, changes in economic activity or 'business conditions' – may be caused by any factor. This view came to be prevalent in economics in the final decades of the twentieth century with the widespread adoption of Equilibrium Business Cycle terminology. According to this, economic dynamics are merely the result of 'shocks', or shifts in underlying conditions. The clear conclusion from this is that there is no systematically recurring business cycle, merely a series of unforeseen accidents after which equilibrium is resumed.

The difficulty with these approaches is that, in a diversified economy, one would expect different responses to 'shocks' by different industries, according to the nature of their exposure to the 'shock'. In other words, one would expect successive changes in equilibrium brought about in succession by shifts in different industries. This is the process that Schumpeter called 'creative destruction': that is, a process in which some industries or firms are expanding, and some are declining, both doing so continuously.

However, concurrent booms and slumps in different industries also happen in the real world. The rationale for business cycle theory lies in the fact that, in a boom, firms and industries *in general* expand output and employment, and enjoy increasing profits, and this is followed by a phase in which firms and industries, with marginal exceptions, reduce their output and employment, and find difficulty in selling their output profitably. For this reason Schumpeter argued that the only 'real' business cycles are long ones in which generic technological innovations affect a wide range of industries. Similarly, Hawtrey, Hayek and Keynes argued that the business cycle had to be due to monetary conditions, because these are the only conditions that affect all industries. The challenge to general equilibrium comes about because general equilibrium presupposes a fixed amount of resources used in the economy. But in a boom the resources used in the economy are expanding, while in a slump they appear to be contracting. This is inconsistent with the notion that the resources of an economy more or less grow over time, with the increase in labour and capital and their productivity. Equilibrium business cycle theorists cope with this inconsistency by resorting to changes in tastes and preferences, and ad hoc 'shocks'.

The case of 'financial accelerator' models that emerged from New Keynesian general equilibrium in the 1990s took a slightly different approach. Here the cyclical factor is abstracted away as unexplained fluctuations in 'net worth' (assets minus liabilities) that are observed in the course of business cycles. This is essentially correct, but leaves unexplained the one element that needs elucidation in such a business cycle model (see, for example, Bernanke and Gertler, 1989).

Among mathematical economists, the real reason for the reluctance of equilibrium theorists to step up to the challenge of the business cycle is that the business cycle is profoundly problematic for economists who need determinate systems of equations in order to arrive at their equilibrium. The business cycle presumes change in economic activity and business cycle theory seeks to understand how that change happens, whereas equilibrium means a stable state that is no guide to any different state. In the real world everything is changing every day. Understanding that change requires complex thinking. Equilibrium theorists can only cope with such complexity by simplifying complex, indeterminate systems, to simple, determinate constructs. Business cycle theorists cope with such complexity by identifying the mechanisms of change to show how the state of affairs today gives rise to the state of affairs tomorrow.

The Marshallian substitute for dynamics[1]

One way of dealing with this complexity was the approach of Alfred Marshall. The traditional approach to economic analysis that Cambridge bequeathed to the twentieth century, and in which Keynes was brought up, was partial equilibrium. This is now standard in all economics textbooks and needs little introduction to economists. It consists of dividing up economic activity into different, but actually simultaneously occurring, 'periods' of activity. In each 'period', the situation in other periods is supposed to be held constant. Thus the shortest period is the market 'day', in which the prices of produced goods are determined by supply and demand in their markets. There is then the 'short period' in which firms determine their profit-maximising levels of output (and employment), given the prices determined in the market 'day'. There is then the 'long period' in which firms determine their scale of production: that is, how much capital equipment they will have or use.

The Marshallian system is an ingenious way of dealing with the complexity of everything happening at once. All variables can change in their respective 'periods' with predictable results. There is an analysis for changes in capital equipment and its productivity; a separate analysis for changes in the labour market; and an analysis of credit with effects on trade and investment. There is even a mathematical appendix in Marshall's *Principles* in which the various 'periods' are brought together to give a general equilibrium. However, this is not the same as an analysis of economic dynamics in which everything is allowed to change because the disequilibrium of today is resolved through the creation of a new disequilibrium tomorrow.

Keynes was also under the influence of Marshall in this regard. In his 'Notes on the trade cycle', Keynes wrote his explanation of the cycle:

> This brings me to my point. The explanation of the *time-element* in the trade cycle, of the fact that an interval of time of a particular order of magnitude must usually elapse before recovery begins, is to be sought in the influences which govern the recovery of the marginal efficiency of capital. There are reasons, given firstly by the length of life of durable assets in relation to the normal rate of growth in a given epoch, and secondly by the carrying-costs of surplus stocks, why the duration of the downward movement should have an order of magnitude which is not fortuitous, which does not fluctuate between, say, one year this time and ten years next time, but which show some regularity of habit between, let us say, three years and five years. (Keynes, 1936, p. 317, italics in the original, perhaps because Keynes realised here that time is not the same as Marshall's 'periods')

Keynes went on to argue that the key variable in the business cycle is what he called the 'marginal efficiency of capital': that is, the expected prospective yield from investment, after deduction of financing costs. He held that this marginal efficiency of capital (mec) fluctuates under the influence of a scarcity of capital in a boom (which increases the mec), and unsold stocks of produced goods in a recession. This fluctuation of the mec then causes the changes in investment that are the root cause of business cycles (Keynes, 1936, pp. 317–18). Keynes's analysis here is complex, because changes in the mec are caused both by changes in stocks (a factor to which Hawtrey attached great significance in his monetary business cycle theory) and by the 'scarcity' of capital. It is intriguing that the rate of interest plays no part in Keynes's argument here.

The Minsky Cycle

Keynes's discussion of the business cycle evoked particular criticism from Hyman P. Minsky, and is the point at which at least one distinguished post-Keynesian has sought to exclude business cycle theory from post-Keynesian economics (Davidson, 2000). For Davidson, Keynes put forward a general theory that demonstrated an under-employment equilibrium whereas business cycle theory knows no lasting equilibrium. By contrast, Hyman Minsky recognised that 'the core of *The General Theory* is the theory of investment and why it is so prone to fluctuate' (Minsky, 1975, p. 94). Minsky criticised Keynes for including the rate of interest in the *supply* price of capital when, in Minsky's view (after Veblen), the proper function of the rate of interest is to discount future returns on investment (1975, pp. 98–9).

Shortly after this, Minsky made his analytical breakthrough into a business cycle theory in which turning points were endogenous, and caused by those changes in investment, rather than exogenous 'displacements', a term he borrowed from Irving Fisher, or what is more commonly called today 'shocks'. The analytical breakthrough came with Minsky's discovery of Kalecki's profits theory, according to which business profits are determined by business investment (in a closed economy with no government – if these limitations are removed, the conclusions are the same but slightly more complicated). This is 'widow's cruse' theory that Keynes himself had advanced in his *Treatise on Money* (Keynes, 1930, p. 139): if workers spend all their income on consumption, then capitalists will receive as sales revenue their (wage) costs of production; to realise money profits, capitalists have to spend over and above their wage costs on investment and their own consumption.

But more than this was necessary to make fully endogenous Minsky's theory of financial fragility. That something is a peculiar property of business investment, in that it takes passive money, sitting in 'hoards', and turns it into income, if the investment is undertaken using the own funds of the investor. If the investment is undertaken using borrowed money, then the process of investment turns credit into income. This ability to convert credit into income for capitalists is shared only by Kalecki's capital tax, used to pay for government expenditure

(Kalecki, 1937). The idea did not come to Minsky from the work of Kalecki, but rather from the German monetary theory that Minsky imbibed from Schumpeter (Toporowski, 2012). It revealed a highly original conclusion to Minsky, namely that investment does not just determine the level of output and employment, as Keynes and Kalecki had argued. It also determines the extent to which, in the economy at large, incomes are able to service debt obligations. A given network of debt structures in an economy at any one time requires a certain nominal value of investment to be undertaken in order that those debts be serviced as required in the debt contracts. A higher level of investment creates additional profits and adds to the equity or reserves possessed by firms. A lower level of investment causes an inability to service debts from income, and hence leads to Ponzi finance, or borrowing to manage existing debt commitments. Debt-financed investment adds to income today, but entails a higher value of investment next year for debt obligations to be covered by income.

Fluctuations in investment therefore appear, in a credit economy, as fluctuations between sound and unsound borrowing. Correspondingly, the banking or financial system moves between good and bad loans in a pro-cyclical way, according to the level of investment. This analysis is the basis of Minsky's 1986 work, *Stabilizing an Unstable Economy*. The book documents Minsky's final break with the partial equilibrium methodology to which Keynes had returned in his *General Theory* and brought Minsky back to business cycle analysis.

Conclusion

The business cycle theory is more than a way of dealing with economic dynamics, as suggested by the traditional approach to the subject, from Harrod to Dynamic Stochastic General Equilibrium. Business cycle theory is a way of incorporating complexity into economic modelling by allowing model parameters to change over the period of a cycle. This is apparent in the contrast between the partial equilibrium approach of John Maynard Keynes, Alfred Marshall and Joan Robinson, and that of Michal Kalecki and Hyman P. Minsky.

The business cycle is a method of economic analysis that challenged general equilibrium analysis in the twentieth century. It is also a challenge to the partial equilibrium that allows for analysis of different or multiple equilibria within a given economy, but cannot show how one conjuncture, or set of economic circumstances, systematically leads to another one in alternations of booms and recessions. The integration of complex financial structures into business cycle analysis remains one of the great unsettled questions of modern financial economics. Despite a revival in the discussion around this question since the 2008 crisis, it remains unsettled, in part because the attendant question of equilibrium refuses to die.

Note

1 The phrase "the Marshallian substitute for dynamics" is due to Leontief (1948, p. 100).

References

Bernanke, B., and M. Gertler (1989). Agency costs, new worth, and business fluctuations, *American Economic Review*, 79, 14–31.

Davidson, P. (2000). There are major differences between Kalecki's theory of employment and Keynes's general theory of employment, interest and money, *Journal of Post Keynesian Economics*, 23, 3–26.

Ferri, P. (2011). *The Macroeconomics of Growth Cycles and Financial Instability*, Cheltenham, UK: Edward Elgar.

Harrod, R. F. (1936). *The Trade Cycle: An Essay*, Oxford: Clarendon Press.

Hicks, J. R. (1950). *A Contribution to the Theory of the Trade Cycle*, Oxford: Oxford University Press.

Kalecki, M. (1933) *Próba teorii koniunktury*, Warszawa: Instytut Badania Koniunktur Gospodarczych i Cen. In J. Osiatyński, ed., *Collected Works of Michał Kalecki*, Volume I, *Capitalism: Business Cycles and Full Employment*, Oxford: Clarendon Press, 1990.

Kalecki, M. (1937). A theory of commodity, income and capital taxation. In J. Osiatyński, ed., *Collected Works of Michał Kalecki*, Volume I, *Capitalism: Business Cycles and Full Employment*, Oxford: Clarendon Press, 1990.

Keynes, J. M. (1930). *A Treatise on Money in Two Volumes*, Volume 1, *The Pure Theory of Money*, London: Macmillan.

Keynes, J. M. (1936). *The General Theory of Employment, Interest and Money*, London: Macmillan.

Kydland, F. E. and E. C. Prescott (1982). Time to build and aggregate fluctuations, *Econometrica*, 50, 1345–70.

Laidler, D. (1991). *The Golden Age of the Quantity Theory of Money*, Princeton, NJ: Princeton University Press.

Lavington, F. (1922). *The Trade Cycle: An Account of the Causes Producing Rhythmical Changes in the Activity of Business*, London: P. S. King.

Leontief, W. (1948). Postulates: Keynes's *General Theory* and the classicists. In S. Harris, ed., *The New Economics*, New York: Knopf.

Minsky, H. P. (1975). *John Maynard Keynes*, New York: Columbia University Press.

Minsky, H. P. (1986). *Stabilizing an Unstable Economy*, New Haven, CT: Yale University Press.

Robertson, D. H. (1915). *A Study of Industrial Fluctuation*, London: P. S. King.

Samuelson, P. A. (1939). Interactions between the multiplier analysis and the principle of acceleration, *Review of Economic and Statistics*, 21, 75–8.

Schumpeter, J. A. (1939). *Business Cycles: A Theoretical, Historical, and Statistical Analysis of the Capitalist Process*, New York: McGraw-Hill.

Toporowski, J. (2012). The monetary theory of Kalecki and Minsky, *Working Papers*, no. 172, Department of Economics, School of Oriental and African Studies, University of London.

Tugan-Baranovsky, M.I. (1894). *Promyshlennye Krizisy v Sovremennoi Anglii.*

6 The asymmetric-information approach and the Great Recession

A critical appraisal

Alessandro Vercelli

Economists and policy-makers 'must be concerned with the design of institutions as well as with operation within a set of institutions' (Ferri and Minsky, 1992). As Minsky foretold (Minsky, 1987), the role and functioning rules of banks changed significantly in consequence of the process of securitisation started in the 1970s, which has transformed the model of banking from the traditional 'originate-to-hold' to a new 'originate-to distribute'. This metamorphosis has deeply altered the institutional structures of the financial system and its policy implications. In particular, the existing thwarting systems proved inadequate to prevent or abort the 2007–8 bank panic that began the Great Recession.

In this chapter we explore the nexus between securitisation and contagion to investigate its crucial impact on the recent subprime crisis. We discuss here exclusively the mainstream contributions focused on the impact of information, or lack of it, on the incentives impinging upon economic behaviour. Though its scope is quite narrow, this literature provided what has become the mainstream approach in academic and governmental institutions: the 'asymmetric-information approach' (from now on AIA) to banking and financial crises.

Both mainstream economics and orthodox finance theory explain, and pretend to predict, economic and financial behaviour as a rational response to market signals. It is therefore natural to look at the role of banking and at the recent banking panic in terms of information and incentives. However, if we look at the economic system in this way – that is, from the point of view of general equilibrium theory – the very existence of banks becomes a puzzle. In a perfectly competitive market where all agents are fully rational and the relevant information available to each of them is complete, why should banks exist? In particular, the supply of loanable funds should match perfectly well the demand for credit directly in the market, guaranteeing the smooth and efficient working of the system without requiring any need of financial intermediation. Therefore the explanation for the role of banks and of their behaviour, including the episodes of panic, must be found in some significant deviation from the assumption that financial markets are efficient and perfectly competitive. In recent decades (since the early 1970s), the crucial deviation from the perfect-competition model introduced to justify the prominent role of banks and to explain (and to some extent forecast) their behaviour is the ubiquitous existence of sizeable asymmetric information (AI) in economic and financial markets. This assumption has been used to explain many stylised facts observed in financial markets under physiological conditions and to account for their pathologies (banking panics, financial crises and their propagation).

In the next section, we briefly recall the basic principles of the asymmetric-information approach (AIA), while in the third section we mention the point of view of the mainstream branch of the AIA (from now on A1), focusing on the recent metamorphosis of the traditional model of commercial banking and the ensuing explanation of the panic of 2007–8. In the fourth section we review at more length the lesser known alternative branch of the AIA (from now on A2) that focuses on the emergence and evolution of a parallel banking system. In the fifth section we discuss the main policy implications of the two main branches of AIA, while in the sixth section we present a few concluding remarks on the strengths and shortcomings of the AIA.

The asymmetric-information approach

The asymmetric-information approach (AIA) recognises a significant impact of the financial side of a given economy on the dynamic behaviour of the economic system (denied by traditional General Equilibrium theory), by focusing on the different quality and quantity of information available to different parties in financial contracts. In particular, borrowers are assumed to have better information than lenders about their genuine financial position and the investment projects to be financed through the loan. This structural information asymmetry is likely to produce significant deviations from optimal equilibrium (see, for example, Mishkin, 1991, pp. 70–1). This depends, first of all, on adverse selection as AI provides a relative advantage to bad-quality borrowers (often called 'lemons' in the AIA literature) over good-quality borrowers, who could thus withdraw from the market (Akerlof, 1970). Since lenders are unable to discriminate correctly between bad and good borrowers, they charge an average rate of interest that, taking account of the effective risk, is too high for good borrowers and too low for bad borrowers. The ensuing distortions of investment imply more systemic risk for the economy as a whole, less aggregate investment, and thus more financial instability and less growth. Lenders react by further increasing the average rate of interest; the latter, however, results in greater adverse selection as well as in credit rationing (Stiglitz and Weiss, 1981). The higher interest rate would not equilibrate the market even in the case of an excess demand for loans but, on the contrary, would further increase disequilibrium. This cumulative out-of-equilibrium process may easily lead to a credit crunch and possibly to a collapse of financial markets (Mankiw, 1986). The exponents of the AIA claim that this cumulative process helps to explain the recurrence of financial fluctuations and their occasional degeneration in episodes of severe financial crisis (see, for example, Mishkin, 1991, p. 71). In addition, the disequilibrating impact of adverse selection is often reinforced by the increase of moral hazard brought about by an increment of AI. Since lenders cannot easily ascertain the quality of the projects of borrowers, the latter have incentives to engage in projects which increase the expected profits but also the risk of default.

The AIA has provided an influential explanation of the prominent role of banks in financial markets. Their main role is seen as their ability to reduce AI, mitigating many problems raised by adverse selection and moral hazard. In particular, according to the traditional model of banking, recently christened 'originate-to-hold', banks have an expertise in collecting information about the reliability of borrowers, exploiting their lower cost of monitoring as compared to individuals and their more efficient enforcement of restrictive covenants (Diamond, 1984). This advantage is enhanced by long-term costumer relationships such as those entertained by local commercial banks with their clients. Summing up, the AIA supports the traditional idea that banks realise an efficient role of intermediation between saving and investment, channelling investible funds in the most profitable directions to promote economic efficiency and growth. However, the problems produced by AI cannot be easily solved through market mechanisms. The main market remedy for the lender relies in the request that the borrower provides an adequate collateral for the loan, which in case of default may cover the value of the loan. This solution, however, requires that the value of the collateral be information-insensitive so that it retains its value in the case of information about unexpected developments in the financial conditions of the borrower and/or of the economy at large. This requires the intervention of specific institutions able to create information-insensitive debt. The private institutions that play this crucial role are banks. In doing this, they also play an active role in the endogenous process of money creation that provides liquidity to the system whenever it is needed. We will see later, however, that banks play this role fairly well only when the markets are characterised by physiological conditions and not when some sort of pathology develops.

The AIA provides many clues not only for explaining the existence and the crucial role of banks in financial markets and in the economy as a whole, but also for explaining financial fluctuations and their recurring degeneration into serious, sometimes devastating, financial crises. The causal mechanisms briefly reviewed above, triggered by an increase in the interest rate producing a self-sustaining feedback with AI, are liable to trigger cumulative processes bringing about recurring fluctuations and, under particular circumstances, financial collapse. Analogously, a stock market crash lowers the value of collaterals, enhancing adverse selection and moral hazard, and this is likely to lead to financial disruption (see Calomiris and Hubbard, 1990; Greenwald and Stiglitz, 1988). This may be induced by any reduction in the net worth of borrowers because they have less to lose by engaging in moral-hazard activities in the hope of defending the declining net worth (Bernanke and Gertler, 1989). Any of the vicious circles mentioned above may be triggered or reinforced by an autonomous increase in AI or by a negative shift in expectations, which may depend in its turn on exogenous factors. In all the cases listed above, the vicious circle generated by AI eventually leads to a reduction in investment, explaining how a financial crisis is transmitted to the real economy.

Coming to the Great Recession originated by the subprime financial crisis in the USA, the AIA splits between two different basic explanations with radically different policy implications. The crucial divergences between them are rooted in a different understanding of the evolution of banking since the early 1980s, and in particular of the crucial role that the process of securitisation came to play. To simplify the analysis we focus on two polar approaches, as represented respectively by Mishkin (A1 or 'the originate-to-distribute hypothesis') and Gorton (A2 or the 'shadow banking system hypothesis'), taking account also of the main contributions of collaborators and followers. The first point of view is discussed in the third section, while the second point of view is discussed in the fourth section.

The process of securitisation as a distortion of the traditional banking system: the 'originate and distribute' hypothesis and the panic of 2008

According to the prevailing view rooted in the AIA, the ultimate cause of the subprime collapse and the ensuing banking crisis is related to the progressive distortion of the crucial role played by banks in the intermediation between lenders and borrowers – a degenerative process going on since the early 1980s. In this view, the process of securitisation progressively transformed the traditional model of banking, epitomised as 'originate-to-hold', into a new model christened 'originate-to-distribute'. In the traditional model, banks originate credit by providing loans to investors, holding the right to receive the future payments by creditors. Within this model, banks are believed to have strong incentives to reduce the problems raised by AI by thoroughly assessing the value and risk of loans and assets, contributing to a beneficial reduction of systemic risk and to a welcome increase in the efficiency of financial markets.

In the new model of banking, the credit originated by banks is securitised and sold to the market. The bank draws significant advantages from this new strategy but produces at the same time negative externalities for the system as a whole, as it shifts the risk to the market, increasing systemic risk. The incentives of banks to assess accurately the reliability of borrowers, the soundness of their investment projects and the risks involved are significantly weakened, since they are not residual claimants on these loans (Gorton, 2009b, p. 27). The banks lose their role of intermediation between lenders and borrowers while, in consequence of this process of disintermediation, the AI in the market tends to increase, enhancing the related pathologies mentioned above. Even the reliability of the balance sheets of banks adopting the new paradigm is jeopardised, since the process of securitisation is largely based on off-balance sheet transactions through Special Purpose Vehicles (SPVs) and conduits established ad hoc. This further contributes to feed AI, strengthening the vicious circle.

This analysis has been adopted by most financial institutions and policy authorities. The Joint Forum (which includes the Basel Committee on Banking Supervision, the International Organization of Securities Commissions, and the International Association of Insurance Supervisors) clearly endorsed this view of the emerging financial crisis in April 2008:

> . . . under the "originate-to-distribute" model, banks frequently no longer have significant retained exposures, nor have they necessarily retained the

> personnel specializing in workouts who can steer creditor negotiations ([BIS, 2008] Credit Risk Transfer, April 2008, p. 20) . . . Since 2005, the growth of CRT continues to provide banks and securities firms with opportunities to profit from originating, structuring and underwriting CRT products. They can earn fees while not having to hold the associated credit risk or fund positions over an extended time period. (quoted from Gorton, 2010, p. 136)

In this view, the originate-to-distribute model of banking creates:

> severe incentive problems, which are referred to as principal–agent problems, or more simply as agency problems, in which the agent (the originator of the loans) did not have the incentives to act fully in the interest of the principal (the ultimate holder of the loan). Originators have every incentive to maintain origination volume, because that would allow them to earn substantial fees, but they had weak incentives to maintain loan quality . . . (Mishkin, 2008)

According to Gorton (2009b, p. 28), 'all the major bank regulators and central bankers appear to subscribe to this view, though their views have differences and nuances' (see also Basel Committee on Banking Supervision, 2008).

The process of securitisation as a crucial component of a parallel banking system: the panic of 2008 and the ensuing run in the repo market

As we mentioned above, one of the most interesting and accurately articulated 'visions' of the origin and deployment of the Great Recession focuses on the relationship between securitisation and contagion in the shadow banking system (see the A2 as developed by Gary Gorton and his collaborators: in particular, Gorton, 2008, 2009; Gorton and Metrick, 2009; Gorton and Pennacchi, 1990, 1993a, 1993b; Gorton and Winton, 2000, 2003). The following synthetic exposition builds freely on their view by summarising, reformulating and extending some of the crucial steps of their argument. The basic idea is that the financial crisis which started in 2007 in the USA has been in its essence a banking panic with many significant analogies with, and a few far-reaching differences from, the banking panics of the past when the banking system as a whole was believed to be, or feared to be, insolvent. In the recent crisis, this panic originated within the shadow banking system when an unexpected exogenous shock (a slowdown in housing prices followed by a significant reduction) affected first the Mortgage Based Securities (MBS) market in early 2007 and then the whole banking system since August 2007.

In order to understand the causal mechanism underlying the process mentioned above, we first have to clarify the nature of traditional banking and that of shadow banking according to the main exponents of the A2. The essence of banking according to Gorton and his collaborators is not that of intermediation between savers and investors, as in the A1, since their relation, especially in financialised capitalism, does not require the intermediation of banks; the essential role of banking is instead that of creating 'a special kind of debt, debt that is immune to adverse selection by privately informed traders' (Gorton and Pennacchi, 1990). . . . "Informationally-insensitive" debt originally was limited to demand deposits. But, demand deposits are of no use to large firms, banks, hedge funds, and corporate treasuries, which may need to deposit large amounts of money for a short period of time' (Gorton, 2009b, pp. 3–4). Firms also do not deposit large sums in banks because the deposit would not be insured. Instead they 'deposit' their short-term liquidity in the sale and repurchase ('repo') market. These deposits are 'insured' by collateralising with bonds, including a growing percentage of securitised products. The depositor may re-use the collateral by 'rehypothecation', where 'rehypothecation is somewhat akin to being able to write checks' (Gorton, 2009b, p. 4). Collateral is a sort of currency for firms, since it not only mitigates default risk but may also be re-used or spent. Repo is thus a form of banking as it creates 'deposits' of money on call (mostly overnight), which are somehow insured by posting collateral which may be rehypothecated with similar multiplicative effects. The progressive growth of the repo market stimulated the parallel growth of wholesale securitisation to satisfy the growing need for collateral for derivative positions and settlement purposes. Securitisation is seen by Gorton as a form of off-balance sheet banking, since SPVs hold loans financed with high-grade debt which is largely informationally insensitive. In particular, it has an information advantage over corporate debt with a similar rate, since the latter is subject to speculation on information about the corporation's performance. Securitised debt is also in demand as collateral because SPVs are 'bankruptcy remote', since the failure of the originator of loans does not affect the investors in securitisation bonds, called 'tranches'.

Shadow banking thus grew out of a symbiotic integration of two forms of banking: the wholesale securitisation system and the repo market. In the decade preceding the subprime crisis, wholesale securitisation and repo banking became organic parts of an alternative banking system, parallel to the regulated banking system, that came to be called 'shadow banking'. The main trouble with shadow banking, as compared with regulated commercial banking, was the fact that its peculiar 'deposits' gave the illusion of being information-insensitive, being 'insured' by the market through the process of collateralisation. However, the crisis of 2007 revealed that such a belief was unfounded. The collaterals proved to be information-insensitive only in periods of financial tranquillity, but they became suddenly information-sensitive, and highly so, as soon as the crisis broke out. This is clearly revealed by the behaviour of repo haircuts:

> [W]hen the depositor deposits money, the collateral may involve a 'haircut' or margin. The haircut is the percentage difference between the market value of the pledged collateral and the amount of funds lent. For example, a haircut of 5% means that a 'bank' can borrow \$95 for each \$100 in pledged collateral. A haircut further protects the depositor against the risk of borrower default by the 'bank'. The size of the haircut reflects the credit risk of the borrower and the riskiness of the pledged collateral. (Gorton, 2009b, p. 30)

The haircut had been zero until early July 2007, showing a widespread trust in the information-insensitiveness of collateral in the US repo market; however, after the housing shock that started to affect mortgage-related assets in early 2007, the haircut began to be perceived as a systemic event. By the end of 2007 the average repo haircut on structured debt had reached the significant level of 9 per cent in the USA. In 2008 it increased rapidly from 10 per cent in January to 15 per cent in June, reaching 24 per cent in August, and jumping to 46 per cent after the bankruptcy of Lehman Bros (see Gorton, 2009b, p. 33). The increasing haircuts may be interpreted as 'withdrawal' of repo deposits from banks, and their continuous and rapid increase to unprecedented values may be interpreted as a bank run in the interbank ('repo') market. The run on repo was analogous to previous banking panics in the USA, before the deposits of commercial banks were insured in 1934. Earlier bank runs happened because deposits were not insured; the recent one happened when the depositors discovered that their deposits, which they had believed to be 'insured' by information-insensitive collaterals, were in fact only partially and very imperfectly covered by collaterals that suddenly proved to be much more information-sensitive than it was previously believed. As Gorton (2009b, p. 37) emphasises:

> A panic is an event where informational debt becomes informationally-sensitive. It is a switch because it becomes profitable to produce private information about the debt . . . This leads to a 'lemon market' in which everyone needs to suddenly produce information to trade . . . This is a devastating regime switch because participants are not prepared to cope with the sudden information requirements for understanding, valuing, and trading securities that are suddenly informationally-sensitive. This makes them illiquid. Not only does information now have to be produced, but the expertise is lacking.

What is worse, much of the required information is not available, particularly about where the exposures to the shock were located. The ensuing panic paralysed the whole interbank market because no one knew which bank was particularly exposed to the shock.

Policy implications of the panic of 2008

The two main branches of the AIA have radically differing policy implications. The 'hold-to-distribute' hypothesis points to the correction of the most significant shortcomings of the new model of banking, mending the distortions of securitisation and shadow banking. Opinions differ, however, on which are the most efficacious and urgent measures to be adopted. Generally speaking, they should go in the direction of an effective repression of shadow banking and the request that all operations, including those that are currently off balance sheet, be rigorously registered in the balance sheets of banks. Notwithstanding that the policy authorities seem to endorse the A1 analysis, they have so far been reluctant to proceed with the necessary energy towards the implementation of these measures, probably because any sort of constraint to financial activity is strongly opposed by financial lobbies. The policy measures adopted so far seem to rely on the combination of two strategies that are well received by financial markets. First of all, central banks provided, and still provide, plenty of liquidity to banks by keeping very low interest rates and by implementing quantitative easing strategies. Second, the revision of the Basel Accord relies mainly on the upgrading of capital requirements for financial institutions. According to AIA, these policy measures should succeed in counteracting the increase in AI brought about by the crisis. This policy strategy, however, is insufficient and questionable (see, for example, Vercelli, 2011).

According to the A2, the modification of the model of traditional banking and its distortions are not considered the crucial cause of the bank panic of 2008 for three basic reasons. First, it is claimed that the process of securitisation, contrary to intentions, succeeded only partly in transferring the risk of loans from the originators (banks) to the buyers (investors). This is clearly shown by a detailed analysis of the subprime chain:

> Significant losses have been suffered by many up and down the subprime chain: originators, securitisation structures and underwriters – firms and individuals – have suffered. The subprime originators/underwriters that went bankrupt include, e.g., Option One, Ameriquest, New Century, and the likes of Citibank, UBS, and Merrill Lynch with billions of write-downs. (Gorton, 2009b, p. 28)

In particular, the originators retained a number of sizeable direct risks. Loans are warehoused before they are securitised, then they are transferred to the underwriters, which must warehouse the MBS tranches; and, in later stages of the process, dealer bankers underwriting the collateralised debt obligations (CDOs) also have to warehouse securitisation tranches. Second, originators of loans (in particular, mortgages) keep a participation in returns or losses that may accrue from the loans originated due to servicing rates and retained interests, particularly in the case of interest-only securities, principal-only securities and residual securities. In addition, some banks keep the most senior portions of CDOs on their balance sheets. Third, the existence of implicit contractual arrangements between buyers of tranches and the SIV sponsor that guarantees them has been empirically documented (Gorton, 2009b, p. 31) and led some SIV sponsors to take these items back on to their balance sheets.

Summing up, the effective practice of securitisation shows that the transfer of risk from the banks originating loans to the investors is only partial. Systemic risk and AI increase as risk is spread in an opaque way over much larger categories of subjects participating in the chain of loans securitisation. None of these subjects retains significant incentives to assess the risk of securitised loans, but, according to the A2, this is by itself insufficient to explain the banking panic triggered by the subprime crisis. In this view, in order to grasp the causes of the latter we have to understand that the process of securitisation has become a crucial component of a parallel banking system which interacts with the traditional one but has a certain degree of autonomy: what has become to be called 'shadow banking'. While 'shadow banking' is seen on the first point of view as a degeneration of the traditional banking system which in principle should be repressed, the second point of view sees it as the banking system of big firms and financial institutions that should be controlled and regulated but not repressed. On this view, the banking panic of 2008 originated not in the traditional banking system but in the shadow banking system.

In order to understand this crucial point, the recent evolution of banking is put into the long-run perspective that, unless we learn from history, we are condemned to repeat past mistakes. Gorton distinguishes two periods: the National Banking Era (1864–1934) following the approval of the National Banking Act, and the Quiet Period (1934–2007). In the National Banking Era, in the absence of a central bank:

> bank themselves developed increasingly sophisticated ways to respond to panics . . . centred on private banks' clearinghouses . . . In response to a panic, banks would jointly suspend convertibility of deposits into currency . . . the clearinghouse would also cease the publication of individual bank accounting information . . . and would instead only publish the aggregate information of all the members. Finally, banks issued loan certificates . . . a kind of deposit insurance. (Gorton, 2009b, p. 19)

This response strategy aimed to make the liabilities of single banks more information-insensitive while also giving tangible protection to clients in the form of loan certificates. Though this strategy was well designed, it did not prevent panics but only reduced their frequency and the impact of their consequences, in particular by preserving single banks from insolvency caused by specific runs. This clearinghouse system evolved continuously, eventually giving birth to the Federal Reserve System created in 1913.

The Great Depression clarified the fact that the self-regulation of markets may succeed in avoiding bank runs in tranquil times but not when the entire system is believed to be insolvent. Therefore in 1934 the crucial decision was taken to provide bank deposits with public insurance and to re-regulate the banking system according to strict rules. This new policy regime inaugurated a 'quiet period' in US banking as a response to the Great Depression. The number of US bank failures, which had increased to the remarkable number of 4,000 per year just before this courageous and controversial decision, suddenly dropped to a number very close to zero – a number that was maintained until the recent crisis (apart from a moderate and short-lived spike from the late 1970s to 1994 (see Gorton, 2009b, fig. on p. 3.). This depends not only on the introduction of public deposits insurance but also on the introduction of severe regulation of the banking system, 1) by segregating commercial banking from investment banking (Glass-Steagall Act, 1933), 2) by limiting entry into the market by rationing banking charters, and 3) by introducing strict supervision, compulsory balance-sheet disclosure, and interest rate ceilings on deposits (Regulation Q).

These measures combined the 'sticks' of regulation and supervision with the 'carrots' of a more valuable bank charter, guaranteeing monopoly rents at the local level. This policy strategy reduced the freedom of choice of bank managers and the degree of competition between banks, but at the same time greatly increased the stability of the financial system. It is possible to argue that what was lost in efficiency because of the policy constraints on competition was more than compensated by the huge positive externalities accruing with financial stability.

The deregulation of financial markets (for example, of interest rate ceilings) progressively introduced in the 1980s, in accordance with the new policy view that became hegemonic in those years, caused bank charter values to decline. In addition, the growing competition from non-banks (e.g. money market mutual funds) induced banks to reduce capital, to increase risk and to rely on financial innovation. Both the systematic process of securitisation and shadow banking can be seen as responses of the banking system to the new policy environment, to preserve the returns on equity in banking. Unfortunately, as we have seen, shadow banking was more profitable for banks but much more vulnerable to panic, since the system of market insurance through collateral that was believed to be information-insensitive turned out to be not at all panic-proof.

According to Gorton, the solution is not 'forcing everything back on balance sheets' (Gorton, 2009b, p. 39), since this would not in itself solve the collateral problem (the scarcity of reliable information-insensitive collateral). A better solution in his opinion would be the adoption of a series of measures meant to create charter value and information-insensitive debt. This is possible only through a strict regulation of whatever subject plays the role of banking (including the emission of securitised products and the creation of repo deposits). This could be obtained by introducing the following measures:

1 Senior tranches of securitisation products should be insured by the state.
2 Government, not rating agencies, should supervise and examine banks, including securitisation.
3 Entry into securitisation should be limited, and any firm that enters should be deemed a 'bank' and be subject to supervision

Points 1 and 2 are instrumental to the creation of reliable information-insensitive debt, while point 3 creates value for the production of information-insensitive debt.

Finally, Gorton emphasises that, contrary to the standard objection raised against points 1 and 3, their adoption would not encourage moral hazard since it would be discouraged by the fear of compromising a valuable charter; on the contrary, as shown by the history of banking in the USA, moral hazard develops in a climate of unfettered competition as a way to defeat competitors.

Criticisms and extensions

In our opinion, each of the two main variants of the AIA captures some significant features of the evolution of the banking system since the early 1980s, and in particular its implications for the 2007–8 bank panic. The A1 analyses the impact on decision-makers of the metamorphosis of banking from the traditional 'originate-to-hold' model to the recent 'originate-to-distribute' model. In particular, it claims that no one within or outside banks retains significant incentives to assess the value and risk of securitised debt. The A2 focuses on the emergence of a parallel banking system tailored to the needs of firms, and clearly analyses its functioning rules. This has allowed the A2 to understand better the origin and early consequences of the bank panic of 2007–8, but the subsequent stages of the financial crisis, its propagation and its degeneration into a Great Recession cannot be fully understood without also taking into account the point of view of A1. A certain degree of complementarity between the two approaches should not be considered surprising, since both are rooted in the AIA and focus on different roles of banking that are not mutually exclusive: the role of intermediation between lenders and borrowers (A1) and the role of creation of information-insensitive debt (A2). Banks play both roles in the financial system and we may conceive them as complementary. However, both branches suffer from the limitations of the common trunk. The main difference between them derives from a diverging view of the role of securitisation and shadow banking in financial markets. The A1 sees securitisation and shadow banking as distortions of the traditional model of commercial banking, while the A2 sees securitisation and its interaction with the repo market as a crucial component of a parallel market system identified with the shadow banking system. The two branches of the AIA draw from their different analyses radically different policy implications. If taken seriously, the A1 should lead to a policy of severe 'financial repression' focused on securitisation and shadow banking to eliminate, or at least mitigate, the distortions of the prevailing model of banking, while according to the A2 shadow banking should not be repressed but strictly regulated. In our opinion, however, this is not possible unless the shadow dimension of the parallel banking system is effaced by the necessary transparency provided by systematic reporting and accounting rigour.

The recent financial crisis has been originated and affected not only by asymmetric information but more generally by the nature and degree of uncertainty, whether asymmetric or not. No doubt asymmetric information is a significant and ubiquitous source of uncertainty but it is not the only one. The spreading of risk across a plurality of unknown and unknowable subjects, which is emphasised by both branches of the AIA, implies that uncertainty over the value and risk of securitised assets is strong (not representable through additive probability distributions) or radical (we just do not know). In addition, information and uncertainty do not exhaust the causes of financial crises and their propagation. This is a common shortcoming of all the branches of the AIA.

The A2 approach to the origin and early developments of the crisis and their policy implications is a useful contribution to the vast but fragmented literature on the origins and early developments of the recent financial crisis. Gorton and his co-authors have succeeded in integrating first-hand knowledge of recent financial practices, an accurate investigation of the empirical evidence and a detailed reconstruction of the history of financial crises and banking panics. In particular, the microeconomic approach usually pursued in finance is extended in a challenging way to the systemic consequences of microeconomic and regulatory decisions, which permits a clearer understanding of the policy implications of the new model of banking. On the other hand, Gorton's arguments are liable to the criticism of implicit theorising, since the relationship between the basic concepts and the subsequent steps of the argument is sometimes insufficiently clarified. The crucial concept that banking is in its essence the creation of information-insensitive debt goes a long way towards the understanding of recent banking practices, but the concept is too narrow. This provides a sharp focus to the argument, but only by clouding relations, which are potentially illuminating, with other theoretical approaches. We may agree that a crucial role of banking has always been the creation of secure debt in the broad sense of shock-insensitive debt; however, the meaning and implications of this are not fully analysed. In particular, Gorton mentions the relationship between the shock insensitiveness of an asset, its liquidity and the risk of holding it, but their crucial relations are not analysed in depth. In addition, although new information is an important source of potential shocks, there are other important shocks that have a different nature: in particular, those triggered by the interaction between the balance sheets of the units that implicitly play an important role in the A2 (see, for example, Koo, 2011). The latter are not information shocks but the consequence of market interaction which is necessarily reflected by accounting figures.

Information sensitiveness, and even more the broader concept of shock sensitiveness, is a concept akin to that of financial fragility: in both cases a small perturbation is sufficient to change the qualitative features or behaviour of economic units (Vercelli, 1991, 2001, 2011). However the financial fragility of a unit depends on the degree of shock-sensitiveness of its balance sheet and therefore on the interaction with all the other units which may affect it (Minsky, 1982a, 1986). As for the financial fragility of the system as a whole, it cannot be assessed through a microeconomic approach applied to a representative unit or by a simple additive aggregation of single units. A satisfactory analysis must take full account of the interdependences between the financial fragility of the single economic units, avoiding the fallacy of composition (Ferri, 2011; Giansante et al., 2012).

The core of the A2 vision combines a view of the symbiotic role of systematic securitisation and of the repo market within the framework of an updated and realistic view of the nature of banking. This interaction may be understood only by delving into the processes of contagion, by focusing first of all on the propagation of the financial crisis from mortgage-related assets to the entire finance and then to the whole economy. Contagion plays a crucial role in this theory, but its role remains in great part implicit. The shock that triggered the crisis (the slowdown in the price of housing at the turn of 2006, followed by its reduction, at first mild and then precipitous) affected at first only the subprime asset classes, whose value significantly declined. The ABX index showed after early 2007 a steady deterioration in subprime fundamentals and a parallel progressive deterioration in subprime-related asset classes and firms (Gorton, 2009b, p. 31).

Subprime mortgage originations in 2005 and 2006 amounted to $1.2, a remarkable sum that, however, would not have been sufficient in itself to trigger a systemic crisis in the USA. The systemic event, however, reflected by the collapse of other asset classes normally unrelated with subprime assets, started only in August 2007 when average repo haircuts, which were still about zero until then, started to rise as described above. The crisis became systemic because no one knew where the increased risk related to mortgage asset classes was located. Therefore when this risk was perceived to have overcome the safety threshold set by the decision-makers, the consequent panic was referred to the banking system as a whole. So the problem is not only one of asymmetric information but of insufficient information available to decision-makers. The ultimate causes of the crisis are thus related to the strong uncertainty affecting the choices of decision-makers, while asymmetric information is only one aspect of it.

The run on repo deposits revealed by the growing haircuts which occurred in the second half of 2007 triggered a well-known process of propagation that had been experienced in earlier financial crises, at least the most serious ones: a variant of the Fisherian process of debt deflation as updated by Minsky (see Fisher, 1933; Minsky, 1982b) . The main dealers found it more and more difficult to refinance their positions and found themselves over-indebted; in order to reduce their indebtedness, they had to sell part of their assets, even those that were originally unrelated to mortgage collateral. The market values of all these assets declined progressively, compelling the main dealers of securitised products in the repo market to downsize their activity. This vicious circle eventually propagated to all the economic units holding assets that underwent a significant loss of value (most financial assets under these circumstances). The process of slow but progressive build-up of bank panic emerged in August 2007 and became progressively more intense, culminating in September 2008.

The policy implications drawn from the A2 analysis of the recent banking panic go in a sensible direction: in order to re-establish a period of financial stability comparable with that of the Quiet Period in the USA, we have to sacrifice the myth of perfect competition. In the 1970s and 1980s it was customary to discuss the trade-off between efficiency, promoted by more competition, and financial stability, promoted by strict regulation and severe supervision, in the quest for the right balance between these two objectives. In the 1980s the Gordian knot was cut in the direction of competition and efficiency in the illusion that the evolution of banking, theoretical knowledge and regulation know-how would avoid financial instability. The result was that financial instability increased progressively, as witnessed by the number of severe financial crises experienced in the three last decades (Reinhart and Rogoff, 2009). As for efficiency, there are scanty signs of an improvement, particularly in the sector of support to the real economy, since in recent decades trading and speculation that were more profitable in the short run and were believed to be less risky crowded out credit for firms and households (Orhangazi, 2007). In addition, the progressive disappearance of charter value brought about by the systematic deregulation of financial markets, contrary to what was expected by mainstream economic theory and finance, encouraged moral hazard, predatory lending and corporate irresponsibility, as has been clearly documented by Gorton. The policy perspective advanced by the A2 is questionable, however, in its defence of shadow banking. On this view, the latter should be strictly regulated, like any form of banking, but not outlawed: 'forcing everything back on balance sheet seems like an attempt to return to the Eden of the Quiet Period without recognizing that the world has changed' (Gorton, 2009b, p. 40). This seems to me to contradict Gorton's own theoretical assumptions. If the ultimate problem is asymmetric information, shadow banking is a crucial part of the problem:

> [K]eep in mind that there are no official measures of the size of the repo market, or repo haircuts or rates. There are no data on the identity of repo market participants . . . there are no official measures of collateral usage in derivatives or settlement. There are no official measures of securitization. The shadow banking system was, as they say, 'off the radar screen'. (Gorton, 2009b, p. 42)

How is it possible to regulate shadow banking if all the relevant data are missing, or are unreliable estimates? How could airport traffic operators regulate traffic and keep safety without radar? How could regulators supervise banking without access to reliable balance sheets? How reliable may balance sheets be considered if off-balance sheet posting is allowed? In conclusion, complete transparency is necessary to complete the information of all the agents, in order to overcome excessive liquidity preference and other anomalies which are typical of strong uncertainty, and to avoid asymmetric information and its disruptive consequences.

References

Akerlof, G. (1970). The market for 'lemons': quality uncertainty and market mechanism, *Quarterly Journal of Economics*, 84, 3, 488–500.

Bank for International Settlements (2008). *Credit Risk Transfer: Developments from 2005 to 2007*, Consultative Document, April.

Basel Committee on Banking Supervision (2008). *Liquidity Risk: Management and Supervisory Challenges*, February.

Bernanke, B. and M. Gertler (1989). Agency costs, net worth, and business fluctuations, *American Economic Review*, 79, 14–31.

Calomiris, C. W. and R. G. Hubbard (1990). Firm heterogeneity, internal finance, and 'credit rationing', *NBER Working Papers*, no. 2497.

Diamond, D. W. (1984) Financial intermediation and delegated monitoring, *Review of Economic Studies*, 51, 393–414.

Ferri, P. (2011). *Macroeconomics of Growth, Cycles and Financial Instability*. Cheltenham, UK: Edward Elgar.

Ferri, P. and H. P. Minsky (1992). Market processes and thwarting systems, *Structural Change and Economic Dynamics*, 3, 79–91.

Fisher, I. (1933). The debt-deflation theory of the great depression, *Econometrica*, 1, 337–57.

Giansante, S., Chiarella, C., Sordi, S. and Vercelli, A. (2012). Structural contagion and vulnerability to unexpected liquidity shortfalls, *Journal of Economic Behavior and Organization*, 83, 558–69.

Gorton, G. (2008). The panic of 2007. In *Maintaining Stability in a Changing Financial System*, Proceedings of the 2008 Jackson Hole Conference, Federal Reserve Bank of Kansas City, 2008.

Gorton, G. (2009a). Information, liquidity, and the (ongoing) panic of 2007, *American Economic Review, Papers and Proceedings*, 99, 567–72.

Gorton, G. (2009b). Slapped in the face by the invisible hand: banking and the panic of 2007, Social Science Research Network working paper, available at SSRN: http://ssrn.com/abstract=1401882.

Gorton, G. (2010). *Slapped by the Invisible Hand: The Panic of 2007*, Oxford: Oxford University Press.

Gorton, G. and A. Metrick (2009). The run on repo and the panic of 2007–2008, Yale University working paper.

Gorton, G. and G. Pennacchi (1990). Financial intermediaries and liquidity creation, *Journal of Finance*, 45, 49–72.

Gorton, G. and G. Pennacchi (1993a). Money market funds and finance companies: are they the banks of the future? In M. Klausner and L. White, eds., *Structural Change in Banking*, Homewood, IL: Irwin, pp. 173–214.

Gorton, G. and G. Pennacchi (1993b). Security baskets and index-linked securities, *Journal of Business*, 66, 1–29.

Gorton, G. and A. Winton (2003). Financial intermediation. In G. Constantinides, M. Harris and R. Stulz, eds., *The Handbook of the Economics of Finance: Corporate Finance*, Amsterdam: Elsevier Science, pp. 431–534.

Greenwald, B. and J. E. Stiglitz (1988). Money, imperfect information, and economic fluctuations. In M. Kohn and S. C. Tsiang, eds., *Expectations and Macroeconomics*, Oxford: Oxford University Press, pp. 103–40.

Koo, R. (2011). The world in balance sheet recession: causes, cure, and politics, *Real-World Economics Review*, 58, 19–37.

Mankiw, N. G. (1986). The allocation of credit and financial collapse. *Quarterly Journal of Economics*, 101, 455–70.

Minsky, H. P. (1982a). *Can 'It' Happen Again? Essays on Instability and Finance*, Armonk, NY: M. E. Sharpe.

Minsky, H.P. (1982b). Debt-deflation processes in today's institutional environment, *BNL Quarterly Review*, 143, 375–93.

Minsky, H. P. (1986) *Stabilizing an Unstable Economy*, New Haven, CT: Yale University Press.

Minsky, H. P. (1987). Securitization, Handout Econ 335A, mimeo. In Levy Archives.

Mishkin, F. S. (1991). Asymmetric information and financial crises: a historical perspective. In R. G. Hubbard, ed., *Financial Markets and Financial Crises*, Chicago: University of Chicago Press, pp. 69–108.

Mishkin, F. (2008). On leveraged losses: lessons from the mortgage meltdown. Speech at the US Policy Forum, New York, February.

Orhangazy, O. (2007). Financialization and capital accumulation in the non-financial capital sector in *Political Economy Research Institute Working Papers*, no. 149.

Reinhart, C. M. and K. Rogoff (2009). *This Time is Different: Eight Centuries of Financial Folly*, Princeton, NJ: Princeton University Press.

Stiglitz, J. E. and A. Weiss (1981). Credit rationing in markets with imperfect information, *American Economic Review*, 71, 393–410.

Vercelli, A. (1991). *Methodological Foundations of Macroeconomics: Keynes and Lucas*, Cambridge: Cambridge University Press.

Vercelli, A. (2001). Minsky, Keynes and the structural instability of a sophisticated monetary economy. In R. Bellofiore and P. Ferri, eds., *Financial Fragility and Investment in the Capitalist Economy*, Vol. II of *The Economic Legacy of Hyman Minsky*, Cheltenham, UK, and Northampton, MA: Edward Elgar, pp. 33–52.
Vercelli, A. (2011). A perspective on Minsky moments: revisiting the core of the Financial Instability Hypothesis, *Review of Political Economy*, 23, 49–67.

Part III

Formal models of the business cycle

7 A Kaleckian macromodel with memory

Gian Italo Bischi and Ahmad Naimzada

In a recent paper, Charles (2010) considers a post-Keynesian model, based on Delli Gatti, Gallegati, and Gardini (1993), and proposes a particular form of endogenous propensity to invest, denoted as abnormal, such that a fall in the propensity to invest occurs when capacity utilization (measured as the output–capital ratio) increases. As argued by Charles, this is attributed to strong pressures from shareholders represented by institutions like banks or pension funds in a financial capitalist economy. In fact, such stockholders may refuse the investment policy needed to respond to a rise in output because it threatens the profitability of their assets in the short run, as the decision to invest may involve a prolonged rise in the retention rate, to ensure safe growth through larger internal funds, leading to a decrease in the amount of their dividends. The dynamic model obtained by Charles is expressed by a one-dimensional quadratic map (conjugate to the standard logistic map) that may exhibit persistent cycles and chaotic trajectories as a result of the abnormal behavior.

In this chapter we assume that, instead of being a function of only the current capacity utilization, the (abnormal) endogenous propensity to invest also depends on the previous value through a weighted average: that is, the stockholders are assumed to have a certain degree of memory, which may be interpreted as more prudent behavior. This assumption gives rise to a two-dimensional discrete dynamical system that includes a behavioral parameter that represents the degree of memory (or level of prudence) of the stockholders. The qualitative analysis of this dynamical system shows that memory has a stabilizing role for a weighted average close to a uniform distribution; otherwise, when the weighted average (i.e. the memory parameter) takes extreme values (i.e. consideration of current value prevails or it is too much neglected), the system is destabilized through period-doubling or Neimark–Sacker bifurcations respectively. Through a stability analysis performed by the usual linearization procedure, we analytically prove the occurrence of the local bifurcations that cause stability loss of the unique equilibrium, and the delimitation of the stability region in the space of parameters is obtained. However, a numerical investigation of the global dynamic behaviors of the model clearly shows that further dynamic scenarios must be considered, characterized by coexistence of attracting sets, each with its own basin of attraction, even in the range of stability of the unique steady state. The possibility of coexistence of the locally stable steady state with different cyclic or chaotic attractors that characterize different kinds of long-run behavior, is shown numerically, as well as the structure of the basins of attraction that characterize the path dependence of the model with memory. This is an interesting situation because it gives an intermediate alternative between two antagonistic points of view, one stating stability of the equilibrium (i.e. any perturbation from the stationary equilibrium is recovered by the endogenous dynamics that goes back to the equilibrium in the long run) and the other one stating instability (i.e. any small perturbation from the equilibrium is amplified by the endogenous dynamics, thus leading to a different attractor characterized by endless self-sustained oscillations). In the case of coexistence, a situation is obtained, sometimes denoted by the term "corridor stability" after Leijonhufvud (1973), such that small perturbations are recovered as far as they are confined inside the basin of attraction of the locally stable equilibrium, whereas larger perturbations lead to time evolutions that further depart from the equilibrium and go to the coexisting attractor in the long run, where oscillatory motion prevails (periodic or chaotic). Moreover, the situation may be even more involved when the boundaries that separate the two basins assume a complicated shape (sometimes quite convoluted), as we shall show numerically in the model considered in this chapter.

These dynamic scenarios, together with their economic consequences, clearly show the importance of a global analysis of nonlinear dynamical systems, which can often be performed only through heuristic methods obtained by a combination of analytical, geometrical, and numerical methods. In fact, a study limited to local stability and bifurcations, based on the linear approximation of the model around the equilibrium points, sometimes may be quite incomplete and even misleading, as the example considered in this chapter clearly shows.

The plan of the work is as follows. In the next section we describe the model with memory and we prove analytical results about the role of memory parameter on the local stability of its unique steady state. We then confirm the stability results numerically and we investigate some global properties of the model and the different kinds of disequilibrium dynamics observed. Moreover, the possibility of coexistence of locally stable steady state and different kinds of cyclic attractor is shown numerically, as well as the structure of the basins of attraction that characterize the path dependence of the model with memory.

The model and its local stability properties

We consider a closed economy without government intervention. National income is subdivided into wages and profits:

$$pY = wL + \Pi \tag{1}$$

where $p \geq 0$ is the price level, $Y \geq 0$ is the national output, $w \geq 0$ is the nominal wage rate, $L \geq 0$ is the level of employment and $\Pi \geq 0$ represents the level of gross profits. Firms, assumed to be all identical, set the price by the following markup-pricing equation:

$$p = (1+m)wl \tag{2}$$

where $m \geq 0$ is the fixed markup used by firms and $l \geq 0$ is the fixed labor–output ratio $l = \frac{L}{Y}$. From equations (1) and (2) we get the profit share in terms of nominal income $0 \leq \pi \leq 1$:

$$\pi = \frac{\Pi}{pY} = 1 - \frac{wl}{p} = \frac{m}{1+m} \tag{3}$$

For the sake of simplicity, in the following we assume $p = 1$. The rate of profit r, defined as the fraction of profits in nominal capital stock, can be expressed as:

$$r = \frac{\Pi}{K} = \frac{Y}{K}\frac{\Pi}{Y} = u\pi \tag{4}$$

where K is the capital equipment and u, the output–capital ratio, is a proxy for the rate of capacity use.

We assume that the economy is populated by three kinds of agent: firms, capitalists, and workers. Turning our attention to saving behaviors, we postulate that firms save a portion $0 \leq s_f \leq 1$ of their net profits $(r - id)$, and capitalists save a portion $0 \leq s_c \leq 1$ of their revenues, including distributed dividends $(1 - s_f)(r - id)$ and interest received from firms, id.

Workers are assumed to consume all their income. Thus the global saving function assumes differentiated propensity to save:

$$g^S = \frac{S}{K} = s_f(r - id) + s_c\left[(1 - s_f)(r - id) + id\right] \tag{5}$$

where S is the total saving. Investment demand, as a ratio of capital stock, is given by:

$$g^d = \frac{I}{K} = \alpha + \beta s_f(r - id) \tag{6}$$

where $\alpha \geq 0$ represents animal spirits and $\beta \geq 0$ represents the propensity to invest. Assuming the standard Keynesian adjustment mechanism – that is, output, through the rate of capacity utilization, changes according to the excess of demand in the goods market – we get the dynamic equation:

$$u_{t+1} = u_t + g_t^d - g_t^s$$

where u_t is the output–capital ratio, used as a proxy for the rate of capacity use, at time period t, and πu_t represents the macroeconomic profit rate at time t. So, after some substitutions and straightforward algebraic manipulations, the same difference equation proposed by Charles (2010) is obtained:

$$u_{t+1} = \left[\alpha - s_f(\beta_t + s_c - 1)id\right] + \left\{1 - \pi\left[s_f(1 - \beta_t) + s_c(1 - s_f)\right]\right\} u_t \tag{7}$$

In Charles (2010) the propensity to invest is endogenized by assuming:

$$\beta_t = \beta_1 - \beta_2 u_t \tag{8}$$

with $\beta_i > 0$, i = 1,2, in order to indicate that a rise in the rate of capacity utilization causes a fall in the propensity to invest. As argued in Charles (2010), this apparent paradox is explained by incorporating the presence of stockholders, represented by institutions like banks and pension funds, which may refuse the investment policy needed to respond to a rise in output because it threatens the profitability of their assets in the short run. For example, the decision to invest may perfectly involve an immediate and prolonged rise in the retention rate, to ensure safe growth through larger internal funds. This is unacceptable for shareholders with short-term views since it would mechanically diminish the amount of their dividends. In a financial capitalist economy, the primacy of stockholders is such that they have the capability to ask for abnormal requests, and postponing accumulation projects is obviously one of them. Therefore, the existence of omnipotent shareholders explains why an increase in the rate of capacity utilization may lead to a fall in the propensity to invest. Such a situation is denoted by Charles as an "abnormal case."

By reducing the first-order difference equation obtained from (7) with (8) to a quadratic map (conjugate to the standard logistic map), Charles (2010) shows that when firms' managers adopt such abnormal behaviors, the system may exhibit persistent cycles and chaotic trajectories as a result of the increasing pressures from shareholders regarding the propensity to invest. In fact, (7) with (8) becomes a one-dimensional quadratic map, conjugate to the logistic map (see, for example, Devaney, 1987; Lorenz, 1993) well known for its chaotic dynamics.

In this chapter we assume that, instead of being a function of only the current capacity utilization of the economic system, u_t, the endogenous propensity to invest also depends on the previous value u_{t-1}, i.e. the stakeholders have a certain degree of memory. This assumption can be expressed by using the following weighted average to compute the propensity to invest.

$$\beta_t = \beta_1 - \beta_2 \left[(1-\omega) u_t + \omega u_{t-1} \right] \tag{9}$$

where the real parameter $\omega \varepsilon [0, 1]$ represents a memory parameter, as the expression (9) reduces to (8) in the limiting case $\omega = 0$, whereas in the other limiting case $\omega = 1$, the actual value u_t is neglected and only the previous one is considered in the determination of the propensity to invest. Of course, intermediate values of ω represent different kinds of weighted average between the two last observations of u_t, $\omega = 1/2$ corresponding to the case of uniform average.

If we plug (9) into (7) we obtain a second-order difference equation, as u_{t+1} is now influenced by both u_t and u_{t-1}, which can be written as an equivalent two-dimensional discrete dynamical system. In fact, by introducing the new dynamic variables $x_t = u_t$ and $y_t = u_{t-1}$ the model (2) with (9) assumes the form:

$$\begin{cases} x_{t+1} = -\pi B(1-\omega)x_t^2 - \pi B\omega x_t y_t + \left[A + idB(1-\omega)\right]x_t + idB\omega y_t + C \\ y_{t+1} = x_t \end{cases} \tag{10}$$

where the following aggregate parameters have been introduced:

$$A = 1 - \pi\left[s_f(1-\beta_1) + s_c(1-s_f)\right]$$
$$B = s_f\beta_2$$
$$C = \alpha - ids_f(\beta_1 + s_c - 1)$$

By imposing the steady-state condition $u_{t+1} = u_t$ for each t, corresponding to $x_{t+1} = x_t = y_t$, it is straightforward to see that a unique positive equilibrium exists, which does not depend on the memory parameter ϖ and is the same as in the model proposed by Charles:

$$x^* = u^* = \frac{A + idB - 1 + \sqrt{(A + idB - 1)^2 + 4\pi BC}}{2\pi B} \tag{11}$$

whose stability properties are strongly influenced by the memory parameter ϖ, as stated by the following proposition.

Proposition 1. *The equilibrium $E = (x^*, x^*)$ of the dynamical system (10) is locally asymptotically stable if $\varpi_f < \varpi < \varpi_h$ with*

$$\omega_f = \frac{\sqrt{(A + idB - 1)^2 + 4\pi BC} - 2}{A - idB - 1 + \sqrt{(A + idB - 1)^2 + 4\pi BC}} \tag{12}$$

and

$$\omega_h = \frac{2}{A - idB - 1 + \sqrt{(A + idB - 1)^2 + 4\pi BC}} \tag{13}$$

If the memory parameter ϖ exits the stability interval decreasing through the lower bound ω_f then it loses stability through a supercritical flip bifurcation, at which a stable cycle of period two is created, whereas if ϖ exits the stability interval increasing through the upper bound ϖ_h then it loses stability through a supercritical Neimark–Sacker bifurcation at which a stable closed invariant curve is created surrounding E, along which quasi periodic or periodic motion occurs.

Proof. The Jacobian matrix of (10) computed at the equilibrium E becomes:

$$J(E)=\begin{bmatrix} \pi B(\omega-2)x^* + A + idB(1-\omega) & -\pi B\omega x^* + idB\omega \\ 1 & 0 \end{bmatrix} \tag{14}$$

Let $Tr = \pi B(\omega-2)x^* + A + idB(1-\omega)$ and $Det = \pi B\omega x^* - idB\omega$ be, respectively, the trace and the determinant of the matrix $J(E)$. Then the characteristic equation becomes:

$$P(z) = z^2 - Tr \cdot z + Det = 0$$

and a set of sufficient conditions for the stability of E, i.e. for the eigenvalues to be inside the unit circle of the complex plane, is given by:

$$P(1) = 1 - Tr + Det > 0; \quad P(-1) = 1 + Tr + Det > 0; \quad 1 - Det > 0 \tag{15}$$

In our case we have $P(1) = 1 + 2\pi Bx^* - A - idB = \sqrt{(A + idB - 1)^2 + 4\pi BC} > 0$ for each set of parameters, where the expression (11) has been used. Instead, the other two stability conditions become, respectively:

$$\omega > \frac{2\pi Bx^* - A - 1 - idB}{2B(\pi x^* - id)} = \omega_f \quad \text{and} \quad \omega < \frac{1}{B(\pi x^* - id)} = \omega_h$$

where the expressions of the bifurcation values ω_f and ω_h given in the proposition are obtained by inserting (11) inside these expressions. The value of ω at which $P(-1)$ ecomes negative represents a flip (or period-doubling) bifurcation value at which an eigenvalue exits the unit circle through the value -1, and the one at which $1-Det$ becomes negative represents a Neimark–Sacker bifurcation at which a couple of complex and conjugate eigenvalues exit the unit circle of the complex plane (see, for example, Guckenheimer and Holmes, 1983; Lorenz, 1993). We claim numerical evidence for the supercritical nature of these bifurcations, as shown in the next section.

In Figure 7.1 the stability region bounded by the two curves $\varpi = \varpi_h$ (flip bifurcation curve) and $\omega = \omega_h$ (Neimark–Sacker bifurcation curve) is represented by the grey-shaded region in the parameters' plane (β_2, ω) for the same set of parameters used in Charles (2010), namely $\alpha = 0.2$, $i = 0.05$, $d = 0.3$, $\pi = 0.47$, $s_f = 0.8$, $s_c = 0.9$, $\beta_1 = 5.5$.

As can be seen, along the line $\varpi = 0$, at $\beta_2 = 5.5$ the equilibrium loses stability for increasing values of β_2 through a flip bifurcation, followed by the well-known period-doubling route to chaos for further increasing values of β_2. For higher values of the memory parameter ϖ the range of stability of β_2 is increased and it becomes larger and larger for intermediate values of β: that is, for a more uniform memory distribution. However, this is no longer true for high values of

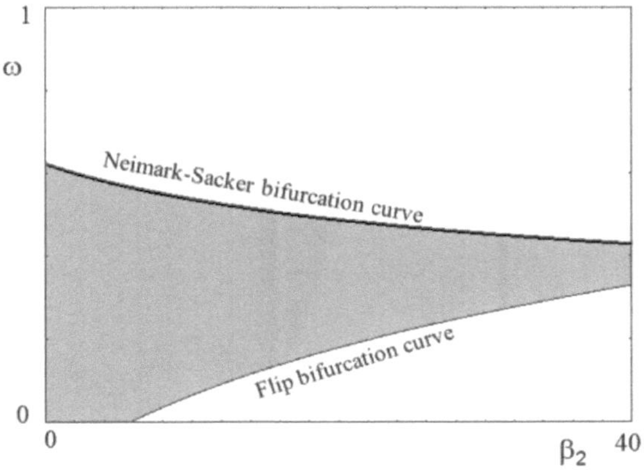

Figure 7.1 Stability region of the equilibrium E, represented by the grey-shaded region in the parameters' plane (β_2, ϖ) for the same set of parameters used in Charles (2010): $\alpha = 0.2$, $i = 0.05$, $d = 0.3$, $\pi = 0.47$, $s_f = 0.8$, $s_c = 0.9$, $\beta_1 = 5.5$.

Source: Authors' computations

ϖ: that is, when in (9) more weight is given to the previous value u_{t-1}. In this case a new phenomenon occurs, strictly related with the memory effect: for increasing values of β_2 the stability of the equilibrium is lost through a Neimark–Sacker bifurcation – quasi-periodic motion around E is observed. Moreover, the range of stability of β_2 is reduced for increasing values of ϖ. It is interesting to observe the qualitative changes in the long-run dynamics when the memory parameter ϖ is increased for a fixed value of β_2. This is shown in the bifurcation diagram of Figure 7.2, obtained for $\beta_2 = 17$ and increasing values of the bifurcation parameter ϖ. This bifurcation diagram clearly shows the stability range of the equilibrium E for intermediate values of the memory parameter ϖ, as well as the two different kinds of local bifurcation through which E loses stability. This bifurcation diagram confirms the results given in the proposition on local stability and bifurcations of the unique equilibrium E.

For increasing values of ϖ in the region $\varpi > \varpi_h$ the amplitude of the quasi-periodic motion increases until the closed invariant curve changes its shape and becomes a chaotic attractors which suddenly disappears, and the generic trajectory diverges. This is caused by global (or contact) bifurcations, as will be shown numerically in the next section. However, other interesting dynamic phenomena will be shown by a global numerical exploration that cannot be revealed by the local stability given in this section.

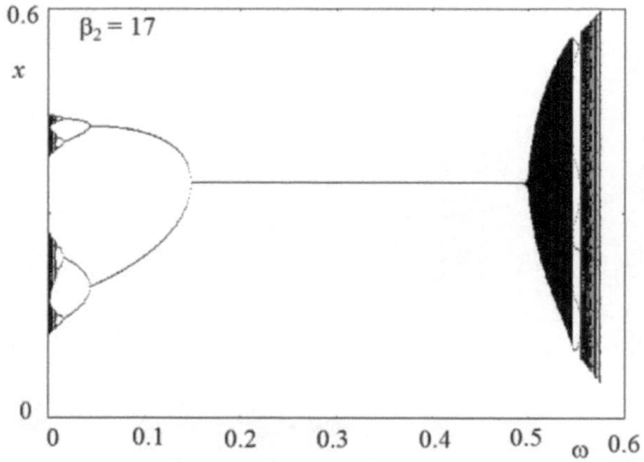

Figure 7.2 Bifurcation diagram, with bifurcation parameter ϖ, obtained with $\beta_2 = 17$ and all the other parameters at the same values as in Figure 7.1. For each value of the bifurcation parameter ϖ a trajectory of the model (10) is generated, starting from the initial condition $(x_0, y_0) = (0.2, 0.2)$.

Source: Authors' computations

Disequilibrium dynamics, multistability, and basins of attraction

In this section we perform some numerical explorations in order to give a more complete view of the global dynamic properties of the model. In fact, the local stability analysis of the previous section, based on the usual linearization procedure that only gives information about the model's behavior in a neighborhood of the equilibrium point, gives no insight into the size and the shape of the basin of attraction of the stable equilibrium: that is, the robustness of its stability with respect to exogenous perturbations. Moreover, for sets of parameters such that the equilibrium point is not stable, we need to analyze the kind of disequilibrium dynamics that prevails, and even when the equilibrium is locally stable we have to check if other coexisting attractors are present far from the equilibrium point: in other words, if other kinds of feasible long-run dynamics can be observed, starting from initial conditions outside of the basin of E.

First of all, Figure 7.3 shows the representations, in the phase space (x,y), of the attractors and the basins of attraction for the same set of parameters used to obtain the bifurcation diagram of Figure 7.2 and three different values of the memory parameter ϖ corresponding to the three different dynamic scenarios stressed in the proposition and shown in the bifurcation diagram: Figure 7.3a, obtained with $\varpi = 0$ (no-memory case), shows a the two-cyclic chaotic attractor whose basin of attraction is represented by the white region, the black one being the basin of infinity – that is, the set of initial conditions that generate diverging

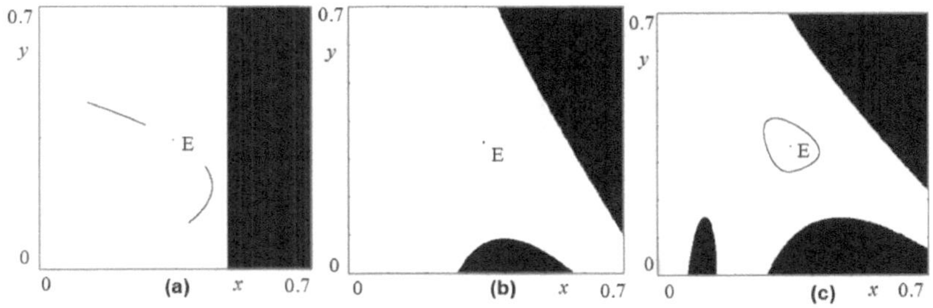

Figure 7.3 Three representations of the phase plane of the model (map) obtained with the same parameters as in Figure 7.2 with $\varpi = 0 < \varpi_f \approx 0.14$ in panel (a); $\varpi = 0.4 \in (\varpi_f, \varpi_h) \approx (0.14, 0.5)$ the stability range, in panel (b); $\varpi = 0.51 > \varpi_h \approx 0.5$ in panel (c). The black region represents the set of diverging trajectories and the white region represents the basin of attraction of the attractor shown: the two-cyclic chaotic set in panel (a), the equilibrium E in panel (b), a stable closed invariant orbit along which quasi-periodic motion occurs in panel (c).

Source: Authors' computations

trajectories; in Figure 7.3b, obtained for $\varpi = 0.4$, the equilibrium point E is the only feasible (i.e. positive and bounded) attractor; in Figure 7.3c, obtained for $\varpi = 0.51$ – that is, just after the Neimark–Sacker bifurcation (occurring at the value $\varpi_h \approx 0.5$ computed according to the proposition) – the stable closed invariant curve is shown, surrounding the unstable equilibrium E, along which the dynamic variable x_t exhibits a quasi-periodic motion.

As the memory parameter ϖ increases, the closed invariant curve enlarges: that is, the amplitude of the oscillations increases, until it reaches the boundary of the basin of attraction, as shown in Figure 7.4, obtained for $\varpi = 0.588$. After the contact between the attractor and the boundary of its basin, the attractor disappears, through a global bifurcation known as final bifurcation (see Mira et al., 1996) or boundary crisis (Grebogi, Ott, and Yorke, 1983). After this global bifurcation the generic trajectory is divergent. This is the reason why the bifurcation diagram shown in Figure 7.2 is interrupted before the bifurcation parameter reaches the value 0.7. Of course, this information cannot be obtained from an analytical study of the linear approximation of the map.

Other surprising dynamic phenomena caused by the presence of the memory can be seen for slightly higher values of the parameter β_2. In fact, the bifurcation diagram obtained for $\beta_2 = 20.5$, shown in Figure 7.5, exhibits the coexistence of two different attractors for intermediate values of the memory parameter ϖ. In fact, such a bifurcation diagram is obtained by taking, for each value of the bifurcation parameter ϖ, two different initial conditions $(x_0, y_0) = (0.3, 0.3)$ and $(x_0, y_0) = (0.02, 0.02)$ respectively, and the asymptotic portions of the corresponding trajectories are represented. As can be seen in the diagram, in the range $\varpi \in (0.17, 0.48)$, i.e. for intermediate values of the memory parameter such that the equilibrium E is locally asymptotically stable according to the proposition of the

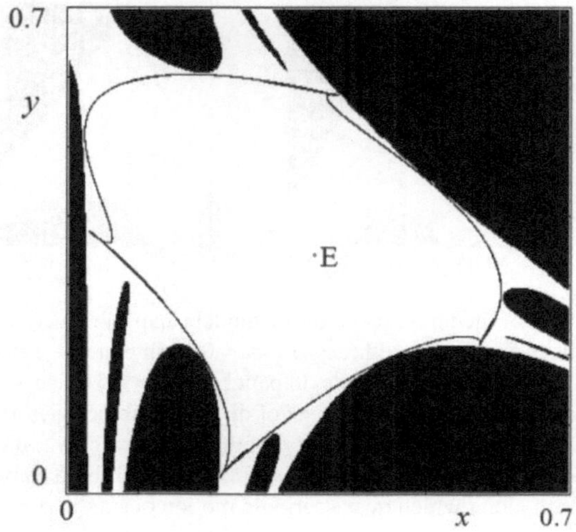

Figure 7.4 The attractor around E for $\varpi = 0.588$ (which is a chaotic attractor at this stage) is very close to the boundary of its basin, and will disappear through a final (or boundary crisis) global bifurcation after a slight increase of the parameter ϖ.

Source: Authors' computations

previous section, a different kind of asymptotic behavior can be obtained, given by oscillatory (periodic or chaotic) motion, represented by an alternative attractor with its own basin that shares the phase plane with the basin of the locally stable equilibrium. A representation of the two coexisting attractors, as well as their basins, obtained with $\varpi = 0.3$, is shown Figure 7.6, where the basin of E is represented by the white region, the basin of the coexisting bounded attractor (a cyclic chaotic attractor at this stage) by the grey region, and the basin of diverging trajectories by the black region, as usual. It is worth noticing that such a coexistence could not be predicted by any analytical local analysis of the dynamical system, and if the analysis is limited to the proof of the proposition of the previous section, together with its immediate numerical confirmation given by the bifurcation diagram of Figure 7.2 or the numerical simulations of Figure 7.3, then a quite incomplete, and even misleading, description of the dynamic properties of the model considered would be given, stating that the system shows convergence to the unique equilibrium for intermediate values of the memory parameter ϖ. Instead, after our numerical explorations we can state that for a wide range of the parameters of the model (such as the one giving the abnormal propensity to invest β_2) the local stability of the equilibrium E guarantees that the system will

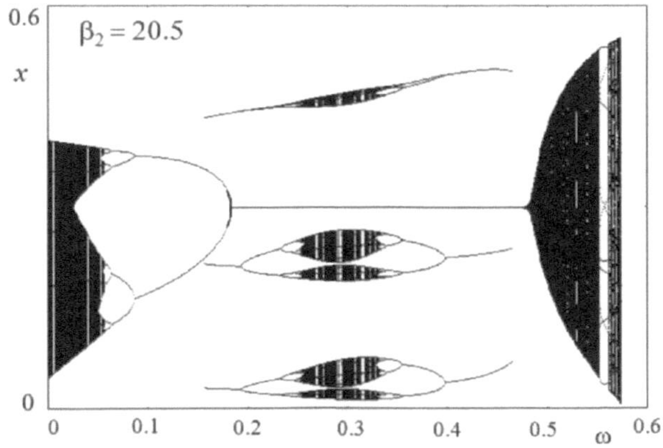

Figure 7.5 Bifurcation diagram, with bifurcation parameter ϖ, obtained with $\beta_2 = 20.5$ and all the other parameters at the same values as in Figure 7.2. For each value of the bifurcation parameter ϖ two trajectories of the model (map) are generated, starting from the initial conditions $(x_0, y_0) = (0.3, 0.3)$ and $(x_0, y_0) = (0.02, 0.02)$ respectively. In the range $\varpi \in (0.17, 0.48)$ the two trajectories converge to different attractors, the equilibrium point E and an oscillatory (periodic or chaotic) one respectively.

Source: Authors' computations

converge to it only if the initial conditions are taken sufficiently close to the equilibrium, and larger perturbations will lead the system to exhibit self-sustained bounded oscillations (periodic or chaotic) in the long run.

This situation has been extensively discussed in the economic literature and has sometimes been called "corridor stability" (see, for example, Leijonhufvud, 1973; Dohtani, Inaba, and Osaka, 2007). This stream of literature stresses the fact that nonlinear dynamic models may have the property that small perturbations are recovered as far as they are confined inside the basin of attraction of a locally stable equilibrium, whereas larger perturbations lead to time evolutions that depart further from the equilibrium and go to the coexisting attractor in the long run. In other words, a neoclassical view of the economic system, spontaneously recovering its equilibrium configuration, prevails if small perturbations are considered, whereas a neo-Keynesian view of amplifications of the perturbations, leading to out-of-equilibrium asymptotic dynamics, prevails when larger perturbations are considered. However, the situation may be even more involved when the boundaries that separate the two basins assume a complicated shape (sometimes quite convoluted). For example, if we consider three different initial conditions with the set of parameters used to obtain the dynamic scenario of Figure 7.6, we obtain

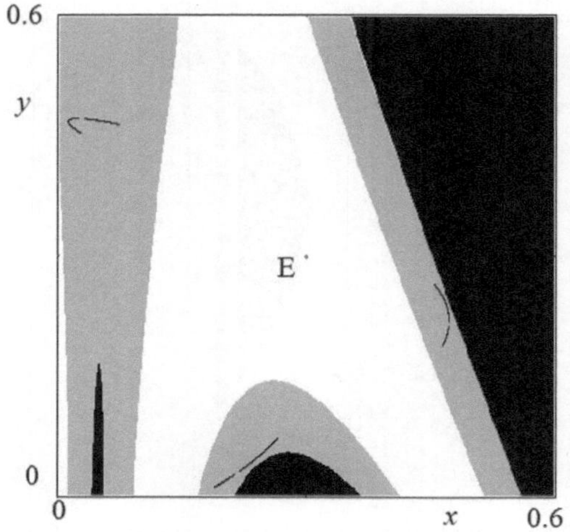

Figure 7.6 Basins of attractions with $\varpi = 0.3$ and all the other parameters as in Figure 7.5. The basins of attraction of the coexisting attractors are represented by different colors: white for the basin of *E*, grey for the basin of the cyclic chaotic attractor, black for the basin of diverging trajectories.

Source: Authors' computations

the usual convergence of a trajectory generated by an initial condition close to the equilibrium, like the one shown in panel (a) of Figure 7.7, and convergence to the chaotic attractor starting from an initial condition taken at a greater distance, like the one shown in panel (b), as well as a counterintuitive situation of convergence starting from an even further initial condition, as in the case shown in panel (c). Of course, all the three asymptotic situations shown in Figure 7.7 can be forecasted on the basis of the basins' representation of Figure 7.7. It is plain that, again, all these typically nonlinear phenomena could not be forecasted on the basis of the analytical results of the previous section. So, such dynamic scenarios, together with their economic consequences, clearly show the importance of a global analysis of nonlinear dynamical systems, which can often be performed only through an heuristic method obtained by a combination of analytical, geometrical, and numerical methods. It is also worth stressing that this path dependence cannot be observed in the model without memory proposed by Charles (2010), corresponding to our limiting case $\varpi = 0$, because in that case the system dynamics are governed by a one-dimensional quadratic map – a typical map with negative Schwartzian derivative and just one critical point, and hence a unique attractor (see, for example, Devaney, 1987).

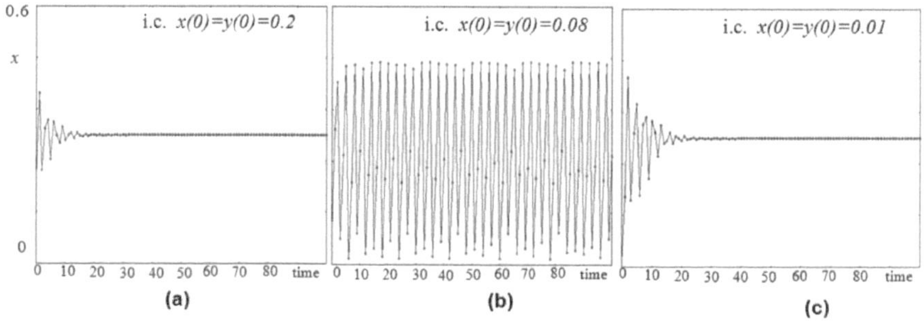

Figure 7.7 Three trajectories of the model versus time, for the same set of parameters as in Figure 7.6, from three different initial conditions: $(x_0, y_0) = (0.2, 0.2)$ in panel (a), $(x_0, y_0) = (0.08, 0.08)$ in panel (b), $(x_0, y_0) = (0.01, 0.01)$ in panel (c).

Source: Authors' computations

Conclusion

We have proposed a modification of the model proposed by Charles (2010) by introducing a memory parameter into the abnormal (that is, negatively sloped) relation between the propensity to invest and the rate of capacity utilization: in other words, instead of a function of only the capacity utilization of the previous period, the propensity to invest has been related to a weighted average of the capacity utilization observed in the last two periods, which transforms the one-dimensional model of Charles into a two-dimensional one. The introduction of memory effects, represented by convex combinations of previous states, has been considered by many authors as a realistic assumption in some economic systems (see, for example, Invernizzi and Medio, 1991). As shown in Aicardi and Invernizzi (1992), sometimes an increasing memory – that is, a larger weight given to the past realizations – has a stabilizing effect. This idea is partially confirmed in the model studied in this chapter, in the sense that starting from a situation of chaotic dynamics with zero memory, as given in the paper by Charles, a situation of stability is reached through a sequence of backward flip (or period-halving) bifurcations. However, we have also proved that the equilibrium loses stability again for further increases in value of the memory parameters through a Neimark–Sacker bifurcation. Indeed, the proposition proved in the second section above essentially states that the unique equilibrium of the model is stable for intermediate values of the memory parameter: that is, for a memory distribution close to a uniform average of the two past values of capacity utilization. This result is quite intuitive, and is also observed in the presence of longer memories, such as the fading memory involving all the states observed in the past, as in the model considered in Bischi and Naimzada (1997). However, as stressed by Hommes et al. (2012), the role of memory and time horizons has hardly been studied in the literature, and its role in a general dynamic framework is not a simple matter. Indeed, even in the case of a short memory, as we considered in the model analyzed in this chapter, things become quite complex, as in some ranges on the parameters such that the equilibrium is locally stable, coexisting periodic and chaotic attractors have been observed numerically, thus giving a strong path dependence. In fact, when the locally stable equilibrium coexists with a different kind of attractor, periodic or chaotic, each with its own basin of attraction, a typical situation of "corridor stability" occurs, as small perturbations (or shocks or historical accidents) around the equilibrium are endogenously recovered by the endogenous dynamics of the system, whereas larger perturbations are amplified by the endogenous dynamics, thus leading to a completely different (and non-stationary) disequilibrium dynamics, so that only an external control policy can force the system back to the original equilibrium. The situation becomes even more involved when the boundaries that separate the two basins assume a complicated (sometimes quite convoluted) shape, as we have shown numerically.

These dynamic scenarios clearly show the importance of a global analysis of nonlinear dynamical systems, which can often be performed only through a heuristic method obtained by a combination of analytical, geometrical, and numerical methods. In fact, an analytical study of the local stability and bifurcations, based on the linear approximation of the model around the equilibrium points, may sometimes be quite incomplete and even misleading.

References

Aicardi, F. and S. Invernizzi (1992). Memory effects in discrete dynamical systems, *International Journal of Bifurcation and Chaos*, 2, 815–30.

Bischi, G. I. and A. K. Naimzada (1997). Global analysis of a nonlinear model with learning, *Economic Notes*, 26, 143–74.

Charles, S. (2010). Explaining persistent cycles in a short-run context: firms' propensity to invest and omnipotent shareholders, *Journal of Post Keynesian Economics*, 32, 409–27.

Delli Gatti, D., M. Gallegati, and L. Gardini (1993). Investment confidence, corporate debt and income fluctuations, *Journal of Economic Behavior and Organization*, 22, 161–87.

Devaney, R. L. (1987). *An Introduction to Chaotic Dynamical Systems,* Menlo Park, CA: Benjamin/Cummings.

Dohtani, A, T. Inaba, and H. Osaka (2007). Corridor stability of the neoclassical steady state. In T. Asada and T. Ishikawa, eds., *Time and Space in Economics*, New York: Springer, pp. 129–43.

Grebogi, C., E. Ott, and J. A. Yorke (1983). Crises, sudden changes in chaotic attractors, and transient chaos, *Physica D*, 181–200.

Guckenheimer, J. and P. Holmes (1983). *Nonlinear Oscillations, Dynamical Systems, and Bifurcations of Vector Fields*, New York: Springer.Hommes, C., T. Kiseleva, Y. Kuznetsov, and M. Verbic (2012). Is more memory in evolutionary selection (de)stabilizing? *Macroeconomic Dynamics*, 16, 335–57.

Invernizzi, S. A. and Medio (1991). On lags and chaos in dynamic economic models, *Journal of Mathematical Economics*, 20, 521–50.

Leijonhufvud, A. (1973). Effective demand failures, *Swedish Journal of Economics*, 75, 27–48.

Lorenz, H. W. (1993). *Nonlinear Dynamical Economics and Chaotic Motion*, 2nd ed., New York: Springer.

Mira, C., L. Gardini, A. Barugola, and J. C. Cathala (1996). *Chaotic Dynamics in Two-Dimensional Noninvertible Maps*, Singapore: World Scientific.

8 The dynamics of the labour market in an agent-based model with financial constraints

Domenico Delli Gatti, Mauro Gallegati and Saul Desiderio

The approach to the labour market that we follow in the present chapter starts from the acknowledgment that any aggregate economic system is more than the algebraic sum of the microeconomic decisions of rational agents. In fact, microeconomic decentralised interactions and out-of-equilibrium transactions are crucial as they create collective arrangements that cannot be directly traced back to individual primitive parameters. In other terms, borrowing concepts and tools from the science of complexity, we rationalise market economies as complex adaptive systems, where bounded-rational agents' micro decisions produce the emergence of *unintended* aggregate outcomes, which in turn feed back on the individual behaviour (downward causation). Basically, we revert to the approach followed by traditional macroeconomics: instead of very sophisticated individual behaviours linked together by a simple macroeconomic structure, we consider simple individual behaviours immersed in a sophisticated environment.

In this view, the stylised facts of the labour market have to be conceived as emergent properties of the system as a whole and must be explained at a higher level (the macroeconomic system) than that of individual purposive actions. As a consequence, partial equilibrium approaches such as search models (e.g. Diamond, 1982) and efficiency wage models (e.g. Shapiro and Stiglitz, 1984) are definitely badly equipped to explain in a satisfactory manner phenomena such as unemployment, since they analyse the labour market without taking into account its interactions with the other parts of the economic system.

Besides overcoming all the limitations that characterise microeconomic and partial equilibrium explanations, our approach also departs also from mainstream macroeconomics, whose methodology, rooted in equilibrium neoclassical microfoundations, does not allow us, in general, to take into account the divergence between individual intentions and aggregate consequences. Furthermore, mainstream models merely focus on the properties of the end-state equilibrium – an exogenously determined situation in which individual actions are mutually compatible by definition. On the contrary, we are interested in the processes and causal relationships that can generate unintended aggregate consequences as a sort of spontaneous, unplanned social order – albeit not necessarily optimal. For this reason, we resort to the agent-based or multi-agent techniques (Judd and Tesfatsion,

2006), which propose themselves as the natural candidates to front the challenges issued by the complexity approach.

In general, in the agent-based approach, computational models are built that try to mimic the functioning of one market in isolation, or of an entire multi-market economy, by simulating the autonomous and decentralised behaviour of microeconomic units (typically firms, workers, consumers, financial intermediaries and so on). In agent-based models, equilibrium is neither assumed from the outset nor imposed by resorting to a fictitious Walrasian auctioneer. Instead, the modeller lets the market behaviour emerge naturally from the local actions of interacting participants. By repeated simulations in a controlled environment, the modeller is able to explore the model features and compare them with real data. As shown in Gaffeo et al. (2008) and Delli Gatti et al. (2011), agent-based models can easily outperform traditional ones in explaining within a unifying framework a wide range of disparate aggregate phenomena, such as fluctuating growth, financial contagion, bankruptcy chains, firms' sizes and growth rate distributions.

The model we present to study labour market dynamics is one of general disequilibrium, where agents interacting on three interconnected markets for labour, consumption goods and credit can fail to coordinate because of persistent uncertainty. In this virtual environment two kinds of uncertainty can be recognised: between-market and within-market. The former arises because price setting is a microeconomic decision taken adaptively only on the basis of the private information available to the single individual, causing transactions to occur at 'false' prices. Thus, the absence of a central auctioneer in general causes individual plans to be incompatible with each other because the aggregate excess demand functions are by and large different from zero. The second kind of uncertainty, as the name suggests, is directly linked to the working of the market microstructure. The markets, in fact, are characterised by continuous decentralised search and matching processes, which may imply individual and, a fortiori, aggregate out-of-equilibrium dynamics even when aggregate excess demand functions are equal to zero and a general equilibrium potentially exists. The search process goes on in each of the markets considered: workers search for a job on the labour market and for consumption goods on the goods markets; firms search for a bank loan on the credit market. Search is costly, so that each searching agent can visit only a finite number of 'providers': firms which provide jobs on the labour market and consumption goods on the goods market; banks which provide loans on the credit market. In each period the identity of the providers that the searcher can visit changes at random so that the network structure is continuously evolving over time, even if the number of providers per searcher is constant. Searching is followed by the matching process, which occurs in a completely decentralised setting: in fact, in our framework there is no 'matching function' – the analytical device that couples agents on the two sides of the market in mainstream search-and-matching models of the labour market – so that transactions can well happen out-of-equilibrium as searchers may visit providers with no excess supply and providers may face insufficient demand.

In a sense, our model is much in the same vein as the post-Walrasian approach (Clower, 1965; Barro and Grossman, 1971). Because of uncertainty, trade generally occurs at disequilibrium prices. Thus, market excess demands (obtained by summing up individual variables) are not independent of current market transactions and current income places a restriction on individual expenditure. One consequence is that money is not simply a veil relegated to determine absolute price levels, but both a medium of exchange used to implement current transactions and a store of value with the role of compensating individual imbalances, such as when an unemployed worker can still act as a consumer by resorting to accumulated savings. The distribution of liquid resources across the agents, therefore, imposes a constraint on individual decisions and concurs to set both prices and quantities. This is the case for workers, whose spending capacity on the consumption goods market is constrained by how much labour they have sold on the labour market, and for firms, whose labour demand is constrained by their proceeds realised as consumption goods sellers.

The possible mismatch between desired plans and available resources is particularly important for firms, as it makes the credit market enter into play. Here we can appreciate the role of uncertainty once again. Because of it, in fact, the validity of the Modigliani–Miller theorem breaks down and firms' financial structure becomes essential in determining firms' credit worthiness and interest rates when they borrow from banks.

Even in the absence of a centralised market-clearing mechanism, our synthetic economy shows a tendency to self-organise towards a spontaneous order which is, however, characterised, depending on the market and the time horizon, by such persistent Keynesian features as involuntary unemployment and unsold production, or excess demands and credit rationing. These phenomena are 'pathologies' in the standard macroeconomic theory: that is, the result of departures from a first-best baseline scenario due to imperfections of one sort or another. In our framework, on the contrary, they are the emerging properties – that is, the 'physiology' – of the macroeconomy.

This work proceeds as follows. The next section provides a general overview of the model, focusing mostly on the labour market. Subsequent sections present the general results and these are followed by a discussion of results from a number of computational experiments aimed at assessing the influence exerted by the labour market parameters on the macroeconomy.

The model

The basic framework we employ is akin to that of Gaffeo et al. (2008) and Delli Gatti et al. (2011), to which we refer for technical details. For the reader's sake, though, in what follows we overview the basics of the model succinctly, placing more emphasis upon the labour market.

A large number of autonomous firms, households (consumers/workers) and banks operate in a fully decentralised manner on the markets for labour, credit and a homogeneous consumption good. Production takes one time period, regardless of the scale of production. Each firm decides the amount of output to produce and the price to charge by taking into account its expected demand and past relative prices. Expectations of future demand are updated adaptively.

Firms post their vacancies at a certain offered wage, and unemployed workers contact a given number of randomly chosen firms to get a job, starting from the one that offers the highest wage. If the firm still has open vacancies, then worker and firm sign a labour contract expiring after a finite number of periods. A worker whose contract has just expired applies also to his or her last employer, in addition to other arbitrarily chosen firms.

Firms then have to pay the wage bill in order to start production. If internal financial resources are in short supply with respect to the wage bill – that is, if there is a financing gap – a firm can borrow from the banking sector. Borrowing firms contact a given number of randomly chosen banks to get a loan. Each bank proposes a contractual interest rate calculated by applying a mark-up on a baseline interest rate set by the Monetary Authority. The mark-up increases with the firm's financial fragility in order to embody an *external finance premium*. Firms start borrowing from the bank that offers the lowest interest rate until all credit supply has been exhausted. After the credit market is closed, if financial resources – both internal and external – are not enough to pay for the wage bill of the population of workers, some workers remain unemployed or are fired.

The market for consumption goods opens after production has been completed. Firms post their prices, and consumers contact a given number of firms to purchase goods, starting to buy from the one that posts the lowest price. Each consumer is allowed to visit a given number Z of firms to assess posted prices. In order to minimise the probability of being rationed, he or she visits the largest firm (in terms of production) visited during the previous round, while the remaining $Z-1$ firms are chosen fully at random. In other words, consumers adopt a sort of Preferential Attachment scheme. Firms that post lower prices tend to attract a larger fraction of consumers and crowd competitors out, gaining the ability to operate in a predominant position in the future. If a firm ends up with excess supply, it gets rid of the unsold goods at zero cost.

Firms collect revenues and calculate gross profits. If gross profits are high enough, they meet their debt commitments, paying back both principal and interest to the banks. If net profits are positive, firms pay dividends to the owners and invest a fraction of net profits in R&D, in order to increase their productivity. Earnings after interest payments and dividends are retained and are employed to increase net worth. Firms and banks are financially viable – and therefore survive – if their net worth is positive. If, on the contrary, net worth is negative, they go bankrupt, shut down and exit the market. Lenders, therefore, have to register a bad debt (that is, a non-performing loan). In this case, a string of new firms/banks equal in number to the bankrupt ones enter the market, and their size at entry is smaller than the average size of survivors.

The labour market

Firms set their labour demand L^d_{it} on the basis of their technology and desired level of production, Y^d_{it}. Production is carried out by means of a constant return to scale technology, with labour L_{it} as the only input:

$$Y_{it} = \alpha_{it} L_{it}, \ \alpha_{it} > 0 \tag{1}$$

where α_{it} is labour productivity.

From equation (1), it follows that the number of job openings set by firm i at time t is simply given by:

$$L^d_{it} = \frac{Y^d_{it}}{\alpha_{it}} \tag{2}$$

At the beginning of time t, the ith firm is provided with an operating workforce $L^\circ_{it} = L_{it\text{-}1} - \hat{L}_{it-1}$, where $\hat{L}_{it-1}$ are the workers whose labour contract has just expired. The firm opens a number of vacancies equal to $V_{it} = L^d_{it} - L^\circ_{it}$ if its desired labour force is larger than the effective one, and zero otherwise (workers with an active contract can be fired only in the case of a firm's financial crisis: that is, when capital is not enough to pay for the wage bill). Meanwhile, we assume that workers supply inelastically one unit of labour per period. Each unemployed worker[1] sends M applications to as many firms: the first one to the firm in which he or she worked in the previous period (if employed), and $M - 1$ at random (M if already unemployed in $t - 1$). Workers are therefore characterised, on the one hand, by a sort of loyalty to their last employer and, on the other, by a desire to insure themselves against the risk of unemployment by diversifying in a portfolio of hiring opportunities.

Firms still characterised by some open job position will communicate its offered wage to workers who contact it, and these will choose to work in the firm offering the highest salary.

Decentralised labour markets (that is, one for each worker) are closed sequentially according to an order randomly chosen at each time step. Given that each worker is allowed to sign one labour contract per period, serious coordination failures could arise as the number of workers actually available does not necessarily correspond to the number of vacancies, especially for firms which are called to hire their workers late in the sequence.

When hired for the first time by a firm, a worker is asked to sign a contract that determines his or her nominal wage level for a fixed number of periods. The wage offered to the worker by firm i in period t is calculated according to the following rule:

$$w^b_{it} = \max\left(\widehat{w}_t, w_{it-\tau}\left(1 + \xi_{it}\right)\right) \tag{3}$$

where $\widehat{w}_t$ is a minimum wage imposed by the law, while $w_{it-\tau}$ is the wage offered to the cohort of workers employed the last time firm i hired (period τ , with $\tau > 0$). Finally, ξ_{it} is an idiosyncratic shock uniformly distributed on the non-negative interval $(0, h_\xi)$. Equation (3) implies that firms revise their wage offer upwards whenever there is the necessity to increase their labour force. Workers who succeed in receiving more than one proposal accept the one paying the higher wage.

The minimum wage is periodically revised upwards, in order to neutralise price inflation. Wages contracted in previous periods that happen to fall below the minimum wage are automatically updated to it. Besides hedging workers against the risk of losing purchasing power due to inflation, the updating of the minimum wage helps to couple firms with their environment. For instance, in periods when the labour market is tight, firms that are hiring increase their output price to preserve profit margins. Higher prices, in turn, drive the minimum wage upwards as an externality. The process works in the opposite way when the market for labour is dull.

The labour market design we choose is consistent with the findings reported by numerous surveys of firms' wage-setting policies. First, there is clear evidence of nominal wage downward rigidity. Firms are particularly resistant to cutting nominal wages even during recessions because they fear that lower wage rates would increase turnover and decrease labour effort (Campbell and Kamlani, 1997; Bewley, 1999). Second, downward rigidity is also observed for the pay of newly hired workers, probably for reasons of perceived equity (Bewley, 1999).

Simulation results

This section reports a general overview of the main results related to the labour market. A thorough exploration of the key properties of the model has been carried out in Delli Gatti et al. (2011), which we refer to for details. We run simulations with the number of workers' applications M set to 4, the labour contract length set to 8 periods and the revision of the minimum wage set to 4 periods. If we assume that one simulation period corresponds to a quarter, this means that labour contracts last 2 years, while the minimum wage is revised annually. Even though we have only made visual attempts to calibrate the model without resorting to real data, our framework displays neither pathological phenomena nor degenerate dynamics.

The time path of aggregate production is characterised by irregular fluctuations, as shown in Figure 8.1(a), and possesses an autocorrelation very close to the actual ones. The model is able to alternate periods of economic growth with phases of recessions within the same non-linear process made up of idiosyncratic shocks combined with adaptive individual behaviours. The way of accounting for business cycles offered by the present model is thus completely different from that provided by dynamic stochastic general equilibrium (DSGE) models, according to which fluctuations in aggregate activity are explained by random changes in such aggregate variables as total factor productivity (TFP) growth (as in RBC-DSGE models) or monetary, investment or mark-up shocks (NK-DSGE approach). In our model, sudden, deep and relatively short recessions are essentially due to the bankruptcies of big firms, which spread through subsequent shockwaves to the economy as a whole. In fact, the bankruptcy of a firm, say A, yields:

1 *A negative demand spillover*. The loss of employment in *A*, in fact, generates a contraction of demand – financed out of the wages previously paid to *A*'s workforce – for the products of other firms, say *B* and *C*. These firms will face a reduction of sales and, other things being equal, of profits. The accumulation of net worth in *B* and *C*, therefore, will slow down and their fragility (and vulnerability to idiosyncratic shocks) will in principle increase.

2 *A non-performing loan*. The bank that has extended loans to *A* will record a bad debt on its balance sheet. The impairment of the net worth, therefore, will cause the bank to reduce the supply of loans in order to meet the target capital requirement ratio. This also means that firms *B* and *C* may eventually face a constraint on the amount of credit they can obtain from the bank.

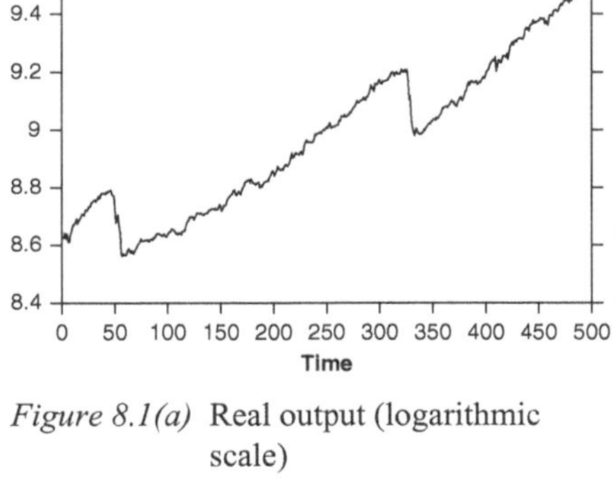

Figure 8.1(a) Real output (logarithmic scale)

Source: Author's computations

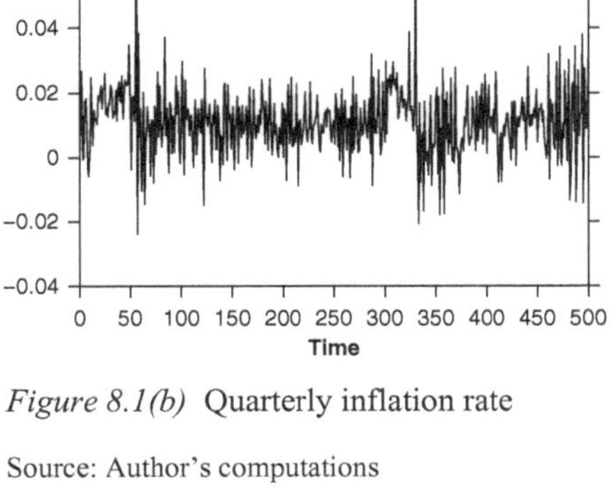

Figure 8.1(b) Quarterly inflation rate

Source: Author's computations

Figure 8.1(c) Unemployment rate

Source: Author's computations

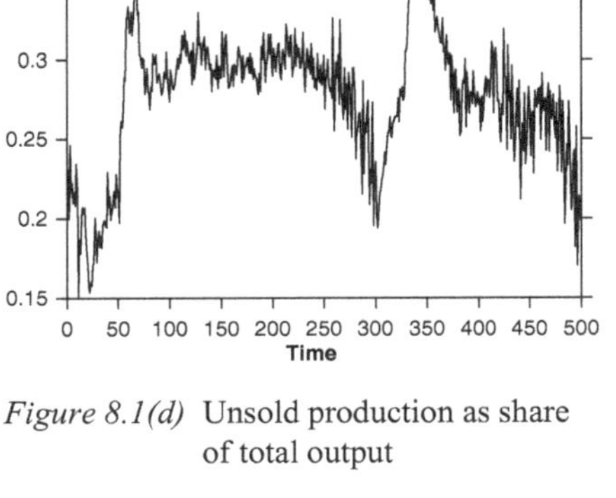

Figure 8.1(d) Unsold production as share of total output

Source: Author's computations

The quarter-to-quarter rate of inflation is on average equal to 1.1 percent (Figure 8.1(b)), and turns occasionally into moderate deflationary episodes, while unemployment rates range between 0.5 percent and 13 percent (Figure 8.1(c)). Panel (c) can be compared with the last panel of Figure 8.1, which reports the series of unsold production as share of total output: the close similarity between their behaviours signals the contemporaneous occurrence of excess supply for both labour and goods, which is a clear symptom of coordination failures. This finding points in the direction of a Keynesian interpretation of unemployment, which we favour with respect to microeconomic explanations such as search costs and sticky wages for the following reasons. Firstly, while search costs may have a role in determining frictional unemployment, we have nonetheless to exclude them from the group of major causes of unemployment because they are not able to explain its large variations. Secondly, although nominal wages are characterised by downward rigidity, real wages are flexible and follow labour productivity (see below) because prices are let free to adjust in any direction. Even sticky wages, therefore, cannot be regarded as the major source of unemployment. As we will see, computational experiments to be conducted in the fourth section will bring about further confirmation of our intuitions about wage flexibility.

Figure 8.2 depicts interesting results that emerge from simulations related to the interplay between labour market and business fluctuations. Panel (a) shows a negative relationship between the rate of wage inflation and the rate of unemployment: that is, a standard, albeit quite flat, Phillips curve. The negative correlation between the two variables is not very strong (−0.37) but is statistically significant. Panel (b) shows a negative relationship between the output growth rate and the unemployment growth rate – namely, an Okun curve (correlation of −0.67). A third emerging regularity regarding the labour market is the Beveridge curve reported in panel (c), showing a negative relationship between the rate of vacancies (here approximated by the ratio between the number of job openings and the labour force at the beginning of a period) and the rate of unemployment. In this case the goodness of fit is less satisfactory than in the case of the Okun curve, but the negative correlation between the two variables, albeit not so strong (−0.45), is once again statistically significant. In addition, the average real wage and productivity follow a similar pattern so that – as shown in panel (d) – the ratio of the two settles around a long-run constant value of approximately 2/3. Since we do not impose any aggregate equilibrium relationship between the two variables, the (on average) constancy of income shares over time is just an emerging feature produced by the self-organisation of the system.

The model also replicates, at least qualitatively, well-known empirical regularities concerning job flows. We find that unemployment is positively correlated to long-term unemployment,[2] which means that higher unemployment rates are associated with longer unemployment duration and with lower turn-over rates among workers. Moreover, layoffs and hirings (that is, job destruction and job creation) have strong positive correlation both in levels and in differences. Finally, layoffs show higher volatility and are more correlated to unemployment than hirings (Blanchard and Diamond, 1990; Davis, Haltiwanger and Schuh,

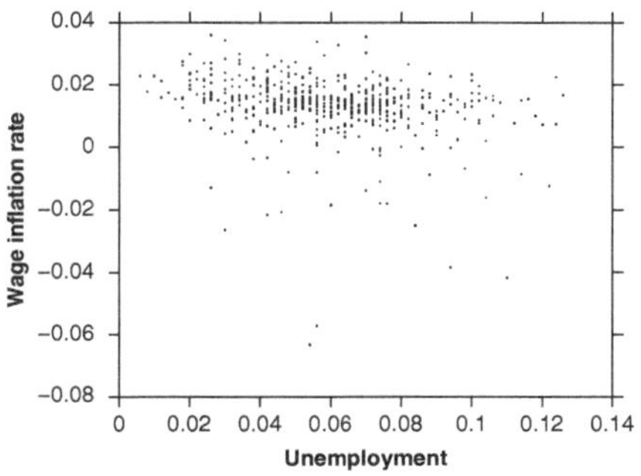

Figure 8.2(a) Phillips curve

Source: Author's computations

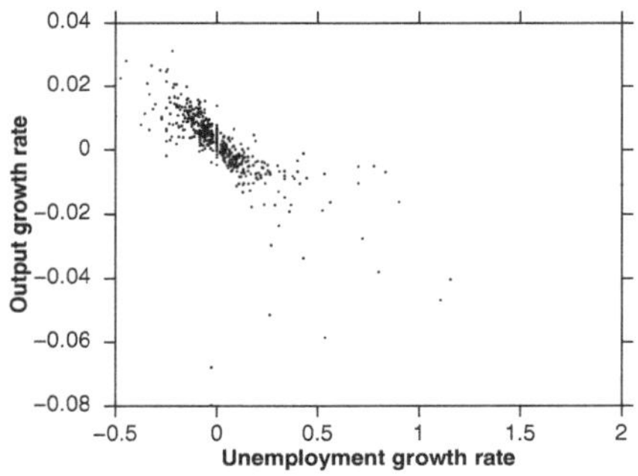

Figure 8.2(b) Okun curve

Source: Author's computations

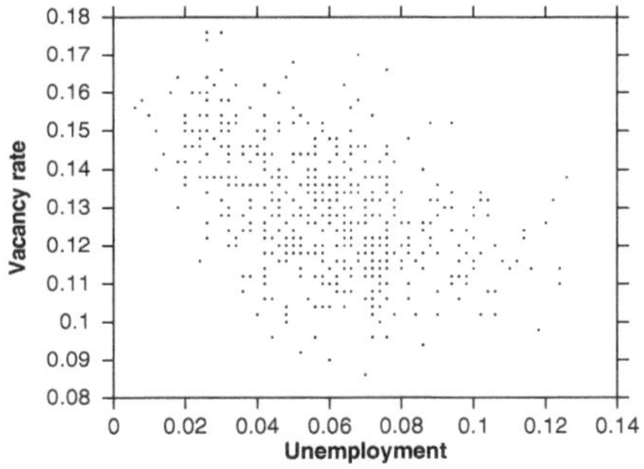

Figure 8.2(c) Beveridge curve

Source: Author's computations

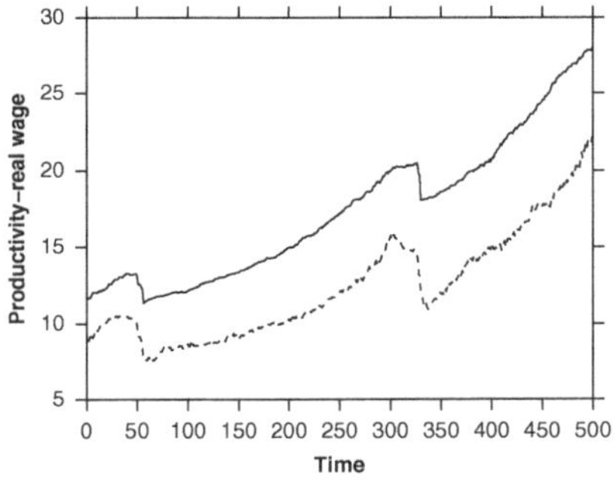

Figure 8.2(d) Productivity and real wage (dashed line)

Source: Author's computations

1996), suggesting that production downscaling might be the major force behind unemployment fluctuations. This corroborates the already proposed Keynesian interpretation of unemployment, whose dynamics must ultimately be determined by the combination of fluctuations in aggregate demand and productivity growth, and not by microeconomic frictions.

The joint emergence of many stylised facts indicates that the complexity approach is indeed a fruitful way to evaluate labour market dynamics. Hence, in the next section we are going to employ the model as a computational laboratory to perform virtual experiments on the labour market.

Experiments on the labour market

This section is devoted to a number of sensitivity analysis exercises involving the principal parameters that regulate the labour market: the number of workers' applications (*M*) and the job contract length. We choose to change one parameter at time, and we run several simulations to quantify how the changes in the value of the input parameter affect the output. For each value we run at least four independent simulations, each one for a different sequence of random numbers. Conclusions are drawn by both visual and statistical inspection.

As a final experiment, we will introduce downward flexibility on nominal wages and assess its influence on unemployment.

Local labour markets

The number of workers' applications M captures the market rigidities due to search costs, basically defining the size of the individual labour markets: the higher M, the higher the probability of the unemployed finding a job. We start our sensitivity experiment by decreasing M from 4 to 3 and 2, discovering that prices, which in the baseline simulation have the tendency to be anti-cyclical and leading, become pro-cyclical and lagging. Aggregate production displays a higher degree of instability because firms have a lower probability of filling their vacancies and consequently of producing planned output. On the other hand, higher search costs increase path-dependency in the labour market. In fact, firms experiencing the 'luck' of filling their vacancies from the early stages of the simulation also have a higher probability of finding the desired workforce in the future thanks to the loyalty-to-last-employer mechanism. Hence, these firms generally perform better than their competitors. The formation of advantaged firms is reflected in the upper tail of firms' size distribution, which appears to scale down more like a Pareto's law. The role of path-dependency is indirectly confirmed as we increase the number of applications (to 5 and 6). Reduced search costs allow workers to come across more job opportunities and make competition on the labour market tougher. All firms, therefore, have the same chance of finding workers and no privileged firm emerges. As a consequence, their size distribution exhibits a thinner upper tail and scales much more as an exponential, or even a uniform. In addition, as one would expect, competition between firms in hiring workers tends to push the real wage up.

Job contract duration

The other relevant parameter, tuning the flexibility of the labour market, is the length of the job contracts signed by firms and workers, which in the baseline simulation we set to 8 periods. In order to control for both a very flexible and a quite rigid labour market, we first decreased it to 6, 4 and 1, and subsequently increased it to 10, 12 and 14. Because we interpret each simulation period as a quarter, the sensitivity experiment thus covers contract durations ranging from one quarter to 3½ years. As a general result, we have found that for intermediate values of the parameter, the model substantially preserves its main statistical properties, whereas degenerate dynamics is produced in the case of extreme values. In particular, when labour contracts are short, the search and matching process between workers and employers occurs more frequently and the network linking them is continuously created and dissolved. The major effect brought about by this continuous reshuffling of workers is a reduced path-dependence, which translates into less pronounced co-movements between relevant macro variables and total output. The unemployment rate and real wages constitute an exception, and basically conserve respectively an anti-cyclical and a pro-cyclical behaviour as in the baseline simulation. Short labour contracts also cause output to become smoother. Consequently, its cyclical component tends to lose the AR(2) structure shown in the baseline simulation, signalling that the labour market is a major source of feedbacks inside our artificial economy.[3] Moreover, the attenuation of path-dependence due to the flexibility of labour contracts causes the bulk of operating firms to distribute more uniformly, consistent with the results reported above. When the labour market is more flexible, the economy is characterised on average by higher levels of unemployment and lower output, revealing the presence of coordination failures on a grand scale due to aggregate demand spillovers. In fact, during periods of declining demand, firms can easily get rid of excess workforce by avoiding the replacement of workers whose contract has expired; the economy, therefore, experiences a sensible reduction in aggregate demand that compels firms to further revise downwards their production plans and labour demand for the subsequent simulation iterations. In contrast, when firms are forced by longer contracts to keep all their workers and also to pay wages during downturns, aggregate demand reduces less, thus preventing the triggering of a vicious circle. Our interpretation of the actual working of this mechanism is further confirmed by pushing it to the extreme: when labour contracts last only one period – that is, when firms are given full freedom to fire – the number of bankruptcies and the unemployment rate reach very high values, and in most of the simulations the whole economy collapses, signalling the presence of fatal market failures.

A completely different story applies when the labour market is rigid (in our case when the job contract duration is equal to 12 periods, or higher). In this case, aggregate time series are often degenerated and simulated co-movements contrast sharply with the ones we calculated for real data of the US economy. The supply side of the model is now the weakest link in the chain: because of long contractual commitments, firms cannot reduce costs by decreasing the production scale when they are financially fragile, and therefore go bankrupt more easily. This leads to an overall macroeconomic breakdown.

Nominal wage flexibility

The basic model assumes the realistic hypothesis of downward rigidity for nominal wages. Most of economic theory holds that this kind of rigidity is at the root of persistent unemployment. Thus, we devote the final experiments to the assessment of the mainstream thesis by introducing full nominal wage flexibility. Basically, we run twenty independent simulations for as many seeds of the random number generator, letting firms reduce their wage offer in the case that their current labour force exceeds labour demand. Results indicate that the new model, as compared with the baseline one, shows a higher average unemployment rate and lower average real GDP growth, inflation and firm default rates. The explanation is straightforward and consistent with previous results. In fact, higher wage flexibility produces two contrasting effects: on one hand, as signalled by the lower inflation rate and firm default rate, it allows firms to reduce the wage bill, and thus costs, when facing periods of weak demand, but on the other hand it reduces workers' income and depresses aggregate demand, offsetting the positive effect exerted on the supply side.

Analogous results are obtained when we remove the automatic adjustment mechanism of the minimum wage (equation 3): if firms are not forced to periodically revise upwards their wage offer, the pure market forces determine nominal wages that are too low from the aggregate point of view, causing the average unemployment rate to be higher than in the baseline model.

Conclusion

In the approach followed in this chapter, stylised facts about the labour market are conceived as emergent properties of the auto-organisation of a complex system. In a complex system, heterogeneous micro units provided with limited information and bounded rationality interact locally (without the intervention of a central Auctioneer) on different markets and react to the stimuli coming from the environment that they have contributed to create, in a continuous process of adaptation and discovery. In order to give shape to these ideas, we deployed a general-disequilibrium, agent-based macro model based on adaptive microfoundations, where a large number of firms, households and banks take their price and quantity decisions on the basis of simple rules-of-thumb and on the stock of small amounts of private information. In the absence of a centralised coordination mechanism, individuals are immersed in a truly uncertain environment and may fail to coordinate, producing Keynesian outcomes of persistent underemployment of resources. In spite of this (or, perhaps, in virtue of this), the model exhibits realistic features in several respects related to industrial, long-run and business cycle dynamics. For instance, co-movement analysis reveals a striking similarity between simulated data and US data on business cycle frequencies, while firms' size distributions show positive skewness and growth rates distributed according to Laplace statistics. In addition, and more importantly to our scope, many stylised facts of the labour market are reproduced. In particular, such relationships between business cycles and the labour market as the Phillips curve, the Okun curve and the Beveridge curve jointly emerge from simulations. The model also reproduces typical correlations that can be observed between job flows (job destruction and job creation) and between unemployment rates and unemployment duration.

By a number of Monte Carlo experiments, we performed a sensitivity analysis over different labour market parameters and discovered that unemployment is essentially due to under-consumption, rejecting at the same time conventional 'wisdom' predictions according to which high unemployment rates would be determined by labour market frictions of one sort or another. In particular, we downsized the relevance usually attributed to wage and labour contract rigidity.

In fact, we showed that whenever the degree of flexibility is increased, the overall economic performance worsens because the higher bargaining power granted to firms lowers labour income and consequently depresses demand for consumption goods.

Notes

1 On-the-job search is ruled out.
2 We classify as long-term unemployed all the workers who have been inactive for more than 3 periods: that is, in our interpretation of a period, for more than three quarters.
3 In co-movement analysis, an autoregressive structure of the second order (AR(2)) in the cyclical component of output is a signal of non-linear feedbacks in the economic structure. See Delli Gatti et al. (2011) for details.

References

Barro, R. and H. Grossman (1971). A general disequilibrium model of income and employment. *American Economic Review*, 61, 82–93.

Bewley, T. (1999). *Why Wages Don't Fall during Recessions*, Cambridge, MA: Harvard University Press.

Blanchard, O. and P. Diamond (1990). The cyclical behavior of the gross flows of US workers, *Brookings Papers on Economic Activity*, 2, 85–143.

Campbell, C. and K. Kamlani (1997). The reasons for wage rigidity: evidence from a survey of firms, *Quarterly Journal of Economics*, 112, 759–89.

Clower, R. W. (1965). The Keynesian counter-revolution: a theoretical appraisal. In F. H. Hahn and Brechling, eds., *The Theory of Interest Rates*, London: Macmillan, pp. 103–25.

Davis, S., J. Haltiwanger and S. Schuh (1996). *Job Creation and Destruction*. Cambridge, MA: MIT Press.

Delli Gatti, D., S. Desiderio, E. Gaffeo, M. Gallegati and P. Cirillo (2011). *Macroeconomics from the Bottom-Up*, Milan: Springer.

Diamond, P. A. (1982). Aggregate demand management in search equilibrium, *Journal of Political Economy*, 90, 881–94.

Gaffeo, E., D. Delli Gatti, S. Desiderio and M. Gallegati (2008). Adaptive microfoundations for emergent macroeconomics, *Eastern Economic Journal*, 34, 441–63.

Judd, K. and L. Tesfatsion (2006). *Handbook of Computational Economics*, vol. 2: *Agent-Based Computational Economics*, Amsterdam: North-Holland.

Shapiro, C. and J. E. Stiglitz (1984). Equilibrium unemployment as a worker discipline device, *American Economic Review*, 74, 433–44.

9 Periodic cycles in a behavioural model

Laura Gardini and Fabio Tramontana

The neoclassical hypothesis of the perfect rationality of economic agents is nowadays hardly defensible. On the one hand, we have the fact that two recent Nobel prize winners, Daniel Kanheman and Herbert Simon, have been awarded the prize for their contribution to the understanding of economic agents' decision making; on the other hand, the present financial and economic crisis is a clear example of the consequences of some behaviors that are definitely irrational.

A common research question is: under which circumstances can a boundedly rational economic agent (i.e. one endowed with limited information and/or limited ability to process it) learn rational behavior? Most of the research papers on learning aim to enforce the perfect rationality hypothesis (see, for instance, Lucas, 1987), but there exists a growing strand of the economic literature that emphasizes how the adopted learning mechanism can endogenously generate a failure of the dynamic convergence to the rational choice (see Grandmont and Laroque, 1991; Bullard, 1994; Tuinstra and Wagener, 2007, among others).

An early contribution is the paper by Himmelweit (1976), where a learning mechanism is applied to a set of producers endowed with identical capital equipment. These producers must decide at each time period whether to produce or not on the basis of their past experiences. A one-dimensional piecewise linear discontinuous map explains the dynamics of production. Himmelweit shows that periodic dynamics of production and market price are most likely to occur and she also gives a remarkable explanation of the periodicity of cycles, if we consider the mathematical tools available in 1976 to deal with a piecewise linear map.

Recently the study of discontinuous maps (begun many years ago) has reached achieved results, starting with the rediscovery of the works by the Russian mathematician Leonov (1959, 1962). This can be seen in the papers of Avrutin, Schanz, and Gardini (2010), Gardini and Tramontana (2010) and Gardini et al. (2010). The typical global bifurcation related to this kind of map is the so-called *border collision bifurcation* (henceforth BCB), a term coined by Nusse and Yorke (1992) and Nusse, Ott, and Yorke (1994). This involves the merging (or collapse) of some invariant set, such as a fixed point, the periodic point of a cycle, or the boundary of any invariant set, with the kink point at which the function changes its definition. Recent results are surveyed in Avrutin et al. (2014).

Besides their applications in physics and engineering, in the economic and financial literature there are several models formulated via discontinuous maps. Noteworthy among these papers are the works of Richard Day (Day, 1982; Day and Shafer, 1987; Huang and Day, 1993) and the papers by Piero Ferri and his collaborators (Ferri and Greenberg, 1990, 1992; Ferri, Greenberg, and Day, 2001; Tramontana et al. 2010). Recent developments in the study of discontinuous maps have also facilitated the conclusion of the study of economic models started when these results were unavailable or not well known. This is, for instance, the case with Tramontana, Gardini, and Agliari (2011), who used recent results to complete the analysis of the Bohm and Kaas (2000) growth model.

The aim of the present chapter is similar to that of Tramontana, Gardini, and Agliari (2011) and consists in rediscovering the rather interesting learning in production model of Himmelweit and completing the analysis of the BCB bifurcation occurring in the model. We present the model in the next section, while the study of the map in the whole economically meaningful parameters' plane is carried out in the third section. In the fourth section we conclude by giving an economic interpretation of the results.

The model

We consider the problem that a large number of producers need to face when they must decide, during each time period, whether or not to produce. Himmelweit compares this problem to the one arising in agriculture whenever a producer has to decide whether or not to plant a certain crop, when if the crop is not planted, nothing else is planted.

Producers are characterized by the same cost structure but different past experiences. The output of each producer is a random variable. Let us denote by $p_{i,t+1}$ the probability that the *i*th producer will produce at time $t+1$. This probability changes over time according to the following rule:

$$p_{i,t+1} = \lambda p_{i,t} + (1-\lambda)s_{i,t} \tag{1}$$

where λ is an anchoring parameter common to all producers, while $S_{i,t}$ refers to the experience gained by the *i*th producer during period *t*. In general, different producers are characterized by different initial histories, so the values of $S_{i,0}$ may differ among producers.

Now we have to specify what we mean exactly by the term $S_{i,t}$. What kind of experience are we talking about? Following Himmelweit, we assume that each producer, before making his or her decision for time $t+1$, looks at which choice has been the better one in the previous period, to produce or not. Given that the choice of not producing at all is neither a profit nor a loss, producers check if by producing in period *t* they obtained (or they might have obtained) a profit or a loss. In the case of profit, we expect that $p_{i,t+1} > p_{i,t}$: that is, the probability of producing in the next period is higher than before, and the opposite is the case where the best choice remains not to produce at all. Given this probability, the proportion of total productive capacity in use at a certain time period t is a random variable that we denote by μ_t. By considering a sufficiently high number of producers N, the variance of μ_t can be ignored and we have:

$$\mu_t = \frac{\sum_i p_{i,t}}{N} \tag{2}$$

The demand side of the market is characterized by a demand function $D(N\mu_t)$ that must be compared to the cost of production c in order to determine if producing is profitable or not. We have that if $D(N\mu_t) > c$ then $p_{i,t+1} > p_{i,t}$, otherwise $p_{i,t+1} > p_{i,t}$, with the restriction that $0 \leq p_{it} \leq 1$.

Finally, let us assume that $S_{i,t} = 1$ if $D(N\mu_t) > c$ and $S_{i,t} = 0$ in the opposite case. The probability of producing develops as follows:

$$\begin{cases} p_{i,t+1} = \lambda p_{i,t} + (1-\lambda) & \text{if} \quad D(N\mu_t) > c \\ p_{i,t+1} = \lambda p_{i,t} & \text{if} \quad D(N\mu_t) < c \end{cases} \tag{3}$$

By summing the probabilities (3) of the producers and dividing the sum by N we obtain:

$$\begin{cases} \mu_{t+1} = \lambda \mu_t + (1-\lambda) & \text{if} \quad D(N\mu_t) > c \\ \mu_{t+1} = \lambda \mu_t & \text{if} \quad D(N\mu_t) < c \end{cases}$$

The demand function is a decreasing one and, if the cost of production c is not excessively high, there must exist a threshold level of demand that permits producers to make profits. They make profits if price is high enough or, in other words, if the total output is low enough. Considering this upper threshold for the production an exogenous variable d, we can write down the one-dimensional piecewise linear map describing the dynamics of the proportion of total productivity used at each time period:

$$\begin{cases} \mu_{t+1} = f_L(\mu_t) = \lambda \mu_t + (1-\lambda) & \text{if} \quad \mu_t < d \\ \mu_{t+1} = f_R(\mu_t) = \lambda \mu_t & \text{if} \quad \mu_t > d \end{cases} \tag{4}$$

In the next section we study how the dynamic behavior of the map (equation 4) changes by varying the values of the two parameters of the model.

Study of the map

The map (equation 4) describes how the proportion of the total productive capacity used by the firms changes dynamically. It depends upon two parameters: λ, which measures the resistance to change of the firms with respect to new information, and d, which represents the threshold level of the proportion of used productive capacity – the one in which profits are zero. By definition, both parameters must belong to the interval [0,1] so our research question consists in explaining what occurs for each admissible combination of parameters, which are inside the square $[0,1] \times [0,1]$ in the (d, λ) parameter plane.

We are considering a piecewise linear map with one discontinuity in which both branches of the map are increasing and with a slope of less than 1. The recent rediscovery of the results of Leonov (1959, 1962), improved in Avrutin, Schanz, and Gardini (2010) and in Gardini et al. (2010), permit us to characterize the periodicity regions completely by analytically calculating the borders of the curves and also by explaining the reason behind the appearance of each periodicity region in that particular position of the parameters' plane.

Let us start with some preliminary results. In the parameters' plane we are considering, map (4) does not have fixed points, at least if we do not consider the extreme cases in which $d = 0$ or $d = 1$. These cases are not interesting from the point of view of the economic application because they imply that the firms' choice is not a real choice given that it is always better either to produce or not to produce at all. If we focus on the cases in which $\in]0,1[$, then no fixed point exists.

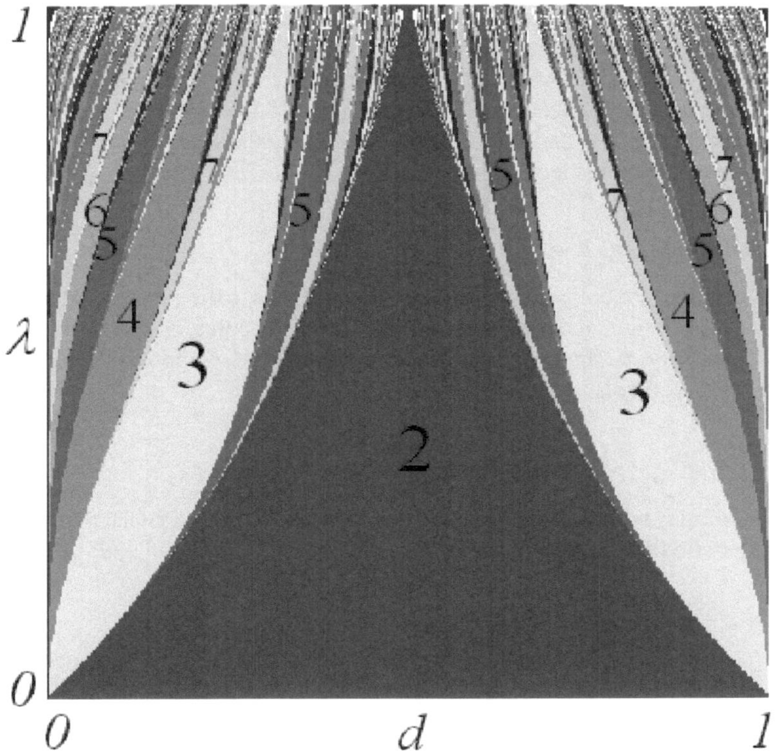

Figure 9.1 Two-dimensional bifurcation diagram

Source: Author's computations

Nevertheless the dynamics are bounded because there exists an absorbing interval $I=[f_R(d), f_L(d)]$ inside which the orbits enter and never escape. So, no divergent trajectories are possible.

We can also prove that each existing cycle must necessarily be stable; in fact, each cycle of period k has a number $r\in(0,k)$ of points located on the right branch (R) of the map and $l=k-r$ points on the left branch (L). The eigenvalue of this generic cycle is given by the product of the slopes of the branches where the points are located, that is:

$$\xi=\left(f_R^{'}\right)^r\left(f_L^{'}\right)^l=\lambda^k$$

and, given the restriction about the values that λ may assume, we know that $0<\xi<1$.[1]

The appearance/disappearance of the cycles is a BCB: that is, typical of piecewise maps. A BCB occurs when a periodic point of a cycle collides with the discontinuity point d. The regions of existence of the cycles are usually determined by subdividing the periodic cycles into classes (called *complexity levels*) related to the symbolic sequence of the cycles. The symbolic sequence of a cycle permits us to characterize where, with respect to the discontinuity, the points of the cycle are located. For instance a 3-cycle of symbolic sequence *RLR* is characterized by 2 points with values higher than the discontinuity and 1 lower than it. Note that the symbolic sequence *RLR* and the sequence R^2L denote the same cycle; the only difference is the point considered first.

Cycles of first complexity level

Cycles having the symbolic sequence LR^n (or RL^n) are called cycles of first complexity level. When the cycle exists, the periodic point on the left side of the discontinuity μ_0 must be the fixed point of the composite function $f_R^n\circ f_L(\mu_0)=\mu_0$, that is:

$$\mu_0=\frac{(1-\lambda)\lambda^n}{1-\lambda^{n+1}} \tag{5}$$

and when it collides with the discontinuity (i.e. $\mu_0=d$) we have a BCB: that is, a border of the periodicity region of the cycle:

$$\Phi_{LR^n}:d=\frac{(1-\lambda)\lambda^n}{1-\lambda^{n+1}} \tag{6}$$

The other BCB occurs when the rightmost point of the cycle (μ_n) collides with the discontinuity. μ_n is the fixed point of the composite function $f_R^{n-1}\circ f_L\circ f_R(\mu)$ through which we get:

$$\mu_n=\frac{(1-\lambda)\lambda^{n-1}}{1-\lambda^{n+1}} \tag{7}$$

and the corresponding BCB curve is:

$$\Phi_{RLR^{n-1}} : d = \frac{(1-\lambda)\lambda^{n-1}}{1-\lambda^{n+1}} \tag{8}$$

These curves are represented in Figure 9.2(a).

With a similar reasoning we can obtain the boundaries of the periodicity regions of cycles of the first level of complexity with symbolic sequence RL^n. We get the equations:

$$\begin{aligned} &\Phi_{RL^n} : d = \frac{1-\lambda^n}{1-\lambda^{n+1}} \\ &\Phi_{LRL^{n-1}} : d = \frac{(1-\lambda)\lambda^n + 1 - \lambda^{n-1}}{1-\lambda^{n+1}} \end{aligned} \tag{9}$$

which are drawn in Figure 9.2(b). Obviously the region of the 2-cycle of symbolic sequence *RL* belongs to both the families.

We have seen that the cycle with symbolic sequence LR^n exists (and is stable) provided that:

$$d \in \left[\frac{(1-\lambda)\lambda^n}{1-\lambda^{n+1}} ; \frac{(1-\lambda)\lambda^{n-1}}{1-\lambda^{n+1}} \right] \tag{10}$$

while a cycle belonging to the family of symbolic sequence RL^n exists (and is stable) as long as:

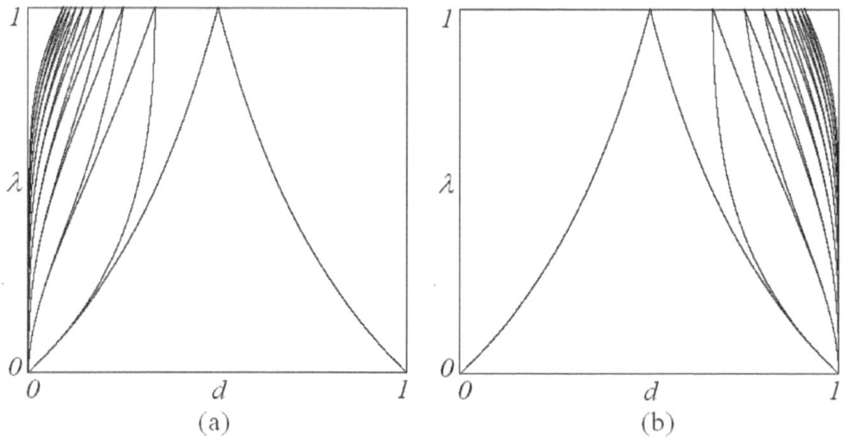

Figure 9.2 BCB curves of first complexity level

Source: Author's computations

$$d \in \left[\frac{(1-\lambda)\lambda^n + 1 - \lambda^{n-1}}{1-\lambda^{n+1}} ; \frac{1-\lambda^n}{1-\lambda^{n+1}} \right] \tag{11}$$

which can be obtained by symmetry with respect to the line $d = 1/2$, starting from those of the symmetric family:

$$\begin{aligned} \frac{(1-\lambda)\lambda^n + 1 - \lambda^{n-1}}{1-\lambda^{n+1}} &= 1 - \frac{(1-\lambda)\lambda^{n-1}}{1-\lambda^{n+1}} \\ \frac{1-\lambda^n}{1-\lambda^{n+1}} &= 1 - \frac{(1-\lambda)\lambda^n}{1-\lambda^{n+1}} \end{aligned} \tag{12}$$

and this explains the symmetry of the periodicity regions with respect to $d = 1/2$.

Cycles of higher complexity level

Cycles of first complexity level do not fill the parameters' space. Between each consecutive pair there exist infinitely many other periodicity regions of higher complexity level. The periodicity of the cycles characterizing these regions follows the so-called *period adding scheme* (or *Farey tree rule*). That is, between two consequent regions of complexity level k we can find two infinite families of periodicity regions of complexity level $k+1$ that accumulate on the two starting regions.

For instance, if we consider the periodicity region of the 2-cycle of symbolic sequence LR (let us call it region Π_{LR}) and the contiguous region of the 3-cycle of first complexity level with symbolic sequence LRR (region Π_{LR^2}), between them we can detect two families of periodicity regions of second degree of complexity, $\Pi_{LR\left(LR^2\right)^m}$ and $\Pi_{(LR)^m LR^2}$, for any $m \geq 1$, accumulating on the regions Π_{LR^2} and Π_{LR}, respectively.

The BCB curves forming the borders of the periodicity regions of the second complexity level can be obtained starting from the equations of the BCB curves of the first complexity level.

Let us consider the region between the curves Φ_{LR^n} and Φ_{RLR^n}. We need to define the composite functions associated with the symbolic sequence of the related colliding points LR^n and RLR^n, say:

$$T_L = f_R^n \circ f_L ; T_R = f_R^n \circ f_L \circ f_R$$

which must be applied to points on the left and on the right of the discontinuity point d, respectively. In this way we obtain two linear maps: $T_L = A_L \mu + B$ and $T_R = A_R \mu + B$, where:

$$A_L = \lambda^{n+1}, A_R = \lambda^{n+2}, B = \lambda^n (1-\lambda)$$

Similarly to what we have seen for the first complexity level BCB curves, we can obtain a family of periodicity regions denoted by the symbolic sequence $T_L T_R^m$ accumulating on Φ_{RLR^n} :

$$\begin{aligned}
\Phi_{T_L T_R^m} &: d = B\frac{1-A_R^{m+1}}{(1-A_R)\left(1-A_L A_R^m\right)} \\
\Phi_{T_R T_L T_R^{m-1}} &: d = B\frac{\left(1-A_R^{m-1}\right)+(1-A_L)\left(1-A_R\right)(A_R^{m-1})}{(1-A_R)\left(1-A_L A_R^m\right)}
\end{aligned} \tag{13}$$

In a similar way we get the family of periodicity regions with symbolic sequence $T_R T_L^m$ accumulating on the curves Φ_{LR^n} and Φ_{LRL^n}. In Figure 9.3 the BCB curves corresponding to $n = 1, \ldots, 8$ and $m = 1,2,3$ are drawn in gray.

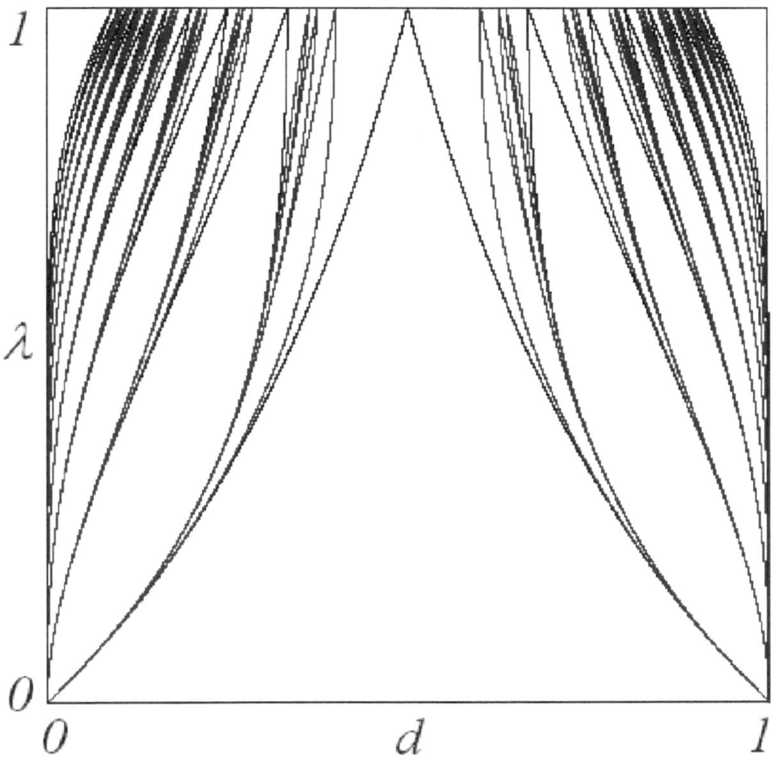

Figure 9.3 BCB curves of higher complexity level

Source: Author's computations

Functions T_L and T_R can now be used as starting point for the calculation of the BCB curves delimiting the third level of complexity regions, and so on recursively.

The role of parameters: some economic considerations

In the previous section, we fully characterized the feasible parameters' plane. Let us now try to propose an interpretation, from the economic point of view, of the results we have obtained.

The first comment concerns the role of the level of output corresponding to a null profit: that is, our parameter *d*. The value $d = 1/2$ is a threshold value for this parameter. At $d = 1/2$ we have a 2-cycle in which a period with high productivity alternates with a low-productivity period. By reducing the value of *d* we enter into a region of the parameters' plane in which other periodicities are also possible. We are considering the left-hand side of Figure 9.1. In this region, if the anchoring parameter λ is high enough, then periodic cycles of period higher than 2 can be obtained. The period adding scheme that governs the periodicities permits us to know that these cycles are characterized by a higher number of points in the region with low productivity. The same is true when $d > 1/2$, but in these cases periodic cycles are characterized by a higher number of points in the high-productivity regions. In particular, the further the value of *d* is from 1/2 (that is, the closer to 1 or 0), the lower is the threshold value of λ, leading to different dynamics from the 2-cycle.

So the role of *d* is totally consistent with its economic meaning. If the market is such that zero profits are obtained with a low value of output, then we expect that production will be low, and the opposite will be the case when this threshold value is high.

The role of λ is clear as well. When firms are inclined to use new information to take their decisions (that is, λ is low) then high periodicities are possible only for extreme values of *d*. In contrast, when firms are reluctant to use new information (λ is high) then high periodicity cycles are more likely to be the outcome of the dynamic process, especially for extreme values of *d*. Moreover, high values of λ are associated with high sensitivity to changes in market conditions. Looking at the top of Figure 9.1, we can see that even a small change in *d* can cause a change in the periodicity of the cycle, while if λ is low the system is sensitive to changes in *d* only when it assumes extreme values.

Summarizing, thanks to recent developments in the study of piecewise linear maps we have completely characterized the border-collision bifurcations of the system as a function of the parameters. This has permitted us to deepen the analysis of Himmelweit and to increase the understanding of the model from both a mathematical and an economic point of view.

Note

1 We are not considering the extreme cases in which $\lambda = 0$ or $\lambda = 1$ because, as for the other parameter *d*, they are not economically interesting.

References

Avrutin, V., L. Gardini, M. Schanz, I. Sushko, and F. Tramontana (2014). *Continuous and Discontinuous Piecewise-Smooth One-Dimensional Maps: Invariant Sets and Bifurcation Structures*, Singapore: World Scientific Publishing Company.

Avrutin, V., M. Schanz, and L. Gardini (2010). Calculation of bifurcation curves by map replacement, *International Journal of Bifurcation and Chaos*, 20, 3105–35.

Böhm, V. and L. Kaas (2000). Differential savings, factor shares, and endogenous growth cycles, *Journal of Economic Dynamics and Control*, 24, 965–80.

Bullard, J. (1994). Learning equilibria, *Journal of Economic Theory*, 64, 468–85.

Day, R. H. (1982). Irregular growth cycles, *American Economic Review*, 72, 406–14.

Day, R. H. and W. Shafer (1987). Ergodic fluctuations in deterministic economic models, *Journal of Economic Behavior and Organization*, 8, 339–61.

Ferri, P. and E. Greenberg (1990). A wage–price regime switching model, *Journal of Economic Behavior and Organization*, 13, 77–95.

Ferri, P. and E. Greenberg (1992). Technical change and wage-share fluctuations in a regime-switching model, *Journal of Economic Behavior and Organization*, 19, 369–77.

Ferri P., E. Greenberg and R. H. Day (2001). The Phillips curve, regime switching, and the NAIRU, *Journal of Economic Behavior and Organization*, 46, 23–37.

Gardini, L. and F. Tramontana (2010). Border collision bifurcations in 1D PWL map with one discontinuity and negative jump: use of the first return map, *International Journal of Bifurcation and Chaos*, 20, 3529–47.

Gardini, L., F. Tramontana, V. Avrutin, and M. Schanz (2010). Border-collision bifurcations in 1D piecewise-linear maps and Leonov's approach, *International Journal of Bifurcation and Chaos*, 20, 3085–104.

Grandmont, J. and G. Laroque (1991). Economic dynamics with learning: some instability examples. In W. Barnett, C. D'Aspremont, J. Gabszewicz, and A. Mas-Colell, eds., *Equilibrium Theory and Applications*, Cambridge: Cambridge University Press, pp. 247–73.

Himmelweit, S. (1976). A behavioural model of learning in production, *Review of Economic Studies*, 43, 329–46.

Huang W. and R. H. Day (1993). Chaotically switching bear and bull markets: the derivation of stock price distributions from behavioral rules. In R. Day and P. Chen, eds., *Nonlinear Dynamics and Evolutionary Economics*, Oxford: Oxford University Press, pp. 169–82.

Leonov, N. N. (1959). On a positive mapping of a line into itself, *Radiofisica*, 2, 942–56.

Leonov, N. N. (1962). On a discontinuous pointwise mapping of a line into itself, *Doklady Akademii Nauk SSSR*, 143, 1038–41.

Lucas, R. (1987). Adaptive behavior and economic theory. In R. Hogarth and M. Reder, eds., *Rational Choice: The Contrast between Economics and Psychology*, Chicago: University of Chicago Press, pp. 217–42.

Nusse, H. E. and J. A. Yorke (1992). Border-collision bifurcations including period two to period three for piecewise smooth systems, *Physica D*, 57, 39–57.

Nusse, H. E., E. Ott, and J. A. Yorke (1994). Border-collision bifurcations: an explanation for observed bifurcation phenomena, *Physical Review E*, 49, 1073–6.

Tramontana, F., L. Gardini, and P. Ferri (2010). The dynamics of the NAIRU model with two switching regimes, *Journal of Economic Dynamics and Control*, 34, 681–95.

Tramontana, F., L. Gardini, and A. Agliari (2011). Endogenous cycles in discontinuous growth models, *Mathematics and Computers in Simulation*, 81, 1625–39.

Tuinstra, J. and F. Wagener (2007). On learning equilibria, *Economic Theory*, 30, 493–513.

Part IV

Empirical and institutional factors in cycles and growth

10 The time dimension of credit risk

Modelling issues and regulatory implications

Marida Bertocchi and Costanza Torricelli[1]

The time dimension of risk is the relationship between the credit risk and the business cycle.[2] In fact, credit risk is determined both by idiosyncratic risk factors related to the single obligor features and by systematic risk factors affecting the creditworthiness of all the obligors. Systematic risk, being not diversifiable, is of utmost importance in the assessment of credit risk at a portfolio level and is generally dependent on macroeconomic conditions. The time dimension of credit risk might have a quite obvious impact on the stability of the financial system, bringing about systemic implications. Systemic risk can be identified either in a 'vertical perspective' as a contagion among banks, or in a 'horizontal perspective' as the interconnection between the financial system and the real economy (ECB, 2009).

The relationship between credit risk measurement and the business cycle has given rise to a wide literature, which was also fostered by the consultative documents related to Basel II in relation to the 'procyclicality issue' (see Allen and Saunders, 2003, for a survey of the early literature). The last financial crisis has renewed interest in the topic on behalf of both the academic literature and the regulator, thus leading to a reconsideration of the issue in Basel III. The business cycle can enter at different levels by affecting the main risk components which characterise a credit risk measurement framework, i.e. the rating, the probability of default (PD) (and the transition matrices, TM), the loss given default (LGD), the exposure at default (EAD), the correlations among PD, LGD and EAD, and the correlations of PDs across borrowers.

Against this backdrop, the aim of this chapter is to discuss some facets of the time dimension of credit risk. Specifically, we will first discuss the modelling and regulatory issues connected to the rating and the PD estimation, then we will focus on credit risk pricing of a specific asset class: namely, corporate bonds. Finally, we will discuss the appropriate framework to evaluate the cyclical effects of models for pricing credit risk also in connection with bank capital regulation.

Rating and default probabilities: estimation issues and regulatory implications

The existence and the nature of the relationship between the real activity and the default rates (as a measure of materialised risk) is not controversial, as witnessed by a wide literature, which, for different countries and in different periods, tested the relationship between banks' performances and the business cycle (e.g. Leaven and Majnoni, 2003; Ayuso, Perez and Saurina, 2004; Pesola, 2007; Quagliariello, 2007; Marcucci and Quagliariello, 2008; Pederzoli, Torricelli and Castellani, 2010). By contrast, the debate is still open as to the relationship between risk accumulation and economic conditions – a debate which has important implications in terms of risk measurement and management. In fact, while risk is generally considered countercyclical (i.e. higher during recessions and vice versa), some authors believe that risk may be highest at business cycle peaks. In particular, Borio, Furfine and Lowe (2001), well in advance of the last financial crises and the Great Recession that followed, stressed that the high default rates during recessions are just a materialisation of risk building up during booms, especially if a strong expansion combines with the creation of financial imbalances. They also argued that these different views about the risk dynamics over the business cycle ultimately reflect different opinions about the nature of the economic process underlying the business cycle.

In order to appreciate the implications of these different views for credit risk management, let us take the two main and most distant ones: the 'predictability view', i.e. the business cycle is a predictable regular sine wave, and the 'random walk view', i.e. the business cycle is too irregular to be predicted. While in the former view macroeconomic forecasts can be included in a credit risk model, in the latter the current conditions are considered the best forecast for the next period. The direct consequence of these two different views of business cycle dynamics on risk measurement is the timing of the increase/decrease of the risk measure. According to the random walk view, the measured risk reflects the current economic conditions and hence it increases during recessions and decreases during expansions. By contrast, in the predictability view, the risk measure should increase if a recession is going to happen over the credit horizon (and vice versa), and the measured risk can increase during an expansion.

Procyclicality is commonly meant as the phenomenon of business cycle amplification due to the reduction in credit availability in recession periods (and vice versa in expansion periods). Procyclicality is to some degree inherent in bank activitity, but regulations may play a role in exacerbating it by imposing capital requirements on banks' credit exposures. Since the first capital accord known as Basel I, regulation forces banks to hold a capital ratio (i.e. a ratio of capital to the sum of risk-weighted assets) above the solvency coefficient of 8 per cent against credit risk. Basel II (BCBS, 2004), by defining risk-sensitive capital charges, implicitly amplified the procyclical effect of compulsory capital requirements. In fact, with Basel II and particularly in the Internal Rating Based (IRB) approach, the denominator of the capital ratio also changes over time: if the risk-weighted assets increase during recessions, this will enhance the effect of the numerator, implying a further reduction in the capital ratio.

From a macroeconomic point of view, since the Basel II consultative documents were issued, the diffused fear (see, for example, Danielsson et al., 2001) was that a co-movement in capital requirement and the business cycle would induce banks to reduce lending further during recessions due to the high capital requirement with which they had to comply. The opposite would happen in economic booms. This mechanism would eventually exacerbate the business cycle's peaks and troughs. As highlighted by Leaven and Majnoni (2003), the risk of a 'capital crunch', i.e. a situation of simultaneous shortage of capital and contraction in the supply of new loans – can stem from the joint working of high capital requirements and economic slowdown, a situation which the last financial crisis has quite clearly exemplified.

This concern is particularly relevant if the 'random walk view' of the business cycle prevails: a risk-sensitive capital requirement is in fact likely to fluctuate over the business cycle, and it will be higher during recessions and lower during expansions. By contrast, if the 'predictability view' is accepted, the capital requirement can be forced by the regulation to increase at the peak of the business cycle, in anticipation of a recession, and to decrease at the trough, in anticipation of an expansion. This would smooth the business cycle sine wave turning points.

The business cycle can enter at different levels by affecting the main variables that characterise a credit risk measurement framework, but we restrict ourselves here to the two phases characterising a rating system: namely, the *rating assignment*, which classifies obligors by rating classes, and the *rating quantification*, which associates a probability of default (PD) to each rating class. In order to capture the time dimension of risk, either the ratings or the corresponding PDs need to be modelled so as to account for economic conditions prevailing over the credit horizon. In line with the literature, we will refer to the PDs dependent on a particular state of the business cycle as *conditional PDs*, as opposed to the *unconditional PDs* which are independent of the particular state of the business cycle.

The rating assignment and the rating quantification can overlap, since models to estimate the PD of a single obligor can be used both to assign a rating and to contribute to the definition of the PD relative to a certain rating class. In fact, the PDs can be estimated in four different ways by means of: 1) statistical methods based on obligors' specific features (mainly accounting data); 2) structural models based on equity market data; 3) reduced form models (typically modelling the default intensity rather than the annual PD) based on credit spread market data; 4) PDs implied from ratings based on historical default data. In the first three cases, the rating assignment and quantification can overlap, in that a PD estimated for the single borrower can be used both to assign the rating and to calculate the rating class PD as an average.

Moreover, the rating systems can follow a '*point in time*' (*pit*) logic or a '*through the cycle*' (*ttc*) logic. The former assigns ratings according to the ability of the borrowers to fulfil obligations over the credit horizon, and is likely to change over the business cycle; the latter considers this ability independently of the business cycle, i.e. it considers a fixed scenario. Ratings assigned through the cycle are built to be stable over the business cycle, changing only with the idiosyncratic factors. The choice between these two conceptually different rating assignments depends on what type of risk the ratings are meant to represent, i.e. relative versus absolute risk of borrowers. If only the relative riskiness is considered in the rating assignment, ratings represent an ordinal ranking of borrowers, regardless of the dimension of risk. By contrast, ratings accounting for absolute risk consider the actual level of risk and hence also its time dimension, i.e. the way it varies over the business cycle. Ratings assigned *pit* consider the absolute dimension of risk, including the time dimension, and hence they will fluctuate over the business cycle. Ratings assigned *ttc* instead are meant to neutralise the business cycle effects in order to isolate the relative riskiness of borrowers. Amato and Furfine (2003, p. 5) argue that credit ratings 'are intended to distinguish the relatively risky firms (or specific bonds) from the relatively safe' and hence ratings should be assigned *ttc*. Crouhy, Galai and Mark (2001) suggest that *ttc* ratings are preferable for investment (lending) decisions, while *pit* ratings should be used when allocating capital and defining reserves (hence capital requirements).[3]

As for the Basel II, banks adopting the IRB approach are required to use a time horizon longer than one year in assigning ratings and to assess ratings according to the 'borrower's ability and willingness to contractually perform despite adverse economic conditions or the occurrence of unexpected events' (BCBS, 2004, p. 97). It follows that Basel II implicitly requires a *ttc* rating system. Moreover Basel II requires PDs to be estimated as long-run averages, hence tendentially constant. These choices, which are in line with the rating agencies' methodology, respond to the willingness of smoothing capital requirements over the different phases of the business cycle to avoid or reduce the procyclical effect, but they tend to reduce risk-sensitivity.

Concerns about procycliclality of Basel II were often dismissed in the early debate by mantaining that most banks held capital in excess of the regulatory minima, so that the real incidence of this problem would be small, if not negligible. However, we should stress that a few papers in the academic literature have put forward proposals to tackle procyclicality since the publication of the Basel II (consultative) documents.[4] Gordy and Howells (2006) maintain that, in order to smooth these procyclical effects within the IRB structure, three main approaches are possible: smoothing the inputs (mainly PDs) to the capital function; flattening the capital function itself in order to reduce its sensitivity to the risk components; and smoothing directly the output of the capital function. Basel II, by requiring *ttc* ratings and long-run averages PDs, adopts the first solution. Moreover, the final 2004 version flattens the capital formula compared to preliminary verisions available as consultative documents, and hence pursues the second solution as well. However, these two former solutions, by acting on the risk components or on the measure of 'potential loss', determine a loss in transparency since the calculated required capital does not properly represent actual risk in that it neglects its time dimension. By contrast, the third solution, supported by Gordy and Howells

(2006) and Repullo, Saurina and Trucharte (2010), preserves transparency since it acts as a correction on a risk-sensitive calculated capital requirement. This approach is closer in spirit to the alternative of smoothing by means of counter-cyclical buffers, as in the statistical provisioning proposed by the Bank of Spain (Fernández de Lis, Martínez and Saurina, 2000; Fernandez de Lis and Garica-Herrero, 2012). Pederzoli and Torricelli (2005) set up a forward-looking model for time-varying capital requirements, which finds application within Basel II. The model rests on the relationship between default rates and the business cycle: by assuming two regimes, expansion and recession, and by forecasting the associated probabilities, the model defines the default probability for each rating class as the expected value of a default rate whose distribution is a mixture of an expansion and a recession distribution. The application to US data over the forecasting period 1971–2002 shows that the model is able both to preserve the risk sensitivity of the capital requirement and to dampen procyclicality at the same time. Marotta, Pederzoli and Torricelli (2006) check the robustness of the approach proposed by Pederzoli and Torricelli (2005) with Italian data, where alternative business cycle chronologies are used: ISAE (Istituto di Studi e Analisi Economica) and ECRI (Economic Cycle Research Institute). Findings suggest that the model's performance depends on the chronology used.

Following this quite academic debate, the issue of the procyclicality of capital requirements against credit risk became apparent to a broader public with the onset of the 2007–8 financial crisis and the subsequent Great Recession. At the same time, the need to revise Basel II regulation was recognised and this led to the publiction of the new regulation known as Basel III (BCBS, 2010a).

Based on the features and consequences of the financial crisis, Basel III takes both a micro and a macro prudential approach and essentially aims to increase considerably the quality and the level of banks' capital and reduce systemic risk, allowing sufficient time for a smooth transition to the new regime. The first objective is mainly related to the need to take liquidity risk into account, which was highlighted by the financial crises and was essentially neglected by Basel II. The second objective is more clearly connected with the time dimension of credit risk and the procyclicality issue discussed so far. In these connections Basel III promotes two types of capital buffer. The first is a capital conservation buffer[5] that can be used by banks to absorb losses during periods of stress without going below the minimum capital requirements. This will reduce the possibility of a self-reinforcing adverse cycle of losses and credit cutbacks with respect to the previous regulation. Second, and to limit procyclicality, there is a countercyclical capital buffer (CCB), which will build up during periods of rapid aggregate credit growth if, in the judgement of national authorities, this growth is aggravating system-wide risk.[6] Conversely, the capital held in this buffer could be released in the downturn of the cycle. This would, for instance, reduce the risk that available credit could be constrained by regulatory capital requirements. As for the 'horizontal dimension' of credit risk, Basel III allows for a better handling of the systemic risk due to the interlinkages and common exposures across individual institutions, by calibrating standards with respect to the contribution that each institution makes to the system as a whole, not just on a stand-alone basis. This approach implies a special treatment of the systemically important financial institutions (SIFIs), which, under the Basel III framework, should have loss-absorbing capacity beyond the common standards.

Current academic and institutional research has been forstered by these regulatory reforms. As for CCB, some papers (e.g. Behn et al., 2013) are motivated by the debate over the methodology to be used to set it. In fact, while the BCBS (2010b) has developed a methodology based on the ratio of aggregate credit to GDP, the EU Capital Requirements Directive (CRD IV), even if it recognises the importance of such a ratio, specifies that buffer rates should also account for other variables relevant as early warning indicators of financial instability – for instance, different credit variables, or real variables such as the growth in house prices). A critical assessment of the CCB is also provided by Repullo and Saurina (2011), who argue that a mechanical application of the buffer would tend to reduce capital requirements when GDP growth is high and increase them when GDP growth is low, thus exacerbating the inherent procyclicality of risk-sensitive bank capital regulation. Hence they propose a fully rule-based smoothing of minimum capital requirements based on GDP growth.

Pricing credit risk for corporate bond portfolios

The pricing of defaultable or risky bonds has been extensively studied in the last 20 years, leading to a large literature on the subject, which includes, among others, Kim, Ramswamy and Sundaresan (1993), Jarrow and Turnbull (1995), Jarrow, Lando and Turnbull (1997), Nielsen and Ronn (1997), Duffie and Singleton (1999), Crouhy, Galai and Mark (2000), Elton et al. (2001), Schönbucher (2002) and Bielecki, Jeanblanc and Rutkowski (2004). If most of the early literature was related to corporate bonds, the last financial crisis and in particular the sovereign debt crisis in 2011 have brought to the forefront the need for more research on the credit-riskiness of government bonds (see, for example, Bertocchi et al., 2013).

Various factors characterise defaultable bonds with respect to the risk-free bonds and specifically the positive probability of default prior to the bonds' maturity, the estimated loss given default, which depends on the assumption on the recovery rate for the class, and the probability that the bond issuer will migrate from the current rating class to a lower one. As for the latter, the so-called transition risk, it is related to movements from one rating group to another, whereby the classification in rating groups is assigned by a rating agency such as S&P, Moody's or Fitch for different levels of creditworthiness (see Table 10.1).

The credit rating consolidates a large variety of information that needs to be known about the creditworthiness of the security's issuer. It is obtained using qualitative, quantitative and non-public information on a company. The credit rating is crucial when buying bonds issued by companies to determine the likelihood that the company will meet its obligations. A poor credit rating indicates that the company has a high risk of default. A rating change reflects an estimate that the credit quality of the issuer has improved or worsened. The

Table 10.1 Bond rating classes for different agencies

	Moody's	*S&P*	*Description*
Investment grade	Aaa	AAA	Best level of creditworthiness; extremely reliable
	Aa	AA	Very good level of creditworthiness; very reliable
	A	A	Good level of creditworthiness
	Baa	BBB	Lowest rate in investment grade
Speculative grade	Ba	BB	There is a chance to fulfil payments if unexpected events do not take place
	B	B	As above
	Caa	CCC	Risk of bankruptcy, speculative features
	Ca	CC	Highly vulnerable to a payment default
	C	C	Bankruptcy is on the way
	D	D	Default – bankruptcy

Source: Author's own descriptions

risk assessments of credit rating agencies have a great influence on companies' borrowing costs, influencing their access to debt markets, as discussed more extensively in Bertocchi et al. (2013).

In order to price corporate bonds, Duffie and Singleton (1999) develop their reduced-form models on the evidence of positive credit spreads with respect to risk-free bonds, to compensate for extra risk carried by the investment with a specific rating class. The credit spreads are taken as financial measures of the issuer's creditworthiness, and the risk associated with co-movements of the credit spread curves and the risk-free term structure is known as correlation risk (see Kijima and Muromachi, 2000).

Jarrow, Lando and Turnbull (1997) characterise the bankruptcy process as a finite state Markov process in the firm's credit ratings. This approach assumes that the market for default-free and credit-risky securities is complete and no arbitrage opportunities are present. It also assumes that the default-free term structure and the bankruptcy process are independent, which is a reasonable approximation for investment grade debt, but not for speculative grade debt. It also adopts an estimate of historical transition probabilities.

This model implies that, referring to: $p(t, T)$, the price at t of a default-free zero coupon bond with maturity T; $p^i(t, T)$, $i = 1, \ldots K$, the price at t of a risky zero-coupon bond with rating class i maturing at T; τ^i ,the random time at which default occurs for a bond in rating class i; α^i, the recovery rate for class i; and $\tilde{Q}$, the risk-neutral survival probability, the pricing formula for the risky zero-coupon bond is:

$$p^i(t,T) \equiv p(t,T)\left[1 \cdot \tilde{Q}\left\{\tau^i > T\right\} + \alpha^i\left\{1 - \tilde{Q}\left\{\tau^i > T\right\}\right\}\right]$$

The model assumes that the only driver for changes in $\tilde{Q}$ is represented by rating transitions: securities in the same rating class will share the same spread dynamics up to class changes. A set of specific risk premia π^i and the time-homogeneity hypothesis of the transition matrix allow the empirical probabilities to be transformed into neutral ones. The rating transition probabilities for the selected time step are computed as time-equivalent transition matrices using the power transition expansion. Other adjustments of empirical transition matrices are done in Kijima and Komoribayashi (1998) and in Lando and Skodeberg (2002).

We refer to Taboga (2009) and to Aussenegg, Goetz and Jelic (2013) for a discussion on the key drivers of corporate spreads. However, it is worth recalling here that yields of investment grade as well as speculative grade corporate bonds are determined by the joint movement of the term structure of interest rates and the rating class by specific spreads. Individual securities depend in addition on specific idiosyncratic risk factors related to the overall economic sector, the business climate, the geographic region, the liquidity and other factors. Corporate bond spreads reflect the demands of risk premiums by market participants due to any of the above factors.

In the Jarrow model outlined above, the credit spreads s^i (t) are expressed through the recovery rates of class and the risk-neutral transition probabilities. The whole price procedure relies on the estimation of the term structure of risk-free rates and credit spreads. Any model for the term structure may be used for this purpose. For example, Abaffy et al. (2007) use the Black–Derman–Toy model.

Correlation is another important aspect that should be taken into account. Correlations may vary within a business cycle: they are generally higher within the same sector. Incorporating correlations into the model may be done by following the approach of Schönbucher (2002) and estimating them from historical data. Under the assumption of independent binomial processes, the up–down movements of the risk-free rate may be associated over each time increment with up–down movements of the credit spread processes within the current rating class and towards contiguous rating classes. The risky interest *rate* $R^i(t) = r(t) + s^i(t)$ over the maturity $T - t$ will result in a recombining quadrinomial lattice (see Hull and White, 1994; Schönbucher, 2002). To include in the risky rate evolution the likelihood of remaining in the given rating class or moving to a contiguous class, one can assume that rating class transitions are state (spread and risk-free rate) independent, which is consistent with the assumption of independent random movements of the term structure of credit spreads from period to period. Thus the multinomial risky short rate is built as follows. At every time increment a set of branches, which depend on the current rating class, will depart from every state process: $r_h(t + k)$ denotes the state of the risk-free process at time $(t + k)$ after an h-move (h = up, down), $s_l^j(t + k)$ is the state of the spread process at time $(t + k)$ after an l-move (l = up, down) for class j, and $R_{hl}^{ij}(t + k)$ is all the short rates at time $(t + k)$ after an h-move in the risk-free rate and an l-move in the spread and a transition from rating class i to rating class j during the period. Each branch is characterised by the risk-neutral transition probability from rating class i to rating class j divided by 4.

Abaffy et al. (2007) use such a model for pricing representative investment grade risky securities in the period April 2000 to March 2003 and in the industrial sectors of telecommunications, utilities, automotives and financial, which are characterised by high liquidity. They observe that the consideration of transition probabilities and correlations has a minor impact on the computed fair prices with respect to fair prices derived from the case of independent risk-free rate and credit spreads, provided no transition in other rating classes is assumed before maturity. Moreover, the difference between average market prices and theoretical prices is minimised only for BBB-rated bonds, while it remains relevant for other rating classes and independent of specific sectors.

Finally, we recall that defaultable bonds carry both non-diversifiable and specific risk credit risk components that remain the key factors in explaining specific bond dynamics. The approach described above is able to isolate the systemic risk component of credit risk. In order to price single securities, one should add a model to price the idiosyncratic diversifiable risk, which in this context is primarily the liquidity risk.

A framework to evaluate cyclical effects of rating systems and bank capital regulation

Even if the objective of Basel II was 'to develop a framework that would further strengthen the soundness and stability of the international banking system' (BCBS, 2004, p. 14), the literature is virtually unanimous in supporting the idea that Basel II exacerbated the procyclical tendencies of the banking system, with obvious dangers for macroeconomic stability (see, for example, Drumond, 2009). The critics essentially state that risk-sensitive capital requirements, being sensitive to the business cycle, tend to increase during an economic downturn, inducing banks to shrink lending with obvious side-effects for the real economy (including households). In the second section, we discussed different solutions that were proposed to tackle the procyclicality issue well before the last financial crisis (e.g. Pederzoli and Torricelli, 2005; Gordy and Howells, 2006; Repullo, Saurina and Trucharte, 2010; Fernández de Lis, Martínez and Saurina, 2000), and we stressed that the degree of procyclicality of capital requirements depends on the specific provisions of the regulation and the specific type of model used to price credit risk. A few papers have provided an evaluation of the different rating systems and possible capital regulation regimes in terms of procyclicality. Gordy and Howells (2006) compare diverse rating philosophies by considering banks with different exogenous investment strategies, and thus disregard the feedback mechanism of capital requirements on bank lending behaviour and, hence, on the economy. Repullo and Suarez (2013) develop and calibrate a dynamic model of relationship lending to compare the relative performance of several capital regulation regimes. They assume that the business cycle is a Markov process (i.e. it is unpredictable) that determines the probability of defaulting on loans and that banks anticipate shocks and, as a precaution, hold capital buffers. They show that Basel II is significantly more procyclical than Basel I, but makes banks safer and hence dominates Basel I in terms of welfare – except for the small social costs of bank failure.[7] However, their model is a partial equilibrium one, which abstracts from demand-side fluctuations and aggregate feedback effects.

In order to overcome limitations implicit in partial equilibrium models and to analyse the different facets and implications of systemic risk, a general equilibrium approach has to be taken. However, not all general equilibrium models provide the appropriate framework for a comprehensive analysis of financial stability and the procyclicality issue. As Tsomocos (2003, p. 620) pointed out, some:

> minimum structural characteristics should be present in any model attempting to capture fundamental aspects of financial instability. First, it should be multiperiod, with aggregate uncertainty and agent heterogeneity. Second, money and liquidity constraints should be explicit, since financial crises evolve from the nominal sector and subsequently spread to the real economy. Third, since the performance of banks is critical for the study of financial instability a banking sector well integrated in the model is indispensable. Finally, the regulatory framework should be clearly defined for policy and sensitivity analysis of various regulatory regimes.

It follows that Dynamic Stochastic General Equilibrium (DSGE) modelling is not the appropriate set-up, since it does not include financial intermediaries (and their default). In other words, as Goodhart, Tsomocos and Shubik (2013, p. 3) put it: 'Standard DSGE models were in essence real (Real Business Cycle, RBC) models, with the addition of price/wage stickiness (frictions).'

It follows that a strand of literature on financial instability has been developing since the original paper by Tsomocos (2003), where the canonical General Equilibrium with Incomplete Markets (GEI) model is extended with money and default. This set-up allows for the analysis of a competitive banking system and financial instability. Moreover, by introducing capital requirements for the banking sector, short- and medium-term macroeconomic consequences of Basel II can be assessed. In the model, monetary equilibria are shown to exist and financial instability and default emerge as equilibrium phenomena. In sum, the GEI framework is suitable to account for both the vertical dimension of systemic risk (inter-bank market) and the horizontal one (interconnection with the business cycle). This seminal article was followed by many contributions that build on the original model by Tsomocos (2003). Specifically, Goodhart, Sunirand and Tsomocos (2006) begin by introducing the possibility of capital requirement violation and consequent penalties, and a secondary market for the banks' equity. Moreover, they introduce limited access to consumer credit markets, thus allowing for different interest rates across the commercial banking sector. Goodhart, Sunirand and Tsomocos (2004) present a smaller version of Goodhart et al. (2006), which allows for obtaining a numerical solution, while Goodhart, Sunirand and Tsomocos (2005) simplify the non-banking agents' problems to reduced-form equations in order to perform a calibration against real UK banking data. However, these models essentially aim to analyse financial fragility in the banking system and do not assess the relevance of different types of rating system. Catarineu-Rabell, Jackson and Tsomocos (2005) analyse the procyclicality issue by comparing different rating systems from the banks' profitability point of view: within a two-period, two-state GE model with one bank, one corporation and one household, they find that banks would prefer a *pit* rather than a *ttc* rating system, with dangerous consequences in terms of procyclicality. However, the paper does do not account for the heterogeneity of agents, which is an important feature in this context.

To sum up, the models cited above do not allow consideration of either the effects of different rating systems on banks' portfolios (e.g. Catarineu-Rabell, Jackson and Tsomocos, 2005) or contagion effects relevant to financial stability (e.g. Goodhart, Sunirand and Tsmocos, 2005, 2006). In order to fill this gap, Pederzoli, Tornicelli and Tsomocos (2010) propose a general equilibrium model of an exchange economy with money and banks. The model is characterised by heterogeneity of the agents in each of the three sectors considered (the banking sector, the corporate sector and households), limited participation, and includes corporate loans, interbank, and deposit markets; moreover, corporations and households trade perishable goods on the commodity market. While banks maximise a function of their profit, corporations and households aim to maximise their inter-temporal consumption. Default is endogenous and subject to penalty, and banks' portfolios have to comply with risk-sensitive minimum capital requirements in the vein of Basel II. The paper presents comparative statics results comparing a cycle-dependent and a neutral rating system from the point of view of banks' profit maximisation and results suggest that banks' preferences about *pit* or *ttc* rating systems depend on the banks' characteristics and on the business cycle conditions in terms of expectations and reality. In the GEI model, households were only included 'to close the economy' – an assumption that did not allow the proper assessment of the role of households in terms of portfolio decisions such as mortgage choices. Goodhart, Tsomocos and Vardoulakis (2011) introduce another good, specifying a utility that resembles the utility from buying a house, and explicitly model a market for mortgages to buy housing which they pledge as collateral. However, since they do not consider wider asset markets, they exclude capital requirements for banks from the analysis. Given the importance of households as economic agents and the role played by mortgages in the last financial crises, we believe that capital requirements within this wider setting still deserve further research.

To conclude, we must recall that the 2007–8 crisis and the subsequent debate over the need for new regulation, including Basel III, has led researchers in GEI to consider combinations of capital regulations, margin requirements, liquidity regulation and dynamic provisioning. Goodhart et al. (2013) show that a policy featuring margin requirements together with countercyclical capital requirements delivers equal or better outcomes for the economy than does an unregulated financial system.

Notes

1 The authors wish to thank Chiara Pederzoli for helpful comments on the draft of this chapter. The usual caveats apply.
2 The relationship between credit risk and the business cycle is supported both by the empirical evidence (e.g. Nickell, Perraudin and Varotto, 2000; Bangia et al. 2002), which shows the increase in default rates during recessions, and by several theoretical models of the real business cycle, which support a negative correlation between credit risk factors and output (e.g. Williamson, 1987; Kwark, 2002).
3 In fact, the main rating agencies, such as Moody's, Standard & Poor's, follow the *ttc* logic. As for bank practice, many banks use rating systems based on balance-sheet data, which are *pit* and 'backward looking' by nature.
4 It should be noted that, even if some of the academic papers appear to be published as journal articles well after the Basel II document final release, the preliminary (working paper) versions of the same papers were in most cases published much earlier.
5 Comprising common equity of 2.5 per cent of risk-weighted assets, bringing the total common equity standard to 7 per cent.
6 Imposed within a range of 0–2.5 per cent comprising common equity, when authorities judge that credit growth is resulting in an unacceptable build-up of systematic risk.
7 They also show that, for high values of this cost, Basel III points in the right direction, with higher but less cyclically varying capital requirements.

References

Abaffy, J., M. Bertocchi, J. Dupačová, V. Moriggia and G. Consigli (2007). Pricing non-diversifiable credit risk in the corporate Eurobond market, *Journal of Banking and Finance*, 31, 2233–63.

Allen, L. and A. Saunders (2003). A survey of cyclical effects in credit risk measurement models, *BIS Working Papers*, no. 126.

Amato, J. and H. Furfine (2003). Are credit ratings procyclical?, *BIS Working Papers*, no. 1210.

Aussenegg, W., L. Goetz and R. Jelic (2013). Common factors in the performance of European corporate bonds: evidence before and after crisis, *European Financial Management*, forthcoming.

Ayuso, J., D. Perez and J. Saurina (2004). Are capital buffers pro-cyclical? Evidence from Spanish panel data, *Journal of Financial Intermediation*, 13, 249–64.

Bangia, A., F. Diebold, A. Kronimus, C. Schagen and T. Schuermann (2002). Ratings migration and the business cycle, with application to credit portfolio stress testing, *Journal of Banking and Finance*, 26, 445–74.

Basel Committee on Banking Supervision (BCBS) (2004). *International Convergence of Capital Measurement and Capital Standards: a Revised Framework*, Basel: Bank for International Settlements, June (revised June 2006).

Basel Committee on Banking Supervision (BCBS) (2010a). *Basel III: A Global Regulatory Framework for More Resilient Banks and Banking Systems*, Basel: Bank for International Settlements, December (revised June 2011).

Basel Committee on Banking Supervision (BCBS) (2010b). *Guidance for National Authorities Operating the Countercyclical Capital Buffer*, Basel: Bank for International Settlements.

Behn, M., C. Detken, T. A. Peltonen and W. Schudel (2013). Setting countercyclical capital buffers based on early warning models – would it work?, *ECB Working Papers*, no. 1604.

Bertocchi, M., G. Consigli, R. D'Ecclesia, R. Giacometti, V. Moriggia and S. Ortobelli (2013). *Euro Bonds: Markets, Infrastructure and Trends*, Singapore: World Scientific, Chapter 3.

Bielecki, T. R., M. Jeanblanc and M. Rutkowski (2004). Modeling and valuation of credit risk, CIME-EMS Summer School on Stochastic Methods in Finance, Bressanone, July 6–12, 2003.

Borio, C., C. Furfine and P. Lowe (2001). Procyclicality of the financial system and financial stability: issues and policy options. *BIS Working Papers*, no. 1.

Catarineu-Rabell, E., P. Jackson and D. Tsomocos (2005). Procyclicality and the new Basel accord: banks' choice of loan rating system, *Economic Theory*, 26, 537–57.

Crouhy M., D. Galai and R. Mark (2000). Prototype risk rating system, *Journal of Banking and Finance*, 25, 47–95.

Danielsson, J., P. Embrechts, C. Goodhart, C. Keating, F. Muennich, O. Renault and H. S. Shin (2001). An academic response to Basel II. *ESRC, Financial Markets Group, Special Papers*, no. 130.

Drumond, I. (2009). Bank capital requirements, business cycle fluctuations and the Basel accords: a synthesis, *Journal of Economic Surveys*, 23, 798–830.

Duffie, D. and K. J. Singleton (1999). Modeling term structure of defaultable bonds, *Review of Financial Studies*, 12, 687–720.

Elton, E. J., M. J. Gruber, D. Agrawal and C. Mann (2001). Explaining the rate spread on corporate bonds, *Journal of Finance*, 56, 247–78.

European Central Bank (ECB) (2009). The concept of systemic risk, *Financial Stability Review*, December.

Fernández de Lis, S., J. Martínez and J. Saurina (2000). Credit growth, problem loans and credit risk provisioning in Spain, *BIS Papers*, 1, 331–53.

Fernández de Lis, S. and A. Garcia-Herrero (2012). Dynamic provisioning: a buffer rather than a countercyclical tool?, *BBVA Working Papers*, no. 12/22.

Goodhart, C. A. E., P. Sunirand and D. Tsomocos (2004). A model to analyse financial fragility: applications, *Journal of Financial Stability*, 1, 1–30.

Goodhart, C. A. E., P. Sunirand and D. Tsomoco (2005). A risk assessment model for banks, *Annals of Finance*, 1, 197–224.

Goodhart, C. A. E., P. Sunirand and D. Tsomocos (2006). A model to analyse financial fragility, *Economic Theory*, 27, 107–42.

Goodhart, C. A. E., D. P. Tsomocos and A. P. Vardoulakis (2011). Modeling a housing and mortgage crisis, *Central Banking, Analysis, and Economic Policies Book Series*, 15, 215–53.

Goodhart, C. A. E., A. K. Kashyap, D. P. Tsomocos and A. P. Vardoulakis (2013). An integrated framework for analyzing multiple financial regulations, *International Journal of Central Banking*, 9, 109–43.

Goodhart, C. A. E., D. P. Tsomocos and M. Shubik (2013). Macro-modelling, default and money, *LSE Financial Markets Group Special Papers*, no. 224.

Gordy, M. and B. Howells (2006). Procyclicality in Basel II: can we treat the disease without killing the patient?, *Journal of Financial Intermediation*, 15, 395–417.

Hull, J. and A. White (1994). Numerical procedures to implement term structure models II: two factor models, *Journal of Derivatives*, 37–48.

Jarrow, R. A., D. Lando and S. M. Turnbull (1997). A Markov model for the term structure of credit spreads, *The Review of Financial Studies*, 10, 481–523.

Jarrow, R. A. and S. M. Turnbull (1995). Pricing derivatives on financial securities subject to credit risk, *Journal of Finance*, L, 53–85.

Kashyap, A. and J. Stein (2004). Cyclical implications of the Basel II capital standards, *Federal Reserve Bank of Chicago Economic Perspective*, 1st Quarter, 18–31.

Kijima, M. and K. Komoribayashi (1998). A Markov chain model for valuing credit risk derivatives, *Journal of Derivatives*, 97–108.

Kijima, M. and Y. Muromachi (2000). Evaluation of credit risk of a portfolio with stochastic interest rate and default processes, *Journal of Risk*, 3, 5–30.

Kim, I. J., K. Ramswamy and S. M. Sundaresan (1993). Valuation of corporate fixed-income securities, *Financial Management*, 22, 117–31.

Kwark, N. S. (2002). Default risks, interest rate spreads, and the business cycle: explaining the interest rate spread as a leading indicator, *Journal of Economics Dynamics and Control*, 26, 271–302.

Lando, D. and T. M. Skodeberg (2002). Analysing rating transitions and rating drift with continuous observations, *Journal of Banking and Finance*, 26, 423–44.

Leaven, L. and G. Majnoni (2003). Loan loss provisioning and economic slowdowns: too much, too late? *Journal of Financial Intermediation*, 12, 178–98.

Marcucci, J. and M. Quagliariello (2008). Is bank portfolio riskiness procyclical? Evidence from Italy using a vector autoregression, Journal of International Financial Markets, Institutions and Money, 18, 43–63.

Marotta, G., C. Pederzoli and C. Torricelli (2006). Forward-looking estimation of default probabilities with Italian data, *Euro-Mediterranean Economics and Finance Review*, 1, 6–110.

Nickell, P., W. Perraudin and S. Varotto (2000). Stability of rating transitions. *Journal of Banking and Finance*, 24, 203–27.

Nielsen, S. S. and E. I. Ronn (1997). The valuation of default risk in corporate bonds and interest rate swaps, *Advanced Future Options Research*, 9, 175–96.

Pederzoli, C. and C. Torricelli (2005). Capital requirements and business cycle regimes: forward-looking modelling of default probabilities, *Journal of Banking and Finance*, 2, 3121–40.

Pederzoli, C., C. Torricelli and D. Tsomocos (2010). Rating systems, procyclicality and Basel II: an evaluation in a general equilibrium framework, *Annals of Finance*, 6, 33–49.

Pederzoli, C., C. Torricelli and S. Castellani (2010). The interaction of financial fragility and the business cycle in determining banks' loan losses: an investigation of the Italian case, *Economic Notes*, 39, 129–46.

Pesola, J. (2007). Financial fragility, macroeconomic shocks and banks' loan losses: evidence from Europe, *Bank of Finland Research Discussion Papers*, no. 15/2007.

Quagliariello, M. (2007). Banks' riskiness over the business cycle: a panel analysis on Italian intermediaries, *Applied Financial Economics*, 17, 119–38.

Repullo, R. and J. Saurina (2011). The countercyclical capital buffer of Basel III: a critical assessment, *CEPR Discussion Papers*, no. 8304.

Repullo, R. and J. Suarez (2013). The procyclical effects of bank capital regulation, *Review of Financial Studies*, 26, 452–90.

Repullo, R., J. Saurina and C. Trucharte (2010). Mitigating the procyclicality of Basel II, *Economic Policy*, 64, 659–702.

Schönbucher, P. J. (2002). A tree implementation of a credit spread model for credit, *Journal of Computational Finance*, 6, 175–96.

Taboga, M. (2009). The riskiness of corporate bonds, *Banca d'Italia Temi di Discussione*, no. 730.

Tsomocos, D. (2003). Equilibrium analysis, banking and financial instability, *Journal of Mathematical Economics*, 39, 619–55.

Williamson, S. D. (1987). Financial intermediation, business failures, and business cycles, *Journal of Political Economy*, 95, 1196–1216.

11 The Great Recession, housing wealth and consumption in the European countries

Annalisa Cristini[1]

The question of whether housing wealth plays a role in household consumption decisions has been widely debated, especially after the housing market boom in the 1990s and early 2000s and its bust in the Great Recession.

Since private consumption (excluding dwelling purchase) is normally more than 50 per cent of GDP, this issue is extremely relevant for its economic implications and raises specific concerns for monetary and fiscal policy: should central banks take the evolution of house prices into account when setting their policies? Should housing wealth be supported by favourable taxation and dedicated mortgage policies?

Though the wealth effect in consumption has been studied for a long time, housing is a special type of asset and cannot be wholly assimilated to financial wealth; a house is not only an investment: it provides a service and, in many cases, it is a way of transferring wealth across generations. The latter view, in particular, is typical of some countries and can be traced back to social attitudes and cultural aspects, which are among the determinants of home ownership. Indeed, the fraction of homeowners differs markedly across countries, ranging from 40 per cent in Germany to more than 80 per cent in Spain (Figure 11.1).

Since home ownership provides an imputed rent (the housing service), an increase in the value of dwellings should not give rise to an increase in homeowners' consumption, unless the rise in value can be converted to cash, either directly, such as by trading down the ladder (selling the house and buying another of a smaller value) or indirectly, using the dwelling as collateral in order to obtain consumer credit.

Trading down is not a widespread practice and, to the extent that the extra cash is needed in periods of low economic activity, when the housing market may be rather flat, trading may not be easy and may not give rise to a substantial wealth effect. More interestingly, house equity could be used as credit collateral. Indeed, as financial markets developed in the early 1980s, innovative ways to increase credit to households were introduced by linking cash withdrawals to households' most relevant asset: that is, their dwellings (Muellbauer and Murphy, 1990; Aron et al., 2012; Muellbauer, 2010). These financial innovations, their diffusion, and the extent to which they actually allowed consumer credit to proliferate, are also ultimately explained by social and economic institutions and for this reason they are also heterogeneous across countries.

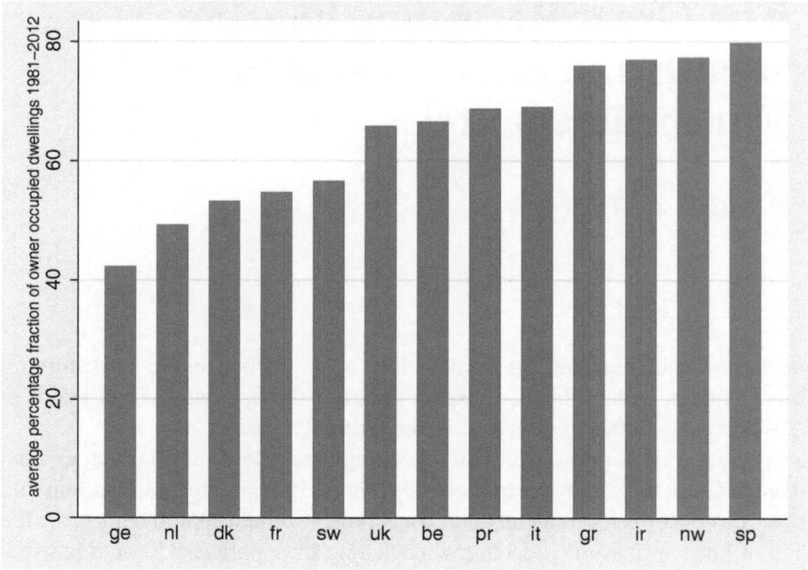

Figure 11.1 Percentage of dwellings occupied by owners. Average 1980–2012.

Source: Author's computations based on HYPOSTAT data

Those countries in which home ownership is traditionally high are not necessarily those in which financial markets have developed most and have allowed homeowners to extract more consumption out of housing. Quite the contrary, where the share of home ownership is traditionally high, housing is viewed as a saving reserve, the main objective of which is to conserve wealth safely across time and transfer it from one generation to the next. On the other hand, it seems that it was exactly where home ownership was not traditionally regarded as a life objective that the housing asset came to be regarded as a vehicle to increase consumption rather than saving, which was possible thanks to a financial system culturally open towards markets.

In the absence of this channel, it is difficult to think of housing wealth as producing a pure wealth effect – a point made by King (1990) and Buiter (2010). In support of this view, Catte et al. (2004) find that the strongest impact on consumption is precisely in those countries where mortgage markets are more 'complete' and provide opportunities for housing equity withdrawal.

To the extent that home ownership may allow consumer credit, it is important to distinguish between homeowners outright and homeowners with mortgages who may actually need to lower their consumption below that of renters. As old homeowners have normally paid the whole mortgage and possess houses larger than those of young homeowners, the extent of the wealth effect is also likely to be related to population demography. Indeed, Campbell and Cocco (2007), using UK microdata, find that the house wealth effect is relevant for old households but not for young ones. Although Cristini and Sevilla (2014) show that this specific result is largely driven by the empirical specification, based on the Euler equation, the role of the population's age composition is also supported by Calomiris, Longhofer and Miles (2012), who find a significant housing wealth effect associated with the population shares of both old homeowners (i.e., people older than 55, for whom a trading-down effect is conjectured) and young homeowners (those aged 20–34, for whom the authors suppose the presence of significant liquidity constraints).

Figure 11.2, based on panels of annual observations on a number of European countries, illustrates the relationship between consumption growth and housing wealth growth: similar to the diagrams presented by Case, Quigley and Shiller (2005), the correlation is positive and stronger than the analogous correlation between consumption growth and the growth of financial wealth.

If one excludes a significant role for both a direct trading-related and an indirect collateral-induced wealth effect, then housing wealth as such should not affect consumption. The co-movement between consumption and housing wealth would then represent only a spurious correlation, the most likely cause of which is the presence of common trends that drive consumption, wealth and income. According to the permanent income hypothesis (PIH), income growth, either expected or unexpected, or both, depending on the type of expectations, could be the kind of common trend that produces the empirical correlation.

It follows that if future income growth were properly controlled for, and housing wealth showed no further impact on consumption decisions, a causal effect of housing wealth on consumption could be excluded and one could conclude that the observed correlation was indeed a spurious one. On the contrary, if wealth and income future prospects were not properly controlled for, current wealth and income will be correlated with the error term and regression estimates would be biased and inconsistent, unless proper instrumental variables (IV) were used.

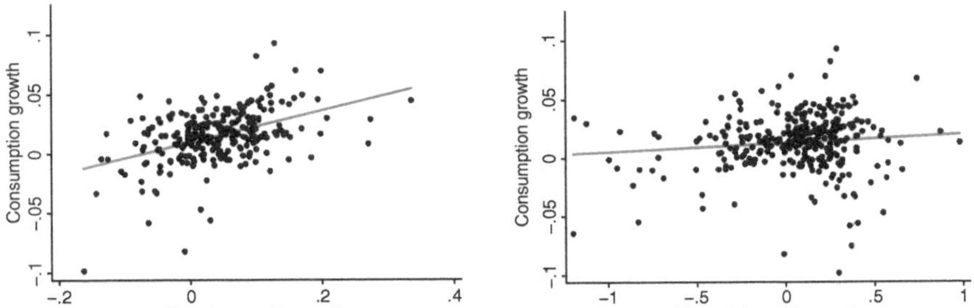

Figure 11.2 Scatter of consumption growth vs. housing wealth growth (left panel) and financial wealth growth (right panel). Country-years, be: 1992–2007; dk: 1991–2012; fr: 1991–2011; ge: 1989–2010; gr: 1995–2010; ir: 1992–2010; it: 1991–2008; nl: 1989–2009; pr: 1992–2011; nw: 1991–2003; sp: 1989–2011; sw: 1991–2012; uk: 1989–2011.

Source: Author's computations based on OECD, World Bank and HYPOSTAT data

From the empirical point of view, the specific aim of testing for a housing wealth effect is entangled with the long-standing debate regarding the estimation of the consumption function itself. There are various possible empirical strategies, ranging from the Euler equation and its random walk hypothesis, to specifications in levels, in first differences and error correction models; in addition, various types of data have been used, from micro household panel data to aggregate time series. Because of these different approaches, it is usually difficult to compare empirical findings, which, with regard to the housing wealth effect, have been all but unanimous. Therefore, the main question set out at the beginning of the chapter is also rather intriguing from the research point of view.

In the following, we exploit the variation of housing wealth across countries and time using time-series panel data on a sample of European countries. Specifically, we construct an index of housing wealth following a procedure similar to the one employed by Case, Quigley and Shiller (2005) and, using the same empirical specifications that they adopt, we estimate a standard consumption function and compare results. In addition, we account for unit roots and endogeneity issues, following the objections put forward by Calomiris, Longhofer and Miles (2009), and present IV estimates. Finally, we suggest the use of Pesaran (2006) common correlation effects (CCE) in order to account for common factors using a flexible approach.

Previous literature using cross-country data

Below we briefly survey the empirical literature on housing wealth effect based on international cross-country data. Our main references are Case, Quigley and Shiller (2005, 2011) and Calomiris, Longhofer and Miles (2009, 2012). Case et al. (2005) compute a housing wealth index for the USA and for fourteen international countries; quarterly data were used for the USA covering the period 1982 Q1 to 1999 Q2, extended from 1978 Q1 to 2009 Q2 in their most recent paper. The data for the international sample could not be updated and the evidence remains based on information up to 1996; in particular, data are annual and available for the following countries: Belgium (1978–96), Canada (1978–93), Denmark (1978–96), Finland (1978–96), France (1982–96), Germany (1991–5), Ireland (1982–7, 1994–5), Netherlands (1978–96), Norway (1980–96), Spain (1975–96), Sweden (1975–96), Switzerland (1991–6), the United Kingdom (1978–96), and the United States (1975–97).

Case et al.'s strategy is to test for the presence of a wealth effect using different empirical specifications; in their original paper they find strong support for a housing wealth effect and little or no evidence of a stock wealth effect: using the international dataset, the elasticity of consumption growth to wealth growth is 0.14, almost five time larger than the same elasticity estimated on the US sample; the relevance of a housing wealth effect is quite robust to various specifications.

These results have been questioned by Calomiris, Longhofer and Miles (2009), who maintain that regressors are likely to be correlated with the residuals and should therefore be instrumented. Indeed, if the LC-PIH holds, residuals comprise innovations in permanent income, but they could also incorporate expected changes in permanent income if the optimisation is not perfect, as well as expected and unexpected changes in transitory income. According to this view, it is possible that house prices, and hence housing wealth, are driven by the same 'common factors' that induce changes in permanent income. Calomiris, Longhofer and Miles (2009) do not consider the panel of international countries and for the panel of US states their results depend on the set of instruments: when lagged wealth, income and consumption are all used as instruments, housing wealth elasticity is as high as 0.167, though smaller in size and significance than the stock wealth elasticity.

A confirmation of the housing wealth effect is found by Catte et al. (2004), who estimate a consumption function separately for a number of international countries. Using OLS and ECM, they find that wealth effects are present in all countries and that the marginal propensity to consume out of housing wealth is in line with or larger than the marginal propensity to consume out of stock wealth.

De Bonis and Silvestrini (2012) use quarterly data from 1997 Q4 to 2008 Q1, for eleven OECD countries: Austria, Belgium, Finland, France, Germany, Italy, Netherlands, Portugal, Spain, the United Kingdom and the United States. They employ a reduced-form consumption function, which includes current income, financial wealth and real wealth. Their main findings indicate that both financial and real wealth are significant, although the former has a considerably larger effect. Their estimated marginal propensities to consume out of wealth are, on an annual basis, 0.4 cents per euro and 3.6 cents per euro, for real and financial wealth, respectively. Their specification does not consider potential endogeneity, although it allows for heterogeneity across countries by using the pooled mean group estimator.

Slacalek (2009) considers a sample of international countries for which he computes a measure of housing wealth in the spirit of Case et al. (2005); following Carroll (2004), he investigates the habit formation of personal consumption, and controlling for this, he estimates the marginal propensities to consume (MPCs) out of financial and housing wealth for single countries and for groups of countries, according to their financial systems. He finds that MPCs are higher in Anglo-Saxon, market-based and non-euro area countries; MPC out of housing wealth is nil in non-Anglo-Saxon countries, in bank-based countries and in the euro area, and relatively lower than the MPC out of financial wealth in the remaining area.

Data

In this chapter, housing wealth is computed in line with the Case et al. approach and is defined as follows:

$$hw_{it} = O_{it} \cdot H_{it} \cdot P_{it}$$

where O_{it} is the occupancy rate of homeowners, defined as the percentage of dwellings occupied by owners and obtained from HYPOSSTA, the European Mortgage Federation. From the same source we obtain the total number of dwellings (H_{it}) and the average house price index 2000 = 100 (P_{it}).

The percentage of owner-occupied dwellings is linearly interpolated, where necessary.[2]

This index of housing wealth is available for Belgium, Denmark, France, Germany, Greece, Ireland, Italy, the Netherlands, Spain Sweden, the UK and Norway;[3] data availability depends on the countries – the longest period is from 1988 to 2012.

We compare this measure with an alternative one available from the OECD household assets dataset, which divides household wealth into financial and non-financial assets and, among the latter, considers 'dwellings'. This measure is available only from 1995 and it is not present for Greece, Ireland, Portugal and Spain. Figure 11.3 compares our preferred measure, based on dwelling ownership rate, with the value of dwellings.

With regard to financial wealth, we compare two alternative measures: market capitalisation, which is the measure used by Case et al. (2005), and household net financial assets. The latter is defined as financial assets (investment fund shares,[4] net equity in life insurance reserves, net equity in pension funds[5]) net of loans; this measure is taken from the OECD household assets dataset; again it is available only from 1995. Market capitalisation is obtained from the World Bank and is defined as the product of market capitalisation, as a percentage of GDP, and GDP in national currency. Figure 11.4 compares the two measures. All wealth variables are in national currency.[6]

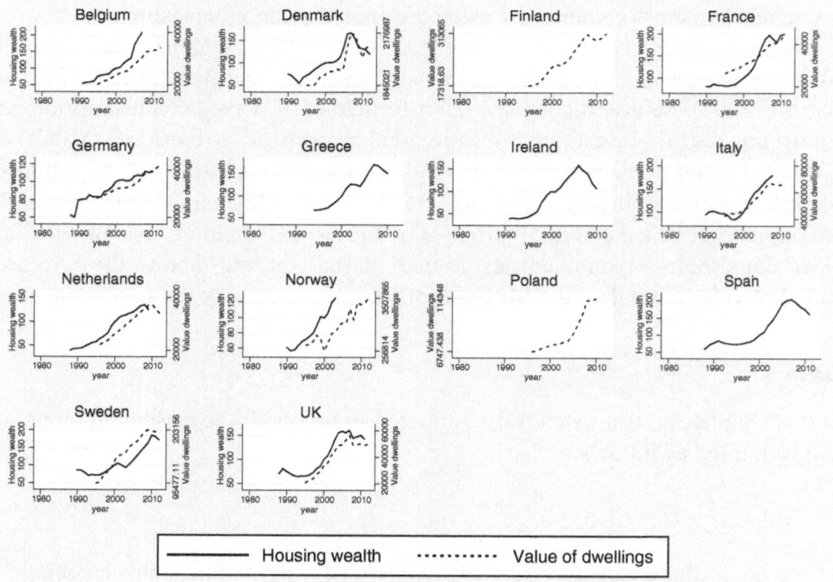

Figure 11.3 Alternative measures of housing wealth

Source: Author's computations based on OECD and HYPOSTAT data

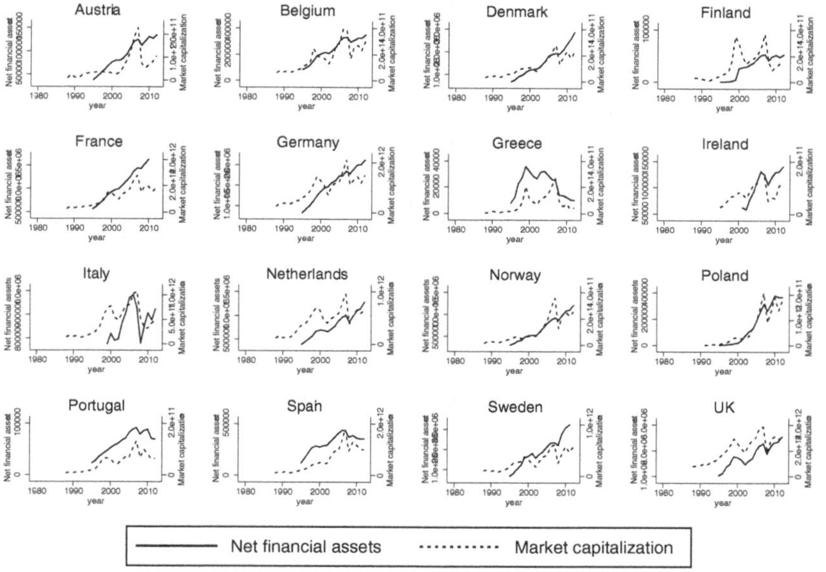

Figure 11.4 Alternative measures of household financial wealth

Source: Author's computations based on OECD and HYPOSTAT data

Income is the gross domestic income, in national currency, available from the OECD.

Consumption is household final consumption expenditure, in national currency, from World Bank data. Unfortunately, aggregate consumption does not distinguish between durable and non-durable consumption. If one assumes that durables depreciate exponentially (Campbell and Mankiw, 1989), then the change in consumption, under PIH, would be a moving average rather than a white noise error, which can be accounted for in the estimation.

Methodology

For the sake of comparison, we follow the empirical specification used by Case et al. (2005) and subsequently adopted by Calomiris, Longhofer and Miles (2009). Case et al. (2005) estimate the following two types of log-linear consumption function:[7]

$$c_{it} = \alpha_1 y_{it} + \alpha_2 fW_{it} + \alpha_3 hW_{it} + d_i + u_{it} \quad (1)$$

$$\Delta c_{it} = \alpha_1 \Delta y_{it} + \alpha_2 \Delta fW_{it} + \alpha_3 \Delta hW_{it} + d_i + u_{it} \quad (2)$$

where subscripts i and t indicate country and year, respectively; d_i are country fixed effects, c is log consumption, y is log disposable income, fW and hW are log financial and log housing wealth respectively; and all variables are measured in per capita real terms.

The difference between (1) and (2) simply rests in using levels versus first differences, which would avoid problems in the presence of integrated variables. In fact, both formulations are rather simple since they do not account for any dynamics; hence they can be regarded as conditional correlations to provide a descriptive view of the overall relationships of interest. In addition, none of the two specifications can be traced to a standard theoretical formulation based on individual optimising behaviour.

1 If one follows the optimisation model, equation (2) could be regarded as a general Euler equation where Δy is included to capture the fraction of individuals that consume on the basis of current income rather than on the basis of their permanent income (Campbell and Mankiw, 1990); according to this specification, the real interest rate should also be present, however, whereas changes in log wealth could be regarded as further elements to test the random walk hypothesis. Following this approach, one would estimate: $\Delta c = f(r, \Delta y, \Delta w)$.
2 The optimising model could also be used to obtain a log-linear consumption function, by combining a log-linear Euler equation and the inter-temporal budget constraint. Since a closed-form solution exists only under restrictive assumptions about the utility function, the resulting consumption function is in fact an approximation. In particular, the inter-temporal budget constraint is linearised using a Taylor expansion and then combined with a log-linear Euler equation. Campbell and Mankiw (1989) show that in this case, log consumption is a function of log wealth and of the real interest rate (unless the inter-temporal elasticity of substitution is unitary); if one accepts the more general Euler equation that accounts for the presence of rule-of-thumb behaving consumers, then Δy will also enter the consumption function via the extended Euler equation. The resulting log-linear consumption would then be a function of the following variables: $c = f(w, r, \Delta y)$.
3 Finally, equation (1) could be regarded as a log transformation of a simple version of the LC-PIH, according to which consumption is a fraction of total wealth, where the latter can be distinguished between human, financial and non-financial wealth; following this specification, however, contemporaneous current income should not be included and residuals should capture only unexpected changes in total wealth and transitory shocks to current income. This specification would determine a consumption function of the following type: $c = f(w)$.

In fact, as suggested by Blinder and Deaton (1985) the use of specific and quite restrictive functional forms obtained from a single optimising individual may not be adequate to represent aggregate consumption functions, particularly as the theoretical restrictions have not been supported by the evidence (Muellbauer, 2010).

Moreover, as long as the objective of the analysis is to go beyond simple correlations and contribute to identifying a potential causal link between housing wealth and consumption, one should account for the potential endogeneity and take care of dynamics.

In time-series panel data, unobserved heterogeneity is common. For example, the choice of how much one should save and/or the type of saving, whether financial or non-financial assets, are partly related to cultural characteristics. To avoid biased and inconsistent estimates, country fixed effects are included in the regression.

More importantly, the error may also comprise unobservable time variant factors which could also violate the condition $E(X_{it}, u_{it}) = 0$, where X_{it} is the vector of r.h.s. variables. Specifically, according to the standard optimising theory of consumption, residuals will contain innovations in permanent income which could be correlated with all contemporaneous regressors included in the equation; in particular, both financial wealth and housing wealth could respond to future (unexpected) prospects that may also drive permanent income; even more so, changes in current income are likely to be correlated with innovation in permanent income. The solution first used by Campbell and recalled by Calomiris, Longhofer and Miles (2009) in their replication of Case et al.'s results is to use instrumental variables. As the latter should be correlated with the endogenous variables but not with the error term, lagged endogenous variables are normally used. In order to prevent correlations in the presence of aggregation and measurement errors, the standard practise suggested by Campbell and Mankiw is to use instruments dated from $t-2$ backwards; this would also take care of MA errors induced, for example, by the presence of durable expenditures in consumption.

Econometric results

Before estimating the model, we test for panel unit roots using the Maddala–Wu (1999) MW test and the Pesaran (2007) CIPS test. The MW test assumes cross-section independence, while the CIPS test assumes cross-section dependence in the form of a single unobserved common factor. In both cases, the tests are provided for specifications with and without trend and using 0–2 lags. Results, reported in the appendix to this chapter, indicate that, except for the case of log real housing wealth with one lag, for which the null of I(1) is rejected according to CIPS and WU with trend, in all other cases and for all other variables the null of unit root could not be rejected.

Results obtained using variables in first differences would then be more reliable because they would be based on stationary time series.[8] Nonetheless, for the sake of comparison, we also run estimation in levels.

Table 11.1 reports results obtained by estimating various specifications of equations (1) and (2), depending on the inclusion of fixed effects and specific time trends; wealth is measured using stock market wealth and housing wealth, as defined by Case et al. (2005). The time-series panel is made up of twelve European countries and the time span is from 1986 to 2012. Tables 11.1(a)–(c) report results obtained using alternative measures of wealth: in Table 11.1(a) financial wealth is from the OECD household wealth dataset; in Table 11.1(b) housing wealth is replaced by the value of dwellings, also from the OECD household dataset;

in Table 11.1(c) both financial and non-financial wealth are measured using the OECD definitions. Notice that in the alternative cases the sample of countries excludes Greece, Ireland and Spain and the time span is from 1996.

Results reported in Table 11.1 confirm the findings of Case et al. (2005): the elasticity of consumption to housing wealth is positive and significant in most cases. In the specification in first differences, and controlling for country and year fixed effects, the estimated elasticity is 0.038; in contrast, stock market wealth is hardly significant and its coefficient is negative when it is – a result also found by Case et al (2011). The income elasticity is around 0.6.

Since stock market capitalisation is only an approximation of household financial wealth, Table 11.1(a) reports the estimated coefficients of interest when stock market wealth is replaced by households' financial wealth. Results are not very different: housing wealth remains significant and the coefficient is slightly larger in size. Financial wealth is still either negative or not statistically significant.

Table 11.1(b) replaces the measure of housing wealth with the value of dwellings owned by the household. The estimated elasticity of consumption to the value of dwellings is 0.16 (an order of magnitude similar to that found by Case et al. (2005) on the international sample) when using first differences and fixed effects. Stock market wealth is not significant but the coefficient is now positive.

Finally, Table 11.1(c) uses financial and non-financial wealth measures taken from the OECD household dataset. In this case financial wealth is also significant and positive: the elasticity of consumption to financial wealth is in the range of 0.06 while the elasticity to non-financial wealth (dwellings) is in the range of 0.28.[9]

These first batteries of estimates suggest that the type of measures used to capture households' wealth make a substantial difference, in terms of magnitudes of the housing wealth elasticity of consumption, and even in terms of statistical significance for financial wealth. Specifically, the stock market development does not seem to be an adequate approximation of the composition of European households' financial wealth.

Before turning to the issues of endogeneity, we look in more detail at the Great Recession period to inquire whether it has strengthened or weakened the links between wealth and consumption.

The Great Recession and the wealth effect

All the channels through which housing wealth may affect consumption are likely to have been upset by the events of the Great Recession. Where the housing bubble had grown most, like in Spain, Ireland and Greece, the dramatic drop in house prices that followed, illustrated in Figure 11.5, is expected to have cut, first of all, the value of collateral for credit consumption. The bursting of the housing bubble also swept across financial assets, reducing financial wealth as well (Figure 11.5).

The turmoil in the housing market hindered transactions and the difficulties encountered in selling a house may have prevented both the possibility of trading down and sustaining consumption through a direct wealth effect, as well as the option, for the unemployed, of moving in search of a new job (Farber, 2012).

Table 11.1 OLS estimates – baseline model. Dependent variable: household consumption

	Levels					*First differences*				
	(1)	*(2)*	*(3)*	*(4)*	*(5)*	*(6)*	*(7)*	*(8)*	*(9)*	*(10)*
Income	0.950***	0.930***	0.851***	0.803***	0.867***	0.691***	0.677***	0.624***	0.660***	0.672***
	(0.01)	(0.03)	(0.05)	(0.05)	(0.07)	(0.04)	(0.04)	(0.07)	(0.05)	(0.07)
Stock market	–0.021**	–0.004	–0.021***	0.004	–0.019***	0.003	0.003	0.003	0.001	0.004
wealth	(0.01)	(0.00)	(0.01)	(0.00)	(0.01)	(0.00)	(0.00)	(0.01)	(0.00)	(0.01)
Housing	0.051***	–0.011	–0.006	0.001	0.038***	0.020	0.025*	0.038**	0.029**	0.036**
wealth	(0.01)	(0.01)	(0.01)	(0.01)	(0.01)	(0.01)	(0.01)	(0.02)	(0.01)	(0.02)
Country fixed effects	No	Yes	Yes	Yes	Yes	No	Yes	Yes	Yes	Yes
Year dummies	No	No	Yes	No	Yes	No	No	Yes	No	Yes
Country time trends	No	No	No	Yes	Yes	No	No	No	Yes	Yes
R^2	0.99	1.00	1.00	1.00	1.00	0.63	0.65	0.69	0.68	0.71
RMSE	0.08	0.02	0.02	0.02	0.02	0.01	0.01	0.01	0.01	0.01
N	217	217	217	217	217	217	217	217	217	217

Countries: be, dk, fr, ge, gr, ir, it,nl, nw, sp, sw, uk; time span: 1986–2012 except for a few countries.
Source: Author's computations based on OECD, World Bank and HYPOSTAT data

Table 11.1(a) OLS estimates – financial wealth. Dependent variable: household consumption

	Levels					*First differences*				
	(1)	*(2)*	*(3)*	*(4)*	*(5)*	*(6)*	*(7)*	*(8)*	*(9)*	*(10)*
Income	0.977***	0.825***	0.863***	0.686***	0.693***	0.630***	0.614***	0.508***	0.607***	0.617***
	(0.01)	(0.05)	(0.07)	(0.06)	(0.10)	(0.05)	(0.06)	(0.09)	(0.06)	(0.10)
Financial	–0.051***	–0.015*	–0.018*	–0.001	–0.043**	–0.003	–0.004	–0.025	–0.012	–0.036*
wealth	(0.01)	(0.01)	(0.01)	(0.01)	(0.02)	(0.01)	(0.01)	(0.02)	(0.01)	(0.02)
Housing	0.014	0.014	0.016	0.042**	0.058***	0.031	0.035*	0.046**	0.033*	0.046**
wealth	(0.02)	(0.01)	(0.02)	(0.02)	(0.02)	(0.02)	(0.02)	(0.02)	(0.02)	(0.02)
Country fixed effects	No	Yes	Yes	Yes	Yes	No	Yes	Yes	Yes	Yes
Year dummies	No	No	Yes	No	Yes	No	No	Yes	No	Yes
Country time trends	No	No	No	Yes	Yes	No	No	No	Yes	Yes
R^2	0.99	1.00	1.00	1.00	1.00	0.58	0.61	0.66	0.69	0.73
RMSE	0.08	0.02	0.02	0.02	0.02	0.01	0.01	0.01	0.01	0.01
N	154	154	154	154	154	154	154	154	154	154

Countries: be, dk, fr, ge, it, nl, nw, sw, uk; time span: 1996–2012 except for a few countries.
Source: Author's computations based on OECD, World Bank and HYPOSTAT data

Table 11.1(b) OLS estimates – wealth from dwellings. Dependent variable: household consumption

	Levels					*First differences*				
	(1)	*(2)*	*(3)*	*(4)*	*(5)*	*(6)*	*(7)*	*(8)*	*(9)*	*(10)*
Income	0.812***	0.469***	0.513***	0.567***	0.500***	0.566***	0.579***	0.589***	0.515***	0.488***
	(0.02)	(0.08)	(0.10)	(0.06)	(0.11)	(0.06)	(0.06)	(0.12)	(0.06)	(0.13)
Stock market	0.022*	0.010	0.012	0.008	0.004	0.004	0.004	0.006	0.003	0.007
wealth	(0.01)	(0.01)	(0.01)	(0.01)	(0.01)	(0.00)	(0.00)	(0.01)	(0.00)	(0.01)
Wealth from	0.128***	0.132***	0.183***	0.112***	0.139***	0.151***	0.132***	0.162***	0.109**	0.167***
dwellings	(0.02)	(0.03)	(0.04)	(0.03)	(0.03)	(0.04)	(0.04)	(0.05)	(0.05)	(0.05)
Country fixed effects	No	Yes	Yes	Yes	Yes	No	Yes	Yes	Yes	Yes
Year dummies	No	No	Yes	No	Yes	No	No	Yes	No	Yes
Country time trends	No	No	No	Yes	Yes	No	No	No	Yes	Yes
R^2	1.00	1.00	1.00	1.00	1.00	0.55	0.57	0.64	0.63	0.67
RMSE	0.07	0.02	0.02	0.01	0.01	0.01	0.01	0.01	0.01	0.01
N	143	143	143	143	143	143	143	143	143	143

Countries: be, dk, fr, ge, it, nl, nw, sw, uk; time span: 1996–2012 except for a few countries.
Source: Author's computations based on OECD, World Bank and HYPOSTAT data

Table 11.1(c) OLS estimates – OECD wealth measures. Dependent variable: household consumption

	Levels					*First differences*				
	(1)	*(2)*	*(3)*	*(4)*	*(5)*	*(6)*	*(7)*	*(8)*	*(9)*	*(10)*
Income	0.846***	0.352***	0.314***	0.445***	0.456***	0.475***	0.473***	0.654***	0.446***	0.658***
	(0.02)	(0.09)	(0.11)	(0.06)	(0.11)	(0.06)	(0.06)	(0.13)	(0.07)	(0.14)
Financial	–0.004	0.044**	0.115***	0.041**	0.009	0.050***	0.048***	0.057*	0.048***	0.073**
wealth	(0.01)	(0.02)	(0.03)	(0.02)	(0.02)	(0.02)	(0.02)	(0.03)	(0.02)	(0.03)
Wealth from	0.112***	0.133***	0.251***	0.159***	0.169***	0.241***	0.244***	0.276***	0.254***	0.305***
dwellings	(0.02)	(0.03)	(0.03)	(0.03)	(0.03)	(0.04)	(0.05)	(0.05)	(0.05)	(0.06)
Country fixed effects	No	Yes	Yes	Yes	Yes	No	Yes	Yes	Yes	Yes
Year dummies	No	No	Yes	No	Yes	No	No	Yes	No	Yes
Country time trends	No	No	No	Yes	Yes	No	No	No	Yes	Yes
R^2	1.00	1.00	1.00	1.00	1.00	0.55	0.56	0.63	0.59	0.66
RMSE	0.07	0.03	0.02	0.01	0.01	0.01	0.01	0.01	0.01	0.01
N	139	139	139	139	139	139	139	139	139	139

Countries: be, dk, fr, ge, it, nl, nw, sw, uk; time span: 1996–2012 except for a few countries.
Source: Author's computations based on OECD, World Bank and HYPOSTAT data

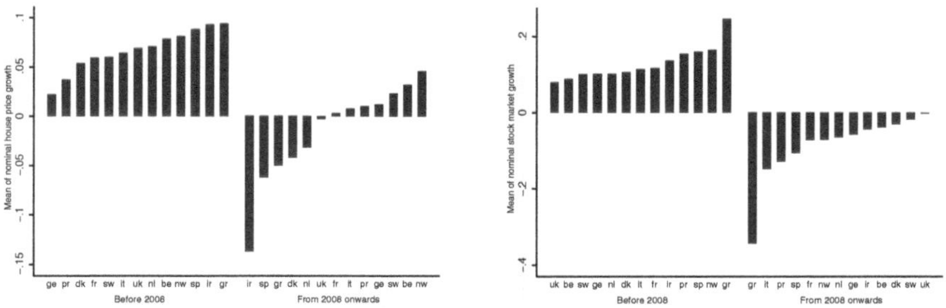

Figure 11.5 Mean of house price growth (left panel) and stock market capitalisation growth (right panel): pre- and post-2008

Source: Author's computations based on OECD, World Bank and HYPOSTAT data

Figure 11.6 illustrates how the scatter graphs of consumption growth and wealth growth change prior to and after the outbreak of the Great Recession in 2008.

From 2008 onwards the correlation between consumption growth and housing wealth strengthens whereas the correlation between consumption growth and stock market wealth growth is similar before and after the Great Recession and the fitted lines remain flat or slightly decreasing in both periods.

The impression conveyed by these figures, according to which the Great Recession is associated with an intensification of the link between housing wealth and consumption, is confirmed by multivariate analysis (Table 11.2). In Table 11.2 we report the results obtained by running the same specifications as Table 11.1 but excluding the years of the Great Recession, from 2008 onwards. Indeed, the elasticity of consumption to housing wealth declines in value and statistical significance (columns 1–5), while the elasticity to stock market wealth remains close to zero. By using the alternative measures of wealth (columns 6–10), the elasticity of consumption to the value of dwellings also declines by 5 percentage points on average, while remaining

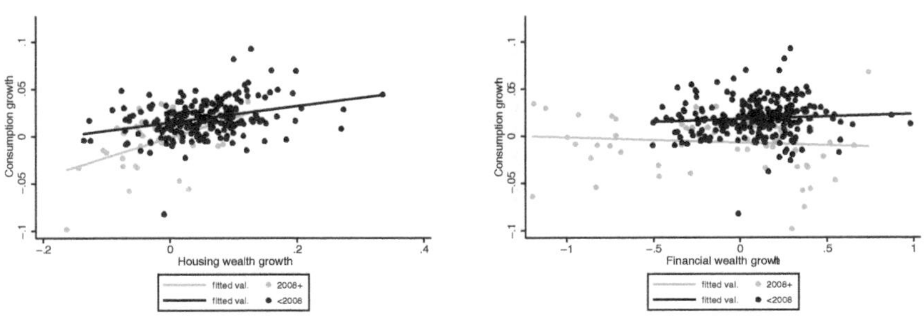

Figure 11.6 Consumption growth vs. housing wealth growth (left panel) and financial wealth growth (right panel): pre- and post- the Great Recession

Source: Author's computations based on OECD, World Bank and HYPOSTAT data

Table 11.2 OLS on first differences excluding the Great Recession (years from 2008 onwards)

	First differences									
	(1)	*(2)*	*(3)*	*(4)*	*(5)*	*(6)*	*(7)*	*(8)*	*(9)*	*(10)*
Income	0.732***	0.693***	0.643***	0.706***	0.689***	0.525***	0.531***	0.583***	0.443***	0.537***
	(0.06)	(0.07)	(0.08)	(0.07)	(0.09)	(0.13)	(0.12)	(0.18)	(0.13)	(0.20)
Stock market	–0.000	0.000	0.002	–0.001	0.001					
wealth	(0.00)	(0.00)	(0.01)	(0.00)	(0.01)					
Housing	0.012	0.017	0.028*	0.026	0.023					
wealth	(0.01)	(0.01)	(0.02)	(0.02)	(0.02)					
Financial						0.030	0.032	0.026	0.013	0.056
wealth						(0.02)	(0.02)	(0.04)	(0.02)	(0.04)
Wealth from						0.206***	0.190***	0.222***	0.225***	0.205***
dwellings						(0.07)	(0.05)	(0.07)	(0.07)	(0.07)
country fixed effects	No	Yes	Yes	Yes	Yes	Yes	No	Yes	Yes	Yes
year dummies	No	No	Yes	No	Yes	No	No	Yes	No	Yes
country time trends	No	No	No	Yes	Yes	No	No	No	Yes	Yes
R^2	0.49	0.52	0.58	0.59	0.63	0.41	0.39	0.50	0.53	0.57
RMSE	0.01	0.01	0.01	0.01	0.01	0.01	0.01	0.01	0.01	0.01
N	187	187	187	187	187	100	100	100	100	100

Source: Author's computations based on OECD, World Bank and HYPOSTAT data

highly statistically significant; in contrast, the elasticity to financial assets declines to a value that is not statistically different from zero.

Though we find confirmation that the Great Recession has sharpened the role of wealth, it remains an open question which channel has induced this increase in responsiveness. Farber (2012), investigating US data, rejects the idea of reduced labour market mobility; since geographical mobility in Europe is even lower, this could be true a fortiori for Europe. Whether the credit channel has played a relevant role remains an open and interesting question.

Endogeneity and instrument reliability

As anticipated, a relevant issue in this literature is the potential endogeneity of wealth and income. Table 11.3 reports IV estimates of the first difference specification using the original measures (as in Table 11.1) and the alternative wealth measures used in Table 11.1(c). Following Calomiris, Longhofer and Miles (2009), instruments are the second and third lags of the three endogenous variables and the dependent variable.

Results indicate a loss of significance across the board, essentially due to a rise in the standard errors. Moreover, income is not generally significant where wealth is, except in regression (9) where results are similar to OLS, showing that consumption elasticity to dwellings is 0.37 and consumption elasticity to income is 0.44. Regression (10) is also rather interesting: the estimated elasticities of consumption to financial and real wealth are similar in value, ranging around 0.3, although the statistical significance is stronger for financial wealth (dwelling is significant at 11.2 per cent); income, however, seems to play no role, which casts doubt on the whole regression.

It is well known that one of the main problems in applied econometrics, and in time series in particular, is to find good instruments. Table 11.4 shows the results of a battery of tests on the instruments used in the IV regressions presented in Table 11.3. The reported diagnostics test the two main properties of a good instrument: exogeneity with respect to the residuals, and correlation with the endogenous variable. In particular, we report the Sargan test for the validity of instruments, which tests the exogeneity of instruments using the over-identifying restrictions, the Shea partial R^2 and the minimum eigenvalue statistic, testing for instrument weakness: that is, for the strength of the correlation between the excluded instruments and the endogenous variables.

While the Sargan test rejects the null of valid instruments only in regressions (2) and (9), the minimum eigenvalue statistics are below any acceptable critical value, suggesting that instruments are so weak as to induce a bias at least 30 per cent as large as that of OLS estimates. Shea partial R^2 are also rather low. On the whole, none of the IV regressions seems sufficiently robust to outperform OLS estimates.

For the time being we can conclude that our data support a strong correlation between consumption and housing wealth, the elasticity of which ranges from 0.04, if wealth is measured using an index similar to Case et al. (2005), to 0.30, if one uses the value of dwellings. The elasticity to stock market wealth is variable: it can be nil or even negative, and it is positive up to a maximum of 0.07 if measured using net household financial assets.

Table 11.3 IV estimates

	First differences									
	(1)	*(2)*	*(3)*	*(4)*	*(5)*	*(6)*	*(7)*	*(8)*	*(9)*	*(10)*
Income	0.555***	0.573***	0.913	0.168	−0.586	0.085	−0.188	0.367	0.445***	0.125
	(0.21)	(0.18)	(0.77)	(0.23)	(0.94)	(0.31)	(0.42)	(0.62)	(0.15)	(0.43)
Stock market	0.024	0.012	0.098	0.013	0.033					
wealth	(0.01)	(0.01)	(0.08)	(0.01)	(0.04)					
Housing	0.087	0.026	0.126	0.024	0.266*					
wealth	(0.07)	(0.05)	(0.22)	(0.08)	(0.15)					
Financial						−0.057	−0.052	0.336**	0.030	0.316**
wealth						(0.11)	(0.12)	(0.13)	(0.04)	(0.13)
Wealth from						0.100	−0.023	0.172	0.368*	0.304
dwellings						(0.14)	(0.20)	(0.25)	(0.22)	(0.19)
Country fixed effects	No	Yes	Yes	Yes	Yes	No	Yes	Yes	Yes	Yes
Year dummies	No	No	Yes	No	Yes	No	No	Yes	No	Yes
Country time trends	No	No	No	Yes	Yes	No	No	No	Yes	Yes
R^2	0.51	0.62	0.14	0.48	0.17	0.10	.	0.38	0.58	0.44
RMSE	0.01	0.01	0.02	0.01	0.02	0.02	0.02	0.02	0.01	0.02
N	186	186	186	186	186	113	113	113	113	113

Notes: Instruments are the second and third lag of the wealth, income and consumption (in first differences) plus trends and dummies present in the regression. In each regression, excluded instruments are therefore 8 and endogenous variables are 3.

Source: Author's computations based on OECD, World Bank and HYPOSTAT data

Table 11.4 Instruments validity and instrument weakness tests

	(1)	*(2)*	*(3)*	*(4)*	*(5)*	*(6)*	*(7)*	*(8)*	*(9)*	*(10)*
Sargan test of over-identifying restrictions (validity of instruments)										
	8.04	12.16*	4.77	7.37	6.94	1.06	1.06	4.65	15.06*	6.72
	(0.15)	(0.03)	(0.44)	(0.19)	(0.22)	(0.96)	(0.96)	(0.50)	(0.01)	(0.24)
Shea Partial R^2										
Income	0.06	0.07	0.02	0.08	0.02	0.08	0.07	0.07	0.19	0.17
Stock wealth	0.06	0.08	0.01	0.07	0.05					
Housing wealth	0.05	0.08	0.01	0.06	0.04					
Financial wealth						0.05	0.06	0.08	0.16	0.11
Wealth from dwellings						0.20	0.15	0.07	0.06	0.16
Minimum eigenvalue statistics										
	0.73	0.05	0.14	0.63	0.30	0.63	0.55	0.53	0.62	0.89

Notes: Each column corresponds to the regression reported in the same column of Table 11.2.
Sargan (Ho: instruments are valid); in parenthesis the p-value. Shea partial R^2 statistic measures the correlation between each endogenous variable and the excluded instruments after partialling out the effect of the included exogenous variable. A small R^2 indicates that the instruments may be correlated more with the exogenous than with endogenous variables. Minimum eigenvalue statistics (Ho: instruments are weak): the critical values for the 2SLS relative bias are the following: 5% (15.18) 10% (9.01) 20% (5.69) 30% (4.46). A value lower than the critical one indicates the bias in 2SLS relative to the bias in OLS estimates.

Source: Author's computations based on OECD, World Bank and HYPOSTAT data

Common trends

The main reason for regressors to be correlated with the residuals, thereby violating the condition for OLS estimates to be unbiased and consistent, is the role of expected and unexpected income growth, which is likely to be correlated with current wealth and income. Though future growth is unobservable, it is reasonable to think that economic integration implies that the expected scenarios would be more and more correlated across countries, especially within Europe. This would imply that future expectations could be captured by common trends, both local and global.

Following this line of reasoning, we estimate a pooled common correlated effect model (CCE) due to Pesaran (2006), where the common trends are captured by the cross-section averages of the dependent and independent variables, which are included as additional regressors, allowing their loadings to differ across countries (Eberhardt, Helmers and Strauss, 2013). This formulation allows sufficient flexibility regarding the nature and type of the (unknown) trends that the cross-section averages are capturing.

Results, reported in Table 11.5, confirm that stock market wealth is not significant for private consumption while housing wealth is, with an elasticity of 0.04 that is

Table 11.5 Common correlation effects

	Original measures		*Household assets measures*	
	Levels	*First differences*	*Levels*	*First differences*
Income	0.848***	0.617***	0.661***	0.562***
	(0.07)	(0.08)	(0.08)	(0.10)
Stock wealth	−0.010	0.000		
	(0.01)	(0.01)		
Housing wealth	0.039**	0.042**		
	(0.02)	(0.02)		
Financial wealth			0.008	0.038*
			(0.01)	(0.02)
Wealth from dwellings			0.078***	0.142***
			(0.02)	(0.04)
Country fixed effects	Yes	Yes	Yes	Yes
Trend	Yes	Yes	Yes	Yes
Common trends	Yes	Yes	Yes	Yes
R^2	1.00	0.88	1.00	0.87
RMSE	0.01	0.01	0.01	0.01
N	217	217	139	139

Common trends are the average trend across countries

Source: Author's computations based on OECD, World Bank and HYPOSTAT data

obtained using the specification both in levels and in first differences. Financial wealth, measured in terms of households' net financial assets, is significant for consumption with an elasticity of 0.04, while dwellings, measured as a part of households' non-financial assets, show an elasticity of 0.14, significant at 5 per cent.[10]

Discussion and conclusion

As the housing market underwent historically large booms and busts, the role of housing wealth in private consumption attracted increasing attention and prompted an interesting debate, especially as empirical findings turned out to be rather controversial.

In this chapter we computed a novel index of housing wealth for a number of European countries and, following the analysis of Case et al. (2005), investigated its relationship with consumption, given income and financial wealth. In addition, to account for integration issues, we compared OLS and IV estimates and presented tests of instrument exogeneity and weakness.

Our results can be summarised as follows: in log-linear consumption functions, independently of whether the specification is in levels or first differences, the estimated elasticity of consumption to real housing wealth is positive and statistically significant. The point estimates vary between 0.03, when the housing wealth index and stock market wealth are used, to 0.28 if housing wealth is measured by the value of dwellings and stock market wealth is replaced by the net value of financial assets. These alternative wealth measures, however, are available for a shorter period of time and fewer countries; when the same sample is used on the original measures, the consumption elasticity of housing wealth increases by only a few percentage points and remains on average around 0.05 (not shown).

On the whole, private consumption appears to be less responsive to financial wealth: when the latter is approximated by stock market capitalisation, the estimated elasticity is virtually nil, whereas it is positive but relatively small if financial wealth is defined in terms of households' net financial assets.

The robustness of OLS estimates was tested using the standard set of instrumental variables adopted in this literature: that is, lagged values of endogenous and dependent variables. Though results are in line with those of Calomiris, Longhofer and Miles (2009) and cast doubt on the causality between housing wealth and consumption, we also find a severe problem of weak instruments, which is likely to introduce a large bias in the 2SLS estimates. As a way out, we estimated a common correlation effect model, which controls for possible common trends in a rather flexible way. To the extent that common trends control for expected and unexpected income growth, this approach can provide consistent estimates; we show that these mostly confirm OLS results.

Finally, the intuition that the house price bust and the loss of real and financial wealth that have characterised the Great Recession could have reinforced the link between wealth and consumption is supported by the data: the consumption elasticity to both housing and financial wealth have increased during the Great

Recession. The extent to which this can be attributed to the drop in collateral housing equity, to the banking sector's reaction to uncertainty in their own balance sheets, or to future scenarios of declining growth, are questions that remain to be answered.

Future research should aim, first of all, to enrich the specifications estimated in this chapter with adequate dynamics: for example, by formulating an error correction model, in order to capture the adjustments of consumption to wealth. Secondly, the flexibility allowed by country-specific common trends may be insufficient to capture institutional differences across European countries; mean group estimators might then be a useful strategy to undertake.

Appendix

Table 11.6 Unit root tests

		MW: Maddala and Wu (1999)				*CIPS: Pesaran (2007)*			
		Specification without trend		*Specification with trend*		*Specification without trend*		*Specification with trend*	
Variable	*Lags*	*Chi Square*	*p-value*	*Chi Square*	*p-value*	*Zt-bar*	*p-value*	*Zt-bar*	*p-value*
lRc	0	25.379	0.385	4.866	1	1.779	0.962	4.862	1
lRc	1	17.503	0.826	10.792	0.99	2.222	0.987	3.222	0.999
lRc	2	18.666	0.77	9.15	0.997	1.699	0.955	4.54	1
lRi	0	39.331	0.025	7.502	0.999	1.927	0.973	6.659	1
lRi	1	25.567	0.375	12.268	0.977	2.473	0.993	3.894	1
lRi	2	26.655	0.321	9.076	0.997	2.047	0.98	6.285	1
lRhW	0	11.692	0.983	25.156	0.397	1.06	0.855	1.018	0.846
lRhW	1	22.657	0.54	68.997	0	−2.753	0.003	−2.674	0.004
lRhW	2	12.155	0.978	30.358	0.173	0.033	0.513	0.049	0.52
lRfW	0	17.782	0.813	13.566	0.956	−0.396	0.346	1.803	0.964
lRfW	1	14.556	0.933	10.137	0.994	−1.033	0.151	0.663	0.746
lRfW	2	16.548	0.867	6.384	1	1.759	0.961	5.489	1

Notes: Null for MW and CIPS tests: series is I(1). The MW test assumes cross-section independence. The CIPS test assumes cross-section dependence is in form of a single unobserved common factor. Group variable: country; number of groups: 13; total number of observations: 265; average number of observations: 20.90. The panel is unbalanced and has gaps.

Source: Author's computations based on OECD, World Bank and HYPOSTAT data

Table 11.7 Summary statistics

	Mean						*Standard deviation*					
	lRc	*lRi*	*lRhW*	*lRdw*	*lRfW*	*lRfA*	*lRc*	*lRi*	*lRhW*	*lRdw*	*lRfW*	*lRfA*
Country												
au						9.201						0.303
be	9.393	10.003	−1.218	10.188	9.419	9.885	0.124	0.163	0.415	0.179	0.454	0.334
dk	11.597	12.284	−1.422	12.196	11.603	12.425	0.113	0.151	0.316	0.055	0.484	0.279
fn				10.095						0.209		
fr	9.423	9.979	−1.171	10.422	9.435	9.661	0.125	0.135	0.369	0.171	0.582	0.222
ge	9.498	10.036	−1.714	10.434	9.058	9.760	0.142	0.157	0.171	0.124	0.493	0.244
gr	9.041	9.386	−0.805		8.128	7.407	0.179	0.168	0.332		0.987	0.542
ir	9.262	9.894	−1.439		9.549	9.919	0.306	0.422	0.520		0.422	0.205
it	9.312	9.842	−0.987	10.895	8.558	9.470	0.141	0.134	0.256	0.176	0.634	0.100
lu				10.226		8.818				0.024		0.867
nl	9.334	10.041	−1.786	10.309	9.916	10.683	0.160	0.189	0.440	0.175	0.503	0.191
nw	11.803	12.568	−1.316	12.609	11.634	11.749	0.157	0.204	0.271	0.100	0.622	0.153
po				9.024		7.335				0.192		1.609
pr	8.822	9.244	−1.089		8.024	8.568	0.201	0.220	0.135		0.676	0.262
sp	9.001	9.512	−0.793		8.966	8.746	0.175	0.208	0.422		0.713	0.195
sw	11.663	12.365	−1.179	11.946	12.222	12.115	0.155	0.181	0.320	0.257	0.557	0.351
uk	9.131	9.594	−1.223	10.566	9.872	10.196	0.254	0.222	0.365	0.334	0.344	0.135

(continued)

Table 11.7 (continued)

	Mean						*Standard deviation*					
	dlRc	*dlRi*	*dlRhW*	*dlRdw*	*dlRfW*	*dlRfA*	*dlRc*	*dlRi*	*dlRhW*	*dlRdw*	*dlRfW*	*dlRfA*
Country												
au						0.058						0.076
be	0.012	0.015	0.083	0.031	0.035	0.060	0.014	0.016	0.068	0.017	0.320	0.100
dk	0.011	0.014	0.021	0.007	0.052	0.058	0.023	0.022	0.099	0.024	0.295	0.053
fn				0.035						0.034		
fr	0.012	0.012	0.043	0.034	0.055	0.049	0.011	0.015	0.058	0.018	0.274	0.042
ge	0.015	0.017	0.026	0.024	0.051	0.047	0.013	0.019	0.061	0.014	0.281	0.040
gr	0.011	0.008	0.050		0.056	−0.021	0.031	0.032	0.067		0.510	0.255
ir	0.022	0.033	0.052		0.048	0.047	0.040	0.040	0.112		0.377	0.125
it	0.012	0.011	0.036	0.027	0.025	−0.011	0.019	0.020	0.061	0.027	0.302	0.078
lu				0.000		0.124				0.029		0.336
nl	0.012	0.016	0.055	0.027	0.041	0.043	0.018	0.018	0.051	0.030	0.317	0.083
nw	0.014	0.019	0.056	0.016	0.070	0.028	0.042	0.020	0.056	0.045	0.377	0.083
po				0.038		0.260				0.039		0.247
pr	0.016	0.018	0.016		0.052	0.038	0.028	0.027	0.035		0.312	0.104
sp	0.014	0.017	0.043		0.061	0.027	0.022	0.021	0.080		0.279	0.119
sw	0.016	0.018	0.032	0.043	0.046	0.078	0.018	0.024	0.073	0.041	0.345	0.112
uk	0.024	0.020	0.031	0.052	0.029	0.025	0.023	0.022	0.076	0.070	0.229	0.104

Source: Author's computations based on OECD, World Bank and HYPOSTAT data

Notes

1 I would like to thank John Muellbauer for a very fruitful discussion and suggestions on an earlier draft of this chapter. Any errors remain my own responsibility.
2 For some countries the share of homeowners is relative to the population. This is also the measure used by Case et al. and more recently by Slacalek (2009), obtained from BIS. For the majority of countries, HYPOSTAT provides information on the percentage of dwellings occupied by owners; for this reason, we use this measure and exclude countries based on the alternative concept of home ownership.
3 We exclude Iceland and Slovenia because too few data are available and Hungary for consistency with the rest of the countries.
4 Not available for Ireland.
5 Not available for the UK.
6 For countries that adopted the euro, all nominal values are in euros; for years prior to the adoption of the single currency, national currencies are translated into euros using the irrevocably fixed 1999 exchange rates.
7 Case et al. also estimate an ECM specification where the long-run consumption is a function of income only.
8 One could also test for a co-integrating vector and eventually use an ECM specification. We do not pursue this exercise in this chapter as we do not estimate error correction models.
9 The different results, and in particular the positive and significant coefficient on financial wealth, are in fact due to the measures used and not the different sample: the initial results are confirmed when using the smaller sample on the original measures.
10 Results are slightly different if the common trend based on the dependent variable is excluded. In this case wealth remains significant only if measured using financial assets, as far as financial wealth is concerned, and dwelling value, as far as housing wealth is concerned. The elasticity of consumption to housing wealth is 0.28 (in the specification in levels) and 0.20 (in the specification in first differences) with respect to an elasticity to financial assets that is 0.04 (specification in levels) and 0.05 (specification in first differences).

References

Aron, J., J. Duca, K. Muellbauer, K. Murata and A. Murphy (2012). Credit, housing collateral and consumption in the UK, US, and Japan, *Review of Income and Wealth*, 58, 397–423.

Attanasio, O. P., L. Blow, R. Hamilton and A. Leicester (2009). Booms and busts: consumption, house prices and expectations, *Economica*, 76, 20–50.

Blinder, A. and Deaton, A. (1985). The time series consumption function revisited, *Brookings Papers on Economic Activity*, 2, 465–521.

Buiter, W. H. (2010). Housing wealth isn't wealth, *Economics: The Open-Access, Open-Assessment E-Journal*, 4.

Calomiris, C., S. Longhofer and W. Miles (2009). The (mythical?) housing wealth effect?, *NBER Working Papers*, no. 1575.

Calomiris, C. W., S. D. Longhofer and W. Miles (2013). The housing wealth effect: the crucial roles of demographics, wealth distribution and wealth shares, *Critical Finance Review*, 2, 49–99.

Campbell, J. Y. and J. F. Cocco (2007). How do house prices affect consumption? Evidence from micro data, *Journal of Monetary Economics*, 54, 591–621.

Campbell, J. Y. and N. G. Mankiw (1989). Consumption, income and interest rates: reinterpreting the time series evidence, *NBER Macroeconomics Annual*, vol. 4, 185–246.

Campbell, J. Y., and N. G. Mankiw (1990). Permanent income, current income, and consumption. *Journal of Business and Economic Statistics*, 8 (3), 265–79.

Carroll, C. D. (2004). Housing wealth and consumption expenditure, mimeo, Johns Hopkins University.

Case, K., J. Quigley and R. Shiller (2005). Comparing wealth effects: the stock market versus the housing market. *Advances in Macroeconomics*, Berkeley Electronic Press, 5: Iss. 1, Article 1, available at: www.bepress.com/bejm/advances/vol5/iss1/art1.

Case, K., J. Quigley and R. Shiller (2011). Wealth effects revisited 1978–2009, *NBER Working Papers*, no. 16848.

Catte, P., N. Girouard, R. Price and C. André (2004). Housing markets, wealth and the business cycle, *OECD Economics Department Working Papers*, no. 394.

Cristini, A. and A. Sevilla (2014). Do house prices affect consumption? A re-assessment of the wealth hypothesis, *Economica*, doi: 10.1111/ecca.12098.

De Bonis, R. and A. Silvestrini (2012). The effects of financial and real wealth on consumption: new evidence from OECD countries, *Applied Financial Economics*, 22, 409–25.

Eberhardt, M., C. Helmers and H. Strauss (2013). Do spillovers matter when estimating private returns to R&D?, *The Review of Economics and Statistics*, 95(2), 436–48.

Farber, H. S. (2012). Unemployment in the Great Recession: did the housing market crisis prevent the unemployed from moving to take jobs?, *American Economic Review*, 102, 520–5.

King, M. (1990). Comments on Muellbauer and Murphy, *Economic Policy* 5, 383–7.

Maddala, G. S. and S. Wu (1999). A comparative study of unit root tests with panel data and a new simple test, *Oxford Bulletin of Economics and Statistics*, 61, 631–52.

Muellbauer, J. (2010). Household decisions, credit markets and the macroeconomy: implications for the design of central bank models, *BIS Working Papers*, no. 306.

Muellbauer, J. and A. Murphy (1990). Is the UK balance of payments sustainable?, *Economic Policy*, 11, 345–83.

Pesaran, M. H. (2006). Estimation and inference in large heterogeneous panels with a multifactor error structure, *Econometrica*, 74, 967–1012.

Pesaran, M. H. (2007). A simple panel unit root test in the presence of cross-section dependence, *Journal of Applied Econometrics*, 22 (2), 265–312.

Slacalek, J. (2009). What drives personal consumption? The role of housing and financial wealth, *B.E. Journal of Macroeconomics*, 9, 1–37.

12 Growth and migration in Italy (1861–1913) interpreted with a dual model of an underdeveloped economy

Giancarlo Graziola

In this chapter I suggest the idea that a return to the model of a dual economy may help economists and economic historians to a clearer understanding of the growth of the Italian economy in the first 50 years after the country's political unification (1861) and the role played by migrations. I begin by reviewing the dual model and then present essential data to check its interpretative relevance. The data collection has been greatly assisted by the recent availability of data provided in the books by Fenoaltea (2011) and Toniolo (2013).

Two models of external and internal migration in an underdeveloped economy

Some essential features of the Italian economy in the second half of the nineteenth century can be captured by the model of a dual economy developed by W. A. Lewis (Lewis, 1954). We shall use this model as formalised by G. Ranis and C. H. Fei (1961) and D. W. Jorgenson (1967),[1] and adapted by us in view of its application to our analysis of Italian migrations in the half-century after Italy's political unification. As is well known, the key assumptions of that model are 1) a backward or agricultural sector with surplus labour relative to land, the only other input; 2) a modern or industrial sector with an unlimited supply of labour and where capital is accumulated; and 3) wages at subsistence levels in both sectors.

Let us begin, however, with a model of growth (Model 1) of an exclusively agrarian economy with surplus labour, subsistence wage and no international trade. Assume that its production function is a standard Cobb–Douglas with constant returns to scale (CRS):

$$Y = e^{\alpha t} L^{a} A^{1-a} \mathit{for} A \leq A^{0}, \alpha > 0, \mathit{and} 0 < a < 1 \tag{1}$$

where Y is agricultural (wheat) output; L land; A agricultural workers; $e^{\alpha t}$ the factor of exogenous and Hicks-neutral technological change; and A^0 the quantity of labour after which its marginal product is zero. If population $P \leq A^0$ then $P = A$ and if $P > A^0$ then $Y = e^{\alpha t} L^{a} (A^{0})^{1-a} = Y^{0}$, a constant, and there will be $R = P - A^0$ redundant agricultural workers. Assuming that L is constant, which is substantially appropriate for Italy in the nineteenth century, and normalising its quantity to 1, the production function simplifies to:

$$Y = e^{\alpha t} A^{1-a} \; for \; A \leq A^0 \tag{1}$$

For ease of exposition we shall assume that the whole of the labour force is made of salaried workers[2] who get a subsistence real wage, w_A, in terms of agricultural output. The output in excess of wages is appropriated as rents by the landowners. This means that rent is simply a surplus, which does not result from any specific maximisation strategy on the part of the landowners.

When $P < A^0$ there is no redundant labour, $A = P$ (disregarding the number of landowners, very small compared to P) and, for any $t = 0$, output is increasing in A (positive marginal product of the agricultural worker) but both output per head, $y = A^{-a}$ and the share of the land rent, LR, in the output are decreasing in A: $LR/Y = A^{-a} - w_A$. When $P \geq A^0$ there is redundant labour, $R = P - A^0$. In this case, for any $t = 0$, output (income) is constant, $Y^0 = [(A^0)^{1-a}]$ (zero marginal product) but output per head of population, $y_A = Y^0/P$, is decreasing, as are $LR\,(= Y^0 - w_A P)$ and $LR/Y^0(= 1 - w_A \frac{P}{Y^0})$.

Lastly one assumes that, with a constant agricultural real wage, the rate of growth of population equals that of output.[3] With this assumption the growth of our economy is obtained from $Y(t) = e^{\alpha t}(A^0)^{1-a}$ simply as:

$$\dot{Y}/Y = P/P = \alpha \text{ and } y = Y/P = \text{constant} \tag{2}$$

Notice that also the productivity of the fixed quantity of land ($L = 1$) and the rents, $LR(t) = e^{\alpha t}[Y^0 - w_A P(0)]$ are growing at the rate α (see Figure 12.1 for an illustration).

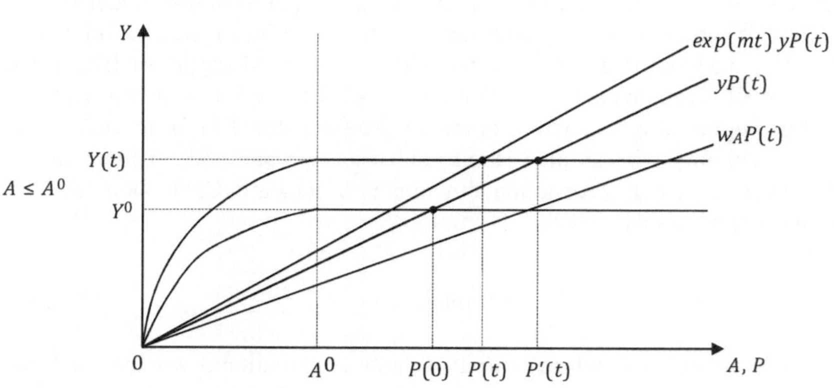

Figure 12.1 Model 1 – an agricultural economy

Source: Author's computations

The economy of Model 1 can be opened by considering the possibility of imports of manufactured (and in particular 'luxury') goods from the landowners at *internationally given* terms of trade between wheat and manufactured goods. This is an addition of no consequence, unlike that of a *permanent* emigration *abroad* of agricultural workers. If this emigration goes on at a positive rate *m* (emigrants/population), equation (2) changes as follows:

$$\dot{Y}/Y = \dot{P}/P = \alpha - \mathrm{m} > 0 \text{ and } \dot{Y}/Y = m \qquad (3)$$

On the assumption that employed and (at least a proportion of) redundant workers are perfect substitutes, permanent emigration will slow down the growth of *P* and redundant workers without affecting that of *Y*: income per head will grow and rents will grow more than they would have done without emigration.

If we keep strictly to the assumptions above, the emigration brings benefits directly to the migrants, whose wages abroad will be (much) higher than that at home, but this is not relevant for the home economy. Here, from what we have just said about the growth of rents, the benefits of migration will go certainly to landowners. However, as happens generally and as it happened on a very large scale in our case, if the permanent migrant is not 'selfish'[4] and sends back remittances to his relatives, these may experience a substantial increase in welfare, spending the remittances on agricultural or manufactured goods imported from abroad. But if we enlarge the interpretation of real wages to cover other types of rural income, we find that the families of the peasants cultivating their plots, and of small tenants and sharecroppers, will enjoy a higher income per head immediately after the departure of their young male members: when they travel abroad, these men will no longer be redundant but instead will be productive.

Though Model 1 of an agricultural or, better, rural economy can claim to be quite an adequate model for explaining external migrations of Italy from the post-unification period to the First World War, it is definitely not suitable for explaining internal migrations in the same period. A possible model for these is a dual economy model. In our Model 2, this economy is characterised by the coexistence of a backward or, more specifically, agricultural sector[5] as in Model 1; and of an advanced or, again more specifically, industrial sector characterised by a technology which uses essentially only capital and labour; the existence of a class of capitalists/entrepreneurs who maximise their profits and reinvest them to expand their businesses; and the existence of an unlimited supply of labour from the backward sector at a constant real wage, in terms of agricultural goods (wheat). The demand for labour, on the other side, is (ultimately) limited at every stage by the stock of capital inherited from the past.

In Model 2 the production function is again a Cobb–Douglas with CRS:

$$X = e^{\beta t} K^{b} M^{1-b} \quad \beta > 0; 0 < b < 1 \qquad (4)$$

where *X* is manufacturing output; *K* is capital, the value of capital goods at constant prices; *M*, employment; and *β*, a rate of technological progress which is again exogenous and Hicks-neutral. Notice, however, that the presence of K in equation (3) allows us to look at that progress as the result of a stream of improvements in the organisation of the production process and/or in the quality of output, whereas the technical progress which brings about improvements in the quality of capital is embodied in the measure of K (see Hulten (1992) for a rigorous and clear treatment of this point). As is frequently done implicitly in verbal presentations of the theory, we assume for simplicity that the industrial good can be either consumed or used as a capital good. So let p_M be the price of X or K, and p_A the price of the agricultural good.

The real wage in terms of agricultural goods in the manufacturing sector, W_M^A, is that wage at which workers are ready to leave the agricultural sector. On the other hand, for the entrepreneurs of the manufacturing sector, the relevant wage is the one in terms of manufactured goods, w_M. Keeping our previous assumption of internationally given terms of trade simplifies radically the determination of the latter, allowing it to be written simply as: $w_M = w_M^A(p_A/p_M)$. Even if having terms of trade given outside the model simplifies its formulation, there remains the question of their constancy or otherwise. The constancy is directly assumed by Jorgenson (1967) in his (closed economy) model, while in the equally closed model of Ranis and Fei (1961), the terms of trade will sooner or later worsen (rise) for the industrial entrepreneurs. This will happen because the growth in the demand for wheat from the (subsistence wages) of workers who have moved into the industrial sector will sooner or later outstrip the growth in the quantity of wheat 'freed' by these formerly redundant workers (more precisely, this will happen when the growth of the dual economy enters phase II – see below and Figure 12.2).[6]

In the real world, the real wage in the modern sector is higher than that in the agricultural sector on account not only of the higher costs of living in the capitalist sector but also of the costs of migration between the two sectors (psychological

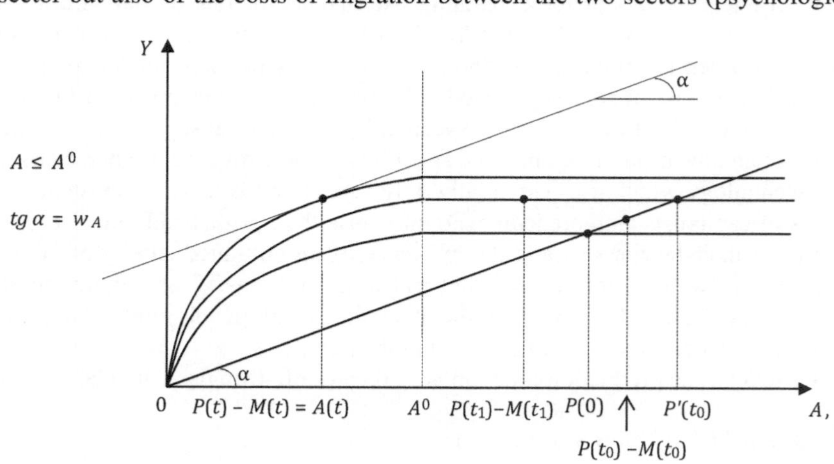

Figure 12.2 Model 2 – a dual economy

Source: Author's computations

costs and travel costs). Moreover, the former could be still higher (namely its value, net of migration costs, could be positive) for the effects of factors such as work experience or 'a difference in conventional standards' (Lewis, 1954). We will ignore these factors for simplicity, and so in Model 2 the real wage in terms of wheat is really uniform between the two sectors of the dual economy.

In a dual economy, accumulation of capital in the industrial sector is the third source of growth besides technological change in the industrial and agricultural sectors. An essential, and simplifying, assumption in the original Lewis formulation of the dual growth model is that the investment is financed entirely by capitalists' profits. This assumption implies that rents and wages are completely spent in consumption but not necessarily that all profits are invested.[7] Ignoring depreciation of capital, nominal profits (setting $t = 0$ so that $X = K^b M^{1-b}$) are given by:

$$\Pi(K,M) = p_M K^b M^{1-b} - r\, p_M K - p_M w_M M \tag{5}$$

where r is the instantaneous rate of interest at which capitalists lend to each other.

From the necessary first-order conditions for a maximum profit, one obtains:

$$(1-b)\frac{X}{M} = w_M \quad \text{and} \quad b\frac{X}{K} = r \tag{6}$$

As is well known, these equations do not in general have a solution, but in our model, where the real wage, W_M, is fixed and employment, M, is a variable, M and r are determined as solutions of equation (6).[8] In this equilibrium, Π is zero and the capitalists obtain only a normal remuneration of their capitals, $rK = bX$.

The equation of the internal motion of the advanced sector is then:

$$K = bX \tag{7}$$

Using the first of (6) to eliminate M from (4) and substituting the result into (7), one obtains the rate of growth of capital as:

$$\frac{\dot{K}}{K} = b\left(\frac{1-b}{w_M}\right)^{\frac{1-b}{b}} \exp(\frac{\beta}{b})\text{t}$$

The rates of growth of M and X are then given by:

$$\frac{\dot{M}}{M} = \frac{\dot{X}}{X} = \frac{\beta}{b} + b\left(\frac{1-b}{w_M}\right)^{\frac{1-b}{b}} \exp(\frac{\beta}{b})\text{t}$$

The accumulation of capital in the manufacturing sector leads to increasing rates of growth of manufacturing output and employment (i.e. a constant labour productivity); the rate of growth of output is higher than the rate of growth of capital, leading to a rising productivity of capital. We are now able to sketch the growth dynamics of a closed dual economy and the implied migration rate. As long as there is redundant labour in the agricultural sector and a constant (agricultural) real wage in both sectors, the rate of population growth remains constant at α, as in Model 1. Initially, the growth of industrial employment at, let us say, a low rate will simply slow down in some degree the growth of surplus labour, as was done by permanent migration abroad in Model 2. Sooner or later, however, an M growing at an increasing rate will outpace the growth of P and force R to decrease towards zero, or P towards A^0. A central feature of the dual growth, in a closed economy, is that the migration of redundant labour from the agricultural to the industrial sector will allow a conversion (1 to 1 in our simplified version of the model) of the agricultural wages in the agricultural sector into agricultural wages in the industrial sector: internal migrants in a way bring their subsistence with them differently from those who migrate abroad. This phase corresponds to 'phase I' of growth in the formalisation of Lewis's model by Ranis and Fei (1961), who call the 'Lewis turning point' (A^0 in Figure 12.1) the point beyond which 'phase II' starts.

During 'phase II' further increases in M imply decreases in the number of agricultural workers, A, with positive marginal productivity. Because of this decrease in A, the internal migration process involves increasing marginal losses of agricultural output, from zero towards the value of the subsistence wage, w_A. The demand for wheat from the industrial wages will no longer be matched by the supply freed up by the emigrated agricultural workers and either 1) technical progress will close the gap, leaving the terms of trade, *PA/PM*, constant; or 2) the wheat demand of manufacturing workers will compete with that of the landowners, increasing the terms of trade, at the expense of the latter; or 3) the real wage in the agricultural sector will end by being made up partly from manufactured good and partly from wheat, while loosely preserving its nature as a subsistence bundle of goods.[9]

As a result of these facts, the labour supply curve for the industrial sector would no longer necessarily be horizontal, but could be upward sloping, slowing down the accumulation of capital.[10] In any case, eventually, a level of employment will be reached at which real wage and marginal product will be equal. At this point agricultural labour would become a scarce factor, like land and capital, and the economy would no longer be dual.

If we stick rigidly to our version of the dual model of growth of a *closed* economy, the benefits of the *internal* migration are very unevenly distributed. The landowners will enjoy increasing rents during 'phase I' and, with constant terms of trade, these increases will continue in 'phase II', given that this ends at the point at which the marginal product of labour equals its subsistence wage (see Figure 12.2). The capitalists/entrepreneurs will benefit from continuously increasing profits, whereas the workers will keep on being paid their subsistence wages. However, if we expand the model to include the possibility that wages in the industrial sector are higher than in the agricultural sector, even after deducting the costs of migration and the higher cost of living in the industrial cities, the workers too will have lasting benefits from migration.

Notice also that in a small, open dual economy, with terms of trade given from the international markets, the wheat for the wages of industrial workers

($= p_A w_A M$) may be imported, with the trade balance kept in equilibrium by the export of the corresponding quantity of industrial goods ($= \frac{p_A w_A^M}{p_M}$). Land rents, $LR = Y^0 - w_A(A^0 + R)$, increase because redundant workers migrating to the industrial sector do not 'carry away' their subsistence.

Finally, let us remind ourselves that the classical model described above is an example of a 'structural' model: that is, a model characterised by a small number of key assumptions which take some economic variables (subsistence wage, redundant labour, saving from profits) as exogenous or given by the social context. However, it is possible to think of other structural models of dual economies based on assumptions different from the classical ones. For example, Jorgenson (1967) presents, in addition to the classical model to which we have made reference above, a neo-classical model of a dual economy. In the latter, the assumptions of a subsistence wage and redundant labour are dropped and replaced by an assumption of a maximum level of output consumed per agricultural worker and the related notion of a surplus, available for the sustenance of manufacturing workers. This structural assumption is the cornerstone of an explanation of a dual growth based again on the mechanisms which allocate the population between the two sectors.

Jorgenson's model is not a purely neoclassical one (e.g. the wage in the agricultural sector is assumed to be proportional to that in the industrial one), unlike that presented in the much more recent Acemoglu (2009), in a chapter on 'Structural transformation and market failure in development'. This model assumes that wages are set competitively in both the advanced, industrial and urban sector and the backward and agricultural sector, but are higher in the former. Capital accumulation takes place only in the modern sector, out of the savings of its individuals, and the dual nature of the economy rests simply on the 'structural' assumption that the rate of migration from the agricultural to the industrial sector does not depend on the gap between their wages but is constrained to some exogenous low level.

Underdevelopment and migration in Italy from unification (1861) to the First World War

Models 1 and 2 presented in the previous section are indeed very streamlined representations of real-world underdeveloped economies, but it must be noted that their very simplicity may suggest what the fundamentals of those types of economy are, and thus help in more detailed researches. The Italian economy after unification, with a GDP per capita of about $1,500 (1990 PPP and prices) was definitely an underdeveloped economy. So were the generality of the world's countries, although some were more developed than others. The GDP per capita of the UK, the then leading economy, was about twice that of Italy, which was lower even than those of the other major European economies (see Figure 12.3). All the other traditional measures of the level of development point in the same direction as GDP per capita and even lower: a life expectancy at birth of only

29 years; a mortality rate in the first year of 290 per thousand; only 1 year of schooling for the population in the 15–64 age bracket; 3,000 hours worked per year (double the rate of today); and a Human Development Index (in 1870) of 50 per cent of that of the other OECD countries (see Brandolini and Vecchi, 2013), a lower percentage than for GDP per capita.

More important for us is the structure of production: in 1861 the agricultural value added was 46 per cent of GDP and the industrial one only 16 per cent (Table 12.1). As for land productivity, it must be kept in mind that Italy was a country more densely populated than most other European countries, but its high rural population/land ratio was matched by a high agricultural output/land ratio.[11] In other words, although Italy was underdeveloped because of a low output per capita, Italian agriculture must have experienced before and after unification some type of technological innovation that kept constant the productivity of an increasing numbers of labourers working on the same quantity of land.

In the half-century between unification and the First World War, Italy started its economic development but at a rather low pace. Table 12.1 shows that GDP and GDP per capita increased by factors of only 2.39 and 1.68, respectively, over the whole period: a period during which the other major economies performed better, as shown in Figure 12.3. Looking at the performance of agriculture, we find that its value added increased by a factor of 1.91, lower than that of GDP.

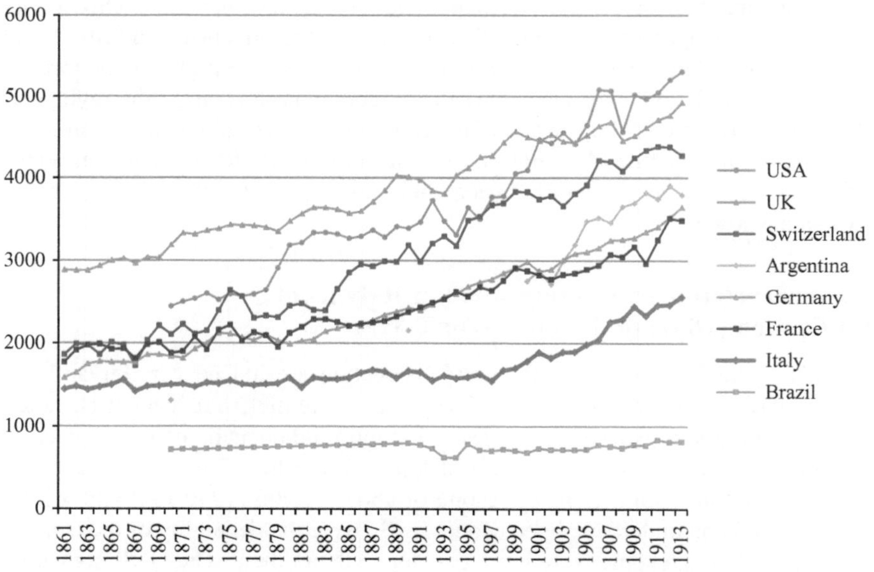

Figure 12.3 GDP per capita for Italy and main countries of its emigration, 1861–1913 (1990 International Geary–Khamis dollars; source: Maddison, 2010).

Source: Author's computations based on Maddison (2010)

Table 12.1 Ten-year growth factors: GDP, agriculture and industry in Italy, 1861–1913

	Agriculture	*Industry*	*GDP*	*Per capita GDP*	*Agriculture/ GDP (%)**	*Industry/ GDP (%)**
1861–1870	1.22	1.07	1.18	1.11	46.0	16.1
1870–1880	1.06	1.20	1.12	1.05	47.6	14.6
1880–1890	1.06	1.30	1.14	1.07	45.1	15.6
1890–1900	1.13	1.15	1.14	1.06	41.9	17.8
1861–1900	**1.55**	**1.92**	**1.71**	**1.32**		
1900–1910	1.10	1.62	1.27	1.18	41.7	18.0
1910–1913	1.12	1.08	1.10	1.08	36.3	23.0
1861–1913	**1.91**	**3.34**	**2.39**	**1.68**		
Average annual growth rate (%)	1.24	2.32	1.67	0.99		

* Initial year

Source: Author's calculations based on Fenoaltea (2012), p. 125

It must be noted that this trend was negatively influenced by 20 years of virtual stagnation from 1870 to 1990. As a result, the share of agricultural value added in GDP decreased significantly by 10 percentage points to 36 per cent. Using the data on the number of workers in agriculture presented in Appendix A5 of Toniolo (2013), we find that their number increased by a factor of 1.24 from 1861 to 2013. This implies that agricultural output per worker has increased by a factor of only 1.54 (= 1.91/1.24) in 49 years, or at an average annual rate of 0.82 per cent. These data suggest that for the whole period 1861–1913 the Italian economy was a predominantly agricultural, underdeveloped economy in which the output of agriculture grew slowly and only a little faster than its population, leaving a very low growth of agricultural output per worker.

This is particularly true for the period from 1861 to 1900, during which agricultural value added per worker grew by a factor of only 1.26 (=1.55/1.23) or at an average rate of 0.48 per cent. From Table 12.2 one can see that the real wages in agriculture increased between 1861 and 1913 more rapidly than agricultural output per worker and indeed by a factor of 1.81, not far from that of agricultural output of 1.91. The explanation of these puzzling data is given by the fact (see note 2) that most Italian agricultural workers were not wage earners, as assumed for convenience in the exposition of Model 1, but peasants, small tenants and so on.

One can conclude that although Model 1, with its constant output per head, is not strictly applicable to the agricultural sector of the Italian economy, it can be taken as a rough approximation to it. It would be better, of course, to have a variant of Model 1 allowing some growth of subsistence incomes and wages over time.

Coming to the industrial sector (the aggregate of manufacturing, construction and utilities), its value added in 1861 was only one-third of the agricultural value added or 16 per cent of GDP, but grew faster at a factor of 2.39 during the period 1861–1913, reaching 23 per cent of GDP in 1913. The factor of growth was a bit higher than its long-term average in the 1880s,[12] with a 10-year value of 1.30, and more

Table 12.2 Growth factors of real wages of unskilled workers (1913 liras/day): Italy, 1861–1913

	Agricultural wage	*Industrial wage*	*Industrial wage / Agricultural wage**
1861–1870	1.02	1.04	1.15
1870–1880	0.94	0.96	1.18
1880–1890	1.24	1.34	1.21
1890–1900	1.15	1.19	1.31
1900–1910	1.23	1.23	1.36
1910–1913	1.07	1.04	1.35
1861–1913	**1.81**	**2.07**	
Average annual growth rate (%)	1.13	1.39	

* Initial year

Source: Author's calculations based on Fenoaltea (2012), p. 125

significantly, also in the 1900s when that value reached 1.62. An indication of the acceleration of industrial growth since the turn of the century is given by the fact that its factor in 1900–13 was 1.74 – only a bit lower than 1.92, the factor of growth in the previous half-century. Again, using the data in Appendix A5 of Toniolo (2013), we find that the factors of growth for the number of industrial workers were 1.92 for the period 1861–1913 and 1.40 for 1861–1900. Thus the dynamics of value added per worker were higher in industry than in agriculture both in the whole period, with a value of 1.74 (= 3.34/1.92) for the former against 1.54 for the latter, and during 1861–1900, with a value of 1.37 (= 1.92/1.40) against a value of 1.26. The figures for industry imply an increase in the annual average rate of growth of industrial labour productivity from 1 per cent in 1861–1900 to 1.8 per cent in 1900–13. As a result of these trends, the ratio of output per worker in industry to that in agriculture stayed roughly constant, increasing only by 8 per cent over 1861–1900 and by 13 percent during 1861–1913. Finally, we note from Table 12.2 that the factor of growth of real industrial wages for 1861–1913 was 2.07 – a higher value higher than that of 1.74 of labour productivity in industry, a puzzling aspect of our data which could be eliminated by assuming that the available data are biased in favour of the most dynamic categories of unskilled wages.

Taken together, the data in Table 12.1 suggest that the process of industrialisation in Italy in the half-century after unification was not really a revolution, but that its acceleration after 1900 transformed an essentially agricultural economy into a dual one, beginning 'phase I' of its development. The data on agricultural and industrial wages are also roughly compatible with the hypothesis in Model 2 that industrial real wages are 'anchored' to agricultural wages.[13]

The dual economy model of the previous section is essentially non-spatial and in its presentation we have talked of migration from the agricultural to the industrial sector only for convenience. In the real world, the spatial dimension of migration is determined ultimately by the factors causing the localisation and concentration of industrial and related service activities. Following the periodisation and model of localisation proposed by A'Hearn and Venables (2013), we note with them that during 1861–90, their first period, the Italian economy was characterised by high internal transport and trade costs so that it did not have a unified national market. The crucial spatial heterogeneity was the natural advantage of the regions of the north, endowed with abundant water resources, which favoured both capitalist agriculture and the textile industries (first silk and then cotton, and so on), and translated into larger local markets, exports and in time higher income per head.[14] The lack of a national market at the beginning of the 1861–1900 period and the slow process of its formation strengthen the pertinence of Model 1 to the Italian economy. In this model there are no basic forces stimulating internal migrations movements but there is room for external migrations in the presence of gaps in incomes per head or real wages between Italy and other countries. As for differences in income per head, they are by now well documented in various studies, among which Maddison (2008) is prominent. International gaps in real wages have been documented in a database assembled by J. Williamson in 1994. From Williamson (1994) we see that Italian real urban unskilled wages were at 22 per cent of US wages in 1870, 24 per cent in 1890 and 33 per cent in 1913. The analogous figures for Argentina and Germany were about double those for the USA. Gomellini and O'Gràda (2013) also inform us that in the 1900s the wage of an unskilled male worker from the Italian south might have been 500 liras, as against $400–500 (about 2,000–2,500 liras) in New York.

These good reasons for emigrating find expression in the data of Table 12.3, from which we see that more than 5.5 million Italians left the country, mainly emigrating to the group of countries shown in Figure 12.3.[15] As the first two rows of Table 12.3 show, migration net of national returning immigrants was much lower in the 1870s, but Table 12.4 shows that the net migration rate has been an increasingly important fraction of the rate of natural increase, rising from 20 per cent in 1872–81 to 40 per cent in 1892–1901, and thus slowing down significantly the effective increase in population growth. In terms of Model 1 this would bring about an increase in income per capita: a movement from $P(0)$ to $P(t)$ instead of a movement to $P'(t)$. Notice that Model 1, in which the increase in income per capita is endogenous, reverses the causality between migration rate and income growth in the origin country. In contrast, in the small number of richer models of Italian migration in the 1861–1913 period (Faini and Venturini, 1994; Hatton and Williamson, 1994; 1998, Chapter 6; Moretti, 1999; Gomellini and O'Grada, 2013), the rate of growth of income per capita is one of the exogenous variables and the migration rate is endogenous.

Starting from the 1890s, a number of factors (progress in transport, etc.) contributed to create a unified national market. The greater size of local markets and, in particular, greater access to markets in the north-western regions of Italy and the reversal of the free trade policy adopted soon after unification (with the introduction of tariffs on industrial goods in 1878 and 1888) allowed the industries of that area to dominate the national market. The subsequent concentration of industrial establishments in the north-west made this area the terminal of an initially local rural–urban migration along the lines of Model 2. The reinforcement of industrial growth in the north-west between 1900 and 1913 encouraged the

Table 12.3 Emigrants and net migration, Italy: 1870–1914

Years	*Emigrants (a)*	*Net migration (b)*	*Rate of permanent emigration (%) (c) = (b)/(a)*	*Net migration rate (in per thousand) (d)*
1870–1874	635,967	–153,970	–24.2	–2.3
1875–1879	527,304	–55,134*	–10.5	–1.2
1880–1884	733,413	..	..	..
1885–1889	1,049,835	..	..	..
1890–1894	1,205,226	..	..	..
1895–1899	1,492,572	..	..	..
1900–1904	2,396,703	..	..	..
1905–1909	3,331,294	–2,436,481	–73.1	–13.2
1910–1914	3,248,515	–2,343,082	–72.1	–14.6
Total 1870–1914	***14,620,829***	..	..	

* Years 1875–6.

(b) Net migration = National returning immigrants – Emigrants.

(d) Net migration/average population (for year at the centre of the period).

Source: Author's calculations based on Istat, *Time Series: Population* (http://timeseries.istat.it/)

first interregional migrations. According to Treves (1976), these were of limited importance but totally directed to the regions of the north and centre of Italy as well as to the regions of the north-west, and especially to Lombardy.

At the same time, it seems that the reinforcement of the growth of GDP per capita after 1900 accelerated the migration process, as shown in Tables 12.3 and 12.4.[16] Migration and growth in this period seem to have become the components of a circular causation process.

Table 12.4 Natural increase and net migration rates: Italy, 1862–1913* (per 1,000 inhabitants)

Years	*Natural increase rate (a)*	*Net migration rate (b)*	*Effective increase rate (c) = (a) + (b)*	*Relative migration rate (d) = (b)/(a)*
1862–1871	6.63	0.06	6.69	0.01
1872–1881	6.86	–1.19	5.67	–0.20
1882–1891	9.86	–2.73	7.13	–0.28
1892–1901	10.17	–4.04	6.13	–0.40
1902–1911	10.22	–1.64	8.58	–0.16
1912–1913	12.74	–10.11	2.63	–0.80

* at current borders

(a) Natural rate (balance) to resident population (yearly arithmetic average).

(b) Net migration/resident population (yearly arithmetic average) (a minus sign means that the number of emigrants exceeds the number of national returning immigrants).

Source: Author's calculations based on ISTAT, *Time Series: Population* (http://timeseries.istat.it/)

Notes

1 See his 'Classical model' of a dual economy.
2 In the period under consideration, the labour force in Italy was composed of workers with a variety of legal relationships with the landowners. Besides the salaried workers there were peasants owning the plots cultivated, large (capitalistic) tenants, small tenants and sharecroppers. Moreover, their numbers varied between Italian regions. The last two categories were the most widespread (Federico, 2002).
3 This assumption could be justified by a pseudo-Malthusian mechanism, which makes the growth of population positively dependent on the growth of income per capita induced by *exogenous* technical change. This could happen, for example, if higher per capita income played a role during the demographic transition, when death rates are falling faster than birth rates. An alternative mechanism, incompatible with our assumption of exogenous technical change, would be that of an *endogenous* technical change induced by an expanding population on an area of fixed size.
4 Fenoaltea (2011, p. 159), makes a distinction between 'permanent' and 'selfish permanent' emigration in his analysis of the relationship between protection and migration in late nineteenth-century Italy. He compares the effects of the latter to that of a plague, which nullify the investment in the human capital of the emigrant. But with redundant workers this effect has already occurred at home.
5 It must be noted that the identification of 'backward' with agriculture and 'advanced' with industry is true only approximately and that it is maintained for simplicity. In the real world, and particularly in Italy in the second half of the nineteenth century, the advanced sector also included capitalist farms, whereas the backward sector included, besides agriculture, not only a host of other rural activities but also industrial and service activities, conducted in a technologically backward environment (even if these activities were highly sophisticated, such as craftsmanship).
6 For a more general model of the determination of the terms of trade between agriculture and industry in a less developed country, which also takes account of demand, see Sah and Stiglitz (1987).
7 This is, of course, the famous classical assumption of Ricardo and the Cambridge School in the 1950s and 1960s. Lewis (1954) also treats the case in which investment is financed by creating money (e.g. banking credit), but in so doing he switches tacitly from a model with one industrial sector to a model with two sectors: one for producing (with labour and capital) a final industrial good, and the other for producing (with labour only) the capital good. Jorgenson (1967) notes that what matters for the dynamics of the accumulation process is that investment is equal to profit, independently of the fact that saving could also be done by landowners turned capitalists.
8 One should note that the national rate of interest is determined independently of the rate prevailing in foreign markets.
9 Here one feels the lack of a theory of demand with which one could specify a real wage in agriculture as $[w_A(p_A, p_M); w_A(p_A, p_M)]$, so that the real wage for the industrial entrepreneurs would be: $w_M = w_A(p_A, p_M)\dfrac{p_A}{p_M} + w_A(p_A, p_M)$. This could increase in time with increasing terms of trade.
10 From (1) we see that $\dot{Y}/Y = a + (1-\beta)\dot{A}/A$. In 'phase II'.
11 Federico (2002) mentions a study by P. O'Brien and L. Prados de la Escosura who found that in 1911 land productivity in Italy was very high by European standards.
12 In passing, we may recall here that in the 1880s Italian industry went through a (relatively) strong expansion of both manufacturing and construction, and fixed investment, facilitated by a credit expansion, which turned into a credit bubble (especially strong in real estate). When this burst, the resulting credit crunch brought about an industrial recession in 1889, which bottomed in 1892 and recovered the 1888 peak in 1896. The

financial collapse of the banking system led to the first major reform of the Italian banking system, with the creation of the Bank of Italy and the setting of the stage for universal German-type banking. Gallegati and Ardeni (1994) suggest that the most plausible interpretation of this story is that based on the hypothesis of financial instability by H. Minsky.

13 On this point, see the comments in Fenoaltea (2011) about his construction of the time series of real wages in agriculture and industry, on which Table 12.2 is based.

14 The south/north ratio in GDP per capita was 98.5 per cent in 1881, but went down to 88 per cent in 1901 and 81.4 per cent in 1911 (see Iuzzolino, Pellegrini and Viesti, 2013).

15 The group looks small but the fact is that Italian migration has been significantly more diversified by country of destination than those of other countries of origin.

16 The causation from growth of income per head to migration has been stressed by Faini and Venturini (1994), while Hatton and Williamson (1998) and Moretti (1999) have stressed the role of the network effect in explaining the migratory boom of 1910–13.

References

Acemoglu, D. (2009). *Introduction to Modern Economic Growth*, Princeton, NJ: Princeton University Press.

A'Hearn, B. and A. J. Venables (2013). Regional disparities: internal geography and external trade. In G. Toniolo, ed., *The Oxford Handbook of the Italian Economy since Unification*, New York: Oxford University Press, pp. 599–630.

Brandolini, A. and G. Vecchi (2013). Standards of living. In G. Toniolo, ed., *The Oxford Handbook of the Italian Economy since Unification*, New York: Oxford University Press, pp. 227–248.

Faini, R. and A. Venturini (1994). Italian emigration in the prewar period. In T. J. Hatton and J. G. Williamson, eds., *Migration and the International Labour Market, 1850–1939*, London: Routledge, pp. 72–90.

Federico, G. (2002). L'agricoltura italiana: successo o fallmento? In P. Ciocca and G. Toniolo, eds., *Storia economica d'Italia. 3. Industrie, mercati, istituzioni. 1. Le strutture dell'economia*, Bari: Editori Laterza, pp. 99–136.

Fenoaltea, S. (2011). *The Reinterpretation of Italian Economic History*, Cambridge: Cambridge University Press.

Fenoaltea, S. (2012). *L'economia italiana dall'Unità alla Grande Guerra*, Rome: UniversItalia.

Gallegati, M. and P. G. Ardeni (1994). Crescita e fluttuazioni nell'economia italiana (1861–1913): Una reinterpretazione, *Politica economica*, 10, 119–53.

Gomellini, M. and C. O'Gràda (2013). Migrations. In G. Toniolo, ed., *The Oxford Handbook of the Italian Economy since Unification*, New York: Oxford University Press, pp. 271–302.

Hatton, T. J. and J. G. Williamson (1994). Latecomers to mass emigration: the Latin experience. In T. J. Hatton and J. G. Williamson, eds., *Migration and the International Labour Market, 1850–1939*, London: Routledge, pp. 55–71.

Hatton, T. J. and J. G. Williamson (1998). *The Age of Mass Migration*, New York: Oxford University Press.

Hulten, C. R. (1992). Growth accounting when technical change is embodied in capital, *American Economic Review*, 82, 964–80.

Iuzzolino, G., G. Pellegrini and G. Viesti (2013). Regional convergence. In G. Toniolo, ed., *The Oxford Handbook of the Italian Economy since Unification*, New York: Oxford University Press, pp. 571–98.

Jorgenson, D. W. (1967). Surplus labour and the development of a dual economy, *Oxford Economic Papers*, 19, 288–312.
Lewis, A. (1954). Development with unlimited supplies of labour, *The Manchester School*, 22, 139–92.
Maddison, A. (2008). *Statistics on World Population, GDP and Per Capita GDP, 1–2008 AD*, http://www.ggdc.net/maddison/oriindex.htm.
Moretti, E. (1999). Social networks and migrations: Italy 1876–1913, *International Migration Review*, 33, 640–57.
Ranis, G. and J. C. Fei (1961). A theory of economic development, *American Economic Review*, 51, 533–65.
Sah, R. K. and J. E. Stiglitz (1987). Price scissors and the structure of the economy, *Quarterly Journal of Economics*, 102, 109–34.
Toniolo, G., ed. (2013). *The Oxford Handbook of the Italian Economy since Unification*, New York: Oxford University Press.
Treves, A. (1976). Le migrazioni interne nell'Italia fascista, Torino: Einaudi.

13 Organisational and technological paradigms

Asynchronised structural breaks, uneven evolution of paradigms and firm growth between complementarities and substitutabilities

Riccardo Leoni

Heterogeneity among firms – in terms of efficiency – has been widely documented in literature. Syverson (2004), for example, demonstrates that within 4-digit SIC industries in the US manufacturing sector, the ratio of total factor productivity among plants at the 90th percentile of productivity distribution is in the order of 2 to 1 with respect to the 10th percentile. By enlarging the range between the two percentiles, the ratio easily arrives at 4. The picture is not very different for other economic systems.[1] It follows that more productive firms are more likely to survive than those with lower productivity: in the American case, the estimates indicate that those that fall below the 20th percentile exit from the market within 5 years.

While the explanations in literature differ, the 'internal' organisation of firms, the quality of the technological capital employed and especially their compatibility are rarely studied. In particular, little attention is paid to analysing the stratifications which are determined over time with respect to the intrinsic characteristics of not only technological and organisational capital but also social capital (knowledge, cognitive skills, interpersonal skills, non-cognitive skills) that crystallise in the routinisation of organisational behaviours.

The stratifications correspond to the different paradigms that follow one another over time. For the sake of space, we here focus only on the technological and organisational paradigms, two essential and complementary factors of economic activity. If a complementarity relation exists between the two factors then relative price is not an applicable tool to assess how the two factors combine; taken in isolation, the two factors are unable to entirely explain the consequences of internal structural breaks on firm economic activity, since the concausal links are lost from sight. In addition, the complementary nature of each factor may be *simultaneous* (which implies that the gains from the simultaneous adoption of two factors are greater than the sum of the gains from the adoption of each factor in isolation) or *sequential* (the gains from the adoption of a factor are greater if another factor has already been adopted compared to situations where it has not been previously adopted). Sequential complementarity may refer to a combination of two or more factors, but also to a combination of two or more elements of a single factor forming a bundle. All these aspects have to be taken into consideration in explaining why two apparently identical competing firms react differently to common shocks. Based on this reasoning, the production function framework is not a suitable tool to enable understanding of these dynamics in their exogenous and endogenous versions. Nor is the vintage capital model of new investment suitable for this purpose, since it is *assumed* that the latest investment always incorporates best-practice technology, meaning that firms are never uncertain about the characteristics of new technologies and that technology has a *unique* meaning, with no discrepancy at all between technology as an artefact and its personal and collective use. The same argument is applicable to organisational features.

We consider Kuhn's scientific paradigm an appropriate tool – with its elements of complementarity such as a set of pieces of knowledge, practical and theoretical know-how, methods and procedures to solve selected problems based on certain principles – to analyse the intrinsic properties of two technologies – namely, electro-mechanical and electronics – and two organisational models: specifically, scientific management and the Ohnism model (all accredited in literature as out-and-out paradigms) to analytically highlight the possible co-evolution or the non-synergistic combination of the two factors. Indeed, a structural break in one of the two factors could give rise to a solution that does not necessarily constitute the best potential and sustainable combination for several reasons: for example, constitutive principles in contradiction not only within the same factors but also between the same devices adopted in different periods of time and for various motives,[2] or adopted without paying specific attention to their complementary (i.e. information imperfections). Other explanations could be prohibitive costs, financial constraints, and several others that will be considered further on in the analysis. When this is the case – namely, when the change processes that a firm faces give rise to spurious combinations (identifiable as 'local' positioning) rather than the full absorption of both complementary paradigms among the factors and complementary ingredients within each factor – resources are wasted and inefficiencies and productivity losses arise. This engenders development paths with either an accumulation or a fragmentation of technological knowledge and organisational competencies resulting in either high or low and stagnant firm growth.

The analysis methodology pursued in this chapter is speculative and empirically oriented, rather than theoretically and mathematically formalised. The chapter is structured as follows: the next section provides the background to the discussion, defining the paradigm and considering the structural breaks and incremental improvements of a given paradigm; the third and fourth sections analyse organisational and technological paradigms from the perspective of their constitutive principles and historical sequences.[3] The fifth section considers the complementarity conditions, and the spurious and pure combination both within and between factors, and outlines the implications for the empirical evaluation of outcomes. The sixth section considers some ambiguities, aporias and methodological doubts that still exist in empirical literature, while the seventh section concludes.

Changes and improvements of the paradigm

Firm efficiency does not grow linearly: it very often progresses with relatively regular and modest changes, at times with larger but discontinuous changes. Sometimes this growth is the result of reactive behaviour to stimuli from the external environment and sometimes it is the result of 'pro-active' behaviour. As a first approximation, paraphrasing Dosi (1983), and borrowing the categories of scientific paradigms from Kuhn (1962), in the case of more or less regular changes we usually speak of movements along the trajectory of a given paradigm that take the form of a moving production possibilities curve and/or the incrementally increasing number of produceable goods. At the origin of discontinuity is almost always the emergence of a new paradigm that gives rise to a significant increase in the variety of products and/or services, or radically new products. The elements that influence these trends differ, but it is clear from literature that in recent decades two factors have attracted the attention of scholars: technology and the ways of organising economic activity in the firm. In this chapter, we concentrate on these two factors by virtue of their intense incidence in this turbulent period of transition we live in.

A paradigm can be defined as a model and a pattern of solutions to *selected* problems, based on *selected* principles and on *selected* materials (Dosi, 1983, p. 83). A change of paradigm therefore implies replacing all the constitutive elements and is hence not directly comparable with previous paradigms.

We here analyse how two technological paradigms – electro-mechanical and electronics – and two organisational paradigms – scientific management and Ohnism – succeeded each another (in combination giving rise to four broadly different outcomes) and as such refer to problems of a technological and organisational nature, while both principles and materials refer to (and are derived from) natural, organisational and anthropological sciences (since re-organisation has to do with human beings).

The transition from one paradigm to another occurs through a process, which makes it difficult to date the occurrence of the event precisely. The movements along a given trajectory – which enter into the *framework* of the underlying principles that are characteristic of the paradigm in question and prescribe the direction – occur as a result of an evolution in *complementary* knowledge, methods, procedures and competencies, in the sense that the development or lack of development of one of these elements can promote or inhibit the development of others. To this must be added the economic forces (e.g. demand-pull, cost-push, market forms), social forces (e.g. the *animal spirits*, learning) and institutional forces that act as real *selective devices* influencing the curvature of the movement in progress, until – according to Freeman and Louçã (2001) – diminishing returns begin to manifest, and progress associated with the paradigm consequently slows down.

According to Kuhn (1962), however, the transition from one paradigm to another does not occur linearly: that is to say, first the falsification of one or more of the elements or the constitutive theories of the paradigm (i.e., results that contradict deeply held expectations) and thereafter the abandonment of the paradigm in favour of a new paradigm that appears capable of providing more accurate and convincing explanations in the context of a wider sphere of phenomena. The new paradigm, which at first sight appears to contrast with the substrate of expectations, generally emerges with difficulty due to resistance to accepting anomalous results. Similarly, this also occurs in relation to the acceptance and subsequent questioning of a theory as a result of unsatisfactory explanations and the failure of activities aimed at resolving the problems, which is followed by a phase where the first draft of a new theory is compared to the old theory, and then at a later date, overlapping theories, up to the definitive prevalence of the new over the old.

The paradigm shift is influenced as much by the evolution of the economic, social and cultural structure and economic factors in the strict sense (income distribution, relative prices, etc.) as by the feedback structure between economic environments, leading towards change and driving the direction of change itself. In turn, however, the incipient paradigm also influences the same economic, social and organisational environment (Perez, 1983). The new paradigm in any case presents a certain degree of independence and autonomy with respect to the evolving structure, and manifests as a cluster of scientific discoveries that pave the way – on the occurrence of a set of additional conditions in relation to the state of the elements that surround an invention (e.g. structural, social, cultural, etc.) – to the innovation phenomenon, intended as families of *radically new* products due to their intrinsic quality, which the market pervasively establishes and progressively implements. These new products, although maintaining their fundamental characteristics to some degree, are refined by continuous improvements guided by the criteria of marketability, cost and capital/labour savings, industrial and social conflicts, and profitability, and derive from different sources (e.g. formal R&D activities, trial and error, innovation learning-based mechanisms, competition-based mechanisms, quality control, public institutions, etc.), giving rise to the aforementioned movement along the new trajectory. In this progression, continuous recombinations of different forms of knowledge, experience and expertise develop, but also new vocabularies, new techniques and new concepts that generate progressive specialisations. These contribute to moving along the trajectory but also to a narrower view that becomes the basis of resistance to any change of perspective, vision or paradigm.

On movements along the development trajectory of a given paradigm, economic literature agrees on the relevance of innovative activities pursued through R&D and market structure, although pointing out that the consistency of progress is conditioned by the nature of the paradigm, expressed by the opportunity, appropriability and cumulativeness of innovative results (Nelson and Winter, 1982; Winter, 1984; Pavitt, 1984; Sutton, 1998).

The ideas and concepts expressed above shed light on how these models have been affirmed in recent times in the sphere of technology and organisation of work activities; two distinct modes of production that can be considered – albeit with some approximation – as two paradigms. We will begin with organisation since the first of the two discontinuities that we examine in this chapter historically manifests itself in this context.

Organisation and human resources management: from the scientific management paradigm to the Ohnist paradigm

The theoretical framework of reference is that of Taylor (1911) and Ohno (1988), the 'engineers' of the two organisational paradigms (or models) that today contend in the field. Although here we do not discuss in detail the origin of the first paradigm, we analyse the constitutive principles of both their structures together with some attempts at modernising and adapting them to the context (defined, in analogy with the conceptual categories mentioned above, as movements along the trajectory). In particular, in the second we highlight the fundamental elements at the base of the now consumed discontinuity compared to the first, along with some protocols that are still being defined (interpreted, again, as movements along the trajectory).

The principles of Taylorist organisation

It is well known that early Taylorism manifested in the industrial life of America in the second half of the 1800s. Scientific management developed after a harsh economic crisis, with recovery linked to a resurgence of efficiency to contain English and German competition, in a context characterised by low-skilled labour but a rapidly expanding market of products. The elimination of machine and worker wastefulness, together with production concentrated on a few types of product, prompted the constant and rapid pace of workshops. Even before the study of the minimum time needed for a good worker to carry out a job, a set of guiding principles had to be devised that would steer the entire organisation, paradigmatically encoded by Taylor:

1 A clear separation of the execution of work, of problem solving and of conception work.
2 The maximum breakdown of executive work to achieve a fragmentation of elementary tasks monitored with 'time-and-motion' studies (TMS) and to establish the minimum amount of time, movements and tools required.
3 The standardisation of these tasks – also taking into account the supposedly limited cognitive ability of workers to repetitively perform excessively long production cycles – and conferring the status of 'one-best-way' to the solution found. Elementary tasks were aggregated to form workstations with minimum technology, simple (fool-proof) and automated workstations assigned to workers with minimum qualifications, remunerable according to time (hour), with the possible addition of wage premia related to results (*output-oriented incentives*) to derive the maximum efforts possible, thus

achieving the containment of both labour and capital costs (the total cost of production).

4 The vertical division of labour by increasingly specialised tasks and functions to improve procedures and methods, supervision of work execution according to a predetermined plan of instructions (inspectors, team leaders with coordination–command–control tasks, maintenance leaders, etc.), product improvement, marketing, and so forth.
5 The aggregation of the various activities (of execution and coordination–command–control) had to follow the principle (*functional*) of information and technology sharing to exploit economies of scale. From this ensued the configuration of units, offices and departments driven by the criterion of command uniqueness. The most notable representation of this organisational configuration is a series of silos where little communication exists between them.

The corollaries of these principles are:

1 Information circulates in a limited way, intended for individual functional areas, flowing downwards from the top of the hierarchy.
2 Production is driven from upstream to downstream based on *ex-ante* expected market demand.
3 Quality control, if and when implemented, is a specialist function on the final product through statistical procedures.

The management techniques, consistent with the principles of the paradigm, consist of:

1 Management-by-objectives (MBO), according to which the objectives are defined in terms of results (output), ignoring or neglecting the operating processes and modes (input).
2 Standard costing, which distinguishes between direct and indirect costs, and imputes indirect costs – to determine total costs – with an average percentage mark-up on direct costs to cover, for example, the depreciation of plants and indirect personnel costs, without, however, taking into account the actual extent of absorption of these factors in the production of individual products.
3 Budgeting, which focuses on the accounting aspects of financial, instrumental and human resources allocated to the functional organisational unit to achieve pre-established targets, exclusively based on the factors of production and costs rather than on results, and analysis efforts concentrated on the effects rather than the causes of the deviations; all without pursuing resource use efficiency, since the efficiency of a task is resolved *ex-ante* by TMS.

According to Simon (1977), given the complexity and the inevitable mutability and uncertainty of the market, firms could respond in two ways: incorporate flexible response mechanisms or try to stabilise and simplify the environment. The response was the homeostatic control of the environment,[4] consistent with the Taylor–Fordist paradigm that enabled decoupling – through redundancy (e.g. stocks of raw materials, semi-finished products in warehouses, spare parts) – of production (denoted by continuous flow) and the market (characterised by changing demand levels). In terms of simplification, the paradigm responded with prices (profitable) affordable to the demand, thanks to cost reductions achieved through economies of scale, which in turn – keeping prices down – would gradually expand market demand but sacrifice its variability.

Not all the elements that characterise the paradigm, including the corollaries and management techniques, were established and formed at the same time. For example, statistical quality controls were implemented in the Bell Labs in the USA in the 1920s (Shewhart, 1931), while thoughts on the connotations of alienation linked to the execution economy, and on how to address these negative aspects, began with Elton Mayo's experiments of worker involvement at the Western Electric Hawthorne plant in the 1920s (Mayo, 1949). The principle of involvement spread with the human relations movement in the 1930s, while the Scandinavian socio-technical system movement focused on the use of autonomous work groups (which we will also address with the Ohnist paradigm) to humanise work and took place in the 1950s with the aim of solving recruitment and retention problems, to increase job satisfaction (which, if maintained over time, should translate into improved job performance) and to reduce turnover and absenteeism (Trist, 1981). The transition from the involvement of the individual worker to that of all workers through their representatives, to motivate them to pro-actively participate at plant level in the early stages of strategic management decision making and organisational changes, found an innovative solution in the German co-determination system, where the emphasis of labour unions shifted from wage bargaining to job saving.

All these innovations, which could be defined as incremental in scope, constitute an advancement at the margin of the paradigm along a trajectory determined by attempts to remedy the occurrence of inconsistencies, inefficiencies, the inevitable differences between intentions (arising from *principles*) and outcomes, without affecting the underlying principles of the paradigm itself. The results of these advancements are not, however, without controversy, starting from the reviews of psycho-sociologist empirical studies (e.g. Kopelman, 1985) that accredited positive outcomes to work quality, work quantity and reduced absenteeism, to those of economists (e.g., Kochan, Katz and McKersie, 1986, p. 87) who argued that 'there is little empirical support to demonstrate that improving individual attitudes and/or motivation produces lasting economic benefits to organisations'. The underlying reason for these ambiguous results probably lies in the difficulty of controlling for the fact that, for the greater motivation of workers to translate into improved performance for the organisation, requires workers to build their broad (polyvalence and polycompetence) competencies *within* the organisation, exercising these in the production of things that have a sense – due to how they themselves contribute to constructively producing them – so as to fruitfully apply their imagination, intuition and the organisational knowledge acquired in a social participatory organisational structure.

The principles of the Ohnist organisation

The paradigm developed by Ohno (the so-called Toyota system) also took its cue from Taylor's need to improve efficiency by eliminating waste, but this time in the presence of a severe shortage of raw materials, a limited internal market and very fragmented demand. The solution was different, however, and was the result of a genuine reversal of thought (Ohno, 1988): production was usually conceived as a flow that runs from 'upstream' to 'downstream'. Reversing the observation point, the production process was conceived as a 'pull operation' from 'downstream' to 'upstream', taking *only* the items needed and *only* when they were needed. Three other pillars were added in this reversal of perspective that created the discontinuity with the previous paradigm: autonomation (combination of autonomy and automation, also defined by Ohno as 'auto-activation'), just-in-time and diversification economies.

First, auto-activation means delegating responsibility for the quality of the product to the worker (line) starting from the elementary tasks themselves, which implies attributing the worker not only the right but also the obligation to take the appropriate time (also stopping the system if necessary) to ensure the maintenance of quality standards at each stage of production. The conceptual framework of this indication prompted Koike (1994) to highlight that the *principle behind* the design of the individual workplace is radically different: more precisely, it involves abandoning the principle of 'separation' of the Taylor mould (whereby the workstation for unusual operations is next to the workstation intended for usual operations), in favour of the principle of 'integration' (according to which every workstation must be able to carry out 'usual and unusual operations'). The consequences of this principle of integration are:

1 Job competencies are broader and more ample since to the execution of operations defined in advance[5] are added maintenance and machine retooling tasks but most of all diagnostic and problem-solving tasks,[6]which in turn help redefine the 'pre-defined tasks' and the 'requested competencies'. This last component ensures the firm a certain dynamic efficiency, as well as an adaptive efficiency, to the extent that the solutions go far beyond fixing errors with respect to expected standards, with variants, options, upgrades and customisations that the market appreciates. We argue that this circularity should nullify (or mitigate) the 'organisational defensive routines' of Argyris and Schön (1978), precisely the organisational behaviours that tend to justify practical actions, thus preventing having to deal with malfunctions and perplexing, threatening or unexpected situations, which effectively reduce the likelihood of productive learning. Linked to higher labour costs are different types of cost-saving due to the greater professionalism of workers including the lesser need for, and use of, specialist workers, quality control (traditionally applied at the end of the work process to the finished product) and other types of cost-saving that we consider hereinafter.
2 Repeated problem-solving tasks (linked to unusual operations) tacitly expand the intellectual skills of workers (Koike, 1994), with the result that

(first) informal learning is associated with (second) additional cost-savings resulting from reduced recourse to formal training.

3 The suggestions system constitutes the workers' legitimacy to exercise self-reflexivity in the cognitive effort to bring continuous improvements (*kaizen*). This exercise adds stimulus to expanding their abilities and can be further strengthened through economic incentives (input-oriented) that acknowledge learning and skill development.[7] These mechanisms help stimulate the firm's dynamic efficiency.

4 Team and production islands[8] constitute another principle of the Ohnist paradigm. Teamwork is defined as a 'productive unit of work' that through the cooperation of participating members – called upon to individually and collectively undertake but also identify flaws and fix them, and to build and share information and knowledge within the team (according to the four phases of Nonaka and Takeuchi, 1995) – must transfer to the team and to the downstream island a (semi) product that varies according to contingencies but is always considered 'work' (or a piece of work) in Arendt's sense (1958), due to the continuous improvement that the individuals and the team as a whole make.[9] This is clearly in conflict with the Taylor principle of repeatedly 'executing' a predefined set of elementary tasks incorporated in the workstation, which results in the provision of 'labour' in the form of mechanical energy. We argue that in terms of meaning, the former condition places the worker in a position to train in a broader cognitive map, to practise self-reflexivity and restrain opportunism (since his first supervisors are his colleague downstream and his team), to activate subjectivity and develop professionalism (see job rotation in the next point) that contribute to shaping his identity, and to build – starting from work activities and operating – a '*vita activa*' with sense and meaning. In contrast, the latter condition places the worker in a state of estrangement and alienation with respect to the orientation of his efforts. The principle of in-line manufacturing and assembly procedures also changes in favour of a 'U'-shaped organisation, interlocking the islands to facilitate 'passing the baton' (the transfer of semi-manufactured goods from one island to a downstream island) and to define the 'productive units of work' to be assigned to teams.

5 Through job rotation (workers moving from upstream to downstream) within and between teams and production islands, the intellectual but also relational skills of workers are continuously stimulated to expand, thereby generating a (second) informal learning mechanism, from which a second cost-saving ensues in terms of formal training. Job rotation constitutes the mechanism of constructing multi-specialisation and multi-functionalism, through which the worker is able to reduce the defects that have eluded the upstream workstations and contribute indirectly to reducing costs.

Second, just-in-time means programming production from 'downstream', starting with orders already placed by customers: namely, products that have *already* been sold. This is achieved by inverting the Taylor–Ford meaning of 'programmed', according to which as much as possible should be produced in a minimum given time, but now attributing it the value of information coming from the market, converted into instructions and then made operational in production programs through the technique of signals (*kanban*) transported backwards from downstream to upstream. These signals indicate the quantity of products, semi-finished products and raw materials that must systematically flow to the downstream stations. Production is thus pulled by 'demand' in terms of quantity, time and types of product required, and leads to the elimination of stocks of materials, semi-finished products and unsold final products.

Third, the concept of a market where every customer seeks a customised product requires 'production-on-demand' with zero buffer stocks. This entails the possibility of producing multiple versions and multiple objects on a given set of machinery and equipment, which requires speeding up changes in installations and moulds, and their frequent repositioning. This goes against the *principle* of mass production (and associated economies of scale) and against 'dedicated' technology (see below). The solution sought in flexible modular technology goes hand in hand with the multi-specialisation and multi-functionalism of workers.

The corollaries of these principles are:

1 Information now travels horizontally, from the customer to line workers with polyvalent competencies to interpret the commercial information reaching them and then transform it into operating programmes by quickly retooling machines for products already purchased by customers. In the Taylor–Fordist system, instead, commercial information initially travels upwards (i.e. up in the hierarchal direction), to be coded and transformed into operational orders that flow downwards to the production lines.
2 Production is pulled upstream from downstream based on orders the firm has received.
3 Immediate deduction of the combination of the just-in-time and *kanban* principles, which is the reconfiguration of the aggregation of assets that shifts from a 'function' (silos) to a 'process' logic, entailing a shift of the entire sequence of activities aimed at customer satisfaction that pass through the old functional areas. The overall organisational area of the process is put in the hands of a manager (process-owner), who reports directly to the top management; engaging, on the one hand, as a real supplier with the customer and market, and on the other, as a real customer with internal (consisting of those few process support activities that the company chooses to preserve) and external suppliers.
4 Quality control is undertaken in the course of the production process at each stage of advancement of the process itself.

The management techniques consistent with the principles of the new paradigm are:

1 Activity-Based Management (ABM), which foresees paying attention to how activities consume resources (in terms of time, materials, etc.) and how they contribute to achieving customer satisfaction, eliminating downtime,

speeding up the production process throughput (lead-time) and the response to market demand (developing and introducing new products: so-called time-to-market), removing those activities that do not generate added value while continuously improving the operating procedures throughout the process. Lead-times, and especially time-to-market (through Concurrent Engineering (CE) in product development),[10] enable the firm to exploit, in the first part of the life of a new product or its innovations and improvements, the higher (lower) income elasticity of demand (price), obtaining revenue[11] that outweighs the cost of additional flexibility, represented by the adjustment costs and sunk costs linked to the potential irreversibility of the choices made *ex-ante*.

2 Activity-Based Costing (ABC), a procedure estimating the costs of products and services based on the amount of resources actually absorbed (space used, raw materials, machine hours and man-hours), avoiding loading prices with inappropriate costs such as those resulting from the underutilisation of plants and machinery. This enables identifying the available resources that are not absorbed in processes, which will subsequently be reconsidered (in the ABM above) for their removal.

3 Activity-Based Budgeting (ABB), which focuses on activities such as value added, and is expressed as units of budget in relation to the cost of activities. Traditional budgeting focuses on monetary inputs rather than on outputs, does not identify product and customer characteristics, does not support continuous improvement and does not identify waste, which are at the core of ABB.

The slow maturation of these principles, corollaries and mechanisms, which were not simultaneously recognised but nevertheless constitute complementary parts, can be seen as an advancement (irregular or accelerating and decelerating) along a trajectory of the new paradigm, which takes the form of a spiral (under the pressure of a constant trade-off between cost and relative returns) as a result of age, selection and intensity of the organisational variables adopted by firms.

Technologies: from the electro-mechanical to the electronic-computing paradigm

Technological innovation implies solving technological or economic problems and entails discovering – in most cases through tacit knowledge – the reason why a given product or machine tool does not work, or why it is relatively expensive, or how to satisfy a potential or actual need, and to create a new solution (Dosi, 1988, p. 1125). This type of activity takes place within a set of scientific principles and heuristic rules, which define and delimit a pattern of solutions to selected techno-economic problems.[12]

Theoretical references to technology in relation to organisation are numerous and more distributed over time, in the sense that the industrial artefact or technological tool takes shape as a result of repeated attempts to achieve increasing levels of precision and functionality with respect to specific requirements and specific functions, and experimenting with different materials. Military requirements for guns have certainly been a good driver of the advancement of metalworking technologies in recent history: the case of North's milling machine in 1818 in the USA is well known, made universal by Howe in 1852 and soon becoming a world standard (Ayres, 1990). The same can be said for the advent of the steam-engine, and the coke-based puddling–rolling process to convert pig iron into bar (wrought) iron for engineering purposes (Ayres, 1990), allowing overtaking of the power of human muscles. The rapid adoption of electric power-generating plants brought about a reduction in the cost (and, subsequently, the price) of electric power, favoured by large (and efficient) steam turbines located at a central power plant, which crowded out the relatively small and inefficient localised (on-site) plants.

The electro-mechanical paradigm

The combination of the theoretical and hands-on aspects of electrical, mechanical and fluid power gave rise to devices that carry out operations with moving parts known as electromechanical parts. An example is the relay device,[13] widely used in complicated subsystems. In general, the growing demand for machinery capable of forming and cutting iron (e.g. rolling mills, lathes, grinding and stamping machines) – equipped with electromechanical devices – led to large-scale production, which led to the greater decomposition of tools (and at a later stage, of products: e.g. reaper, sewing machine, bicycle, typewriter, car, etc.) into a larger numbers of components, in turn requiring the greater specialisation of high-precision machine tools to produce these components (and guarantee the *interchangeability* of each component).

The *principle* that dominated was still that of machine tools *dedicated* to specific operations, exclusively controlled by humans (semi-skilled workers): namely, machine tools with the capacity to perform repetitively a sequence of prescribed actions, usable in industrial production to pursue economies of scale. Soon the use of electromechanical technology as a means of overcoming the limits of human muscles came to substitute these human muscles and *manual abilities*. If manufactured products could previously be easily assembled by one man in a few minutes, and when necessary the components could be *manually fitted* by the same man, production complexity soon began to increase as a result of 1) the increase in product characteristics, 2) the greater decomposition of a given product into many small and simple components (Taylor's principle), and 3) the greater specialisation of high-precision machine tools that guaranteed the standardisation (i.e. interchangeability) of parts and components, which drastically reduced manual fitting and consequently various professional competencies.

All this prompted the use of complex but *standardised subassemblies*, through the agency of inventions such as ball-bearing assembly, spoked wheels, gear changers and roller-chains, and progressively led to significant economies of scale (Giedion, 1969).

In the second half of the 1800s, the car took the place of the gun industry as a technological driver (American Machinist, 1977; Rosenberg, 1976) as a result of two factors: first, the decentralisation of mechanical power from large, immobile central steam engines to small, mobile internal-combustion engines (invented by the Germans) or even more dispersed electric motor drives; and second, the sheer complexity, which required the assembly of a huge number of parts and components (most produced elsewhere) by specialised suppliers and subcontractors. Ford contributed greatly with his moving assembly line ('bringing the work to the man'), which on one hand imposed a mechanical order on the production process, and on the other forced assembly workers to pace their work to the motion of the line. His contribution continued first with the mechanical link between specialised machines (though not originally designed to be compatible) by means of a (dedicated) transfer machine, and second with the organisation of all major machining operations into a single, synchronous line, obtaining a considerable reduction of labour and an increased utilisation of capital. The *sine qua non* condition was standardisation, which implied *dramatically cutting flexibility* to pursue economies of scale by means of mass production.

The microprocessor-based technologies paradigm: from the origin of CIM to ERP and ICT

The increased complexity of production, also due to the increase in product characteristics, was soon transformed into increased demand for a variety of models and products. Mass production at first attempted to contain and counter such demand by decoupling – as mentioned earlier – production and the market. The persistent retail consumer's demand for variety generated tension among manufacturers in search of some feasible solution. Among the many innovations pursued by firms (cutting tools and tool materials, casting and forging technology, powder metallurgy, etc.), the most relevant was certainly the *flexible nature of the technology*. Punched paper or magnetic tape controls for machine tools were the key to opening the door to a new technological paradigm: applied in the first instance to feed data to milling machines (American Machinist, 1977) and accomplished by what was, in fact, rudimentary and highly dedicated digital technology – namely, the numerical control machine (NC). With strong impetus from the development of semiconductor-switching elements, this became the computerised numerical control machine (CNC), which was capable of carrying out a sequence of operations on a single part and using different tools. The simultaneous control of a number of independent stand-alone NC machines by a single computer initially generated *machining centres* (called CAM: computer-aided manufacturing), consisting of (at least) a CNC machine tool, a workpiece store, work- and tool-handling devices, and an automatic control and supervision subsystem. Thereafter it generated *flexible manufacturing systems* (FMS), containing several automated (CNC) machine tools of either a universal or specific type, flexible manufacturing islands and, when necessary, additional manual or automated work stations, as a consequence of the parallel development of software, which cut programming time for CNC and FMS systems. An obvious extension was automatic tool changing to make a group of multipurpose machines producing a wide variety of different products more efficient and improve the cost/performance ratio; this was achieved by incorporating into a single machine tool all the machining operations needed for a given part.

The parallel (albeit autonomous) developments of robots (in the handling process versions, especially welding and assembly) and CAD (computer-aided design) were channelled and absorbed by the increasingly complex and sophisticated FMS, thanks to progressively overcoming problems arising from non-common standards and lack of interfaces in the sphere of material flows and information flows. The reason for these developments was in the first instance a reduction in the use of unskilled and semi-skilled labour, and secondly, the shortening of lead-times from design to production and in perfecting the product design.

The improvement of sensors and actuators made robots and other production equipment more versatile, quicker and more exact than human beings. The advancement of the paradigm, with progress, improvements and incremental innovations, took place on the one hand under the pressure of the level of changes in demand for consumer goods, by the capital equipment itself as well as by the relative prices (i.e. so-called market-mechanism inducements), and on the other hand, from the combination of opportunity, appropriability and complementary technologies incorporated in individual capital equipment.

The substitution of electronic sensors for human eyes and ears, and computers (to some extent, through expert systems) for human brains, at least in certain categories of routine on-line manufacturing operations, and in a wide range of equipment (amongst other things, increasingly small-scale), initiated – from a technological point of view – the transition from the old electro-mechanical paradigm towards a new paradigm founded on microprocessor-based technologies.

The off-line functions directly linked to on-line functions led to the evolution of production into a real *computer integrating manufacturing* (CIM) system, interconnecting hardware and software, starting from ideas up to customers, by means of design, production, production control, quality control, product delivery and so forth. This provided a glimpse of the concept of being able to achieve an 'unmanned factory', able to cope with time-based competition and product variety, two cornerstones of the modern economy. The benefits were fuelled by three expectations: labour and capital saving, increasing capacity and product quality improvement.

The technological determinism (or techno-centric approach) underlying CIM prompted the gradual emergence of several intractable problems over the 1990s, on one hand shattering the illusion that an error-free system could be constructed, capable of managing the unforeseen in its subsequent concatenated and uncontrolled failure, and on the other fostering the emergence of the fragility of the aforementioned production–market decoupling, in the face of the unavoidable and persistent instability of the competitive environment and the uncertainty in production process management.

In relation to the first issue, despite significant advances in this field, technical systems broke down frequently and the costs of such interruptions were high. These systems aimed to ensure the automatic exchange of information without the intervention of a human operator; they were created and developed in a unified and integrated way, compatible with a hierarchical and stable environment (or presumed as such, based on the production–market decoupling), and characterised by aversion towards industrial relations. These systems were certainly adjustable and improvable, but only with the intervention of professional engineers and technicians – who became the de facto repository of production know-how to the detriment of production workers – to assess situations, to interpret the system crashes, to analyse the choices and to make decisions without technological or artificial intelligence apparatuses being able to replace them. The fundamental limitation of CIM was dealing with information in terms of a set of *bits* (binary digits), neglecting the semantic dimension, in line with the mathematical theory of communication that postulated 'semantic aspects of communication are irrelevant to the engineering problem' (Shannon, 1948, p. 379).

In relation to the second issue (the fragility of production–market decoupling), instability and uncertainty required higher levels of delegation and consistent decision-making autonomy to satisfy the changes sought by the market as quickly as possible. However, the very emergence of technological breakdowns at times implied changes in, if not redesigns of, the processes that required a different structure of interdependencies; changes that were diagnosed and implemented by operators who were near the workstations, but who at the same time had to battle with the economy of time.

In any case, investments in capital-intensive and sophisticated technologies were always expected to overcome deep-seated structural problems.

Two events marked a deviation in the evolutionary path of the techno-centred approach: the Japanese approach to CIM, more human-centred; and the taking-off of MRP (Material Resource Planning), which became the modern ERP (Enterprise Resource Planning).

Regarding the Japanese humanising approach, the *principle* is that in the face of instability and uncertainty the most flexible element in the technological system is the people who make it work: that is, the motivation of engineers, technicians and workers on the shop floor who are familiar with the system. From this principle follows a more frugal approach to technology compared to the massive investments of Western companies, preferring – as rule – gradual improvements in the production process and in quality rather than sophisticated installations (Ayres and Ebel, 1990).

As far as the second event (MRP) is concerned, this started as a conventional short-term forecast tool of demand and a computation of all the implications (materials, decisions on whether to make or buy, purchase orders to outside suppliers, etc.), thereafter evolving into a new generation of management software (MRP_II) that included orders and production cycles, and allowed verifying that the production hours needed for work and for the human machine did not exceed availability, to then arrive at the modern ERP: namely, a set of integrated tools for the management of all the information in a productive organisation of goods or services, from research to production, from finance to marketing, and from suppliers to customers. These new management systems have not yet acquired a unanimous definition – with different variations in the last decade from both the conceptual and technological infrastructure perspectives, designed to provide the functional capability required to turn the ERP concept into a reality (see the survey carried out by Nazemi, Tarokh and Djavanshir, 2012). However, empirical literature agrees, based on an analysis of the main software packages in the world market (SAP, Oracle, Baan, Peoplesoft, Edwards, etc.), on accrediting the *principle* underlying the development of these systems, using as a point of reference firm organisational design based on processes (conceived by Ohno) rather than on functions (Taylor) to capture organisation-wide information, with minimum redundancy. This means that a firm seeking sustainable competitive advantages by adopting ERP must re-engineer the entire organisation, from the organisational layout to responsibilities and from coordination mechanisms to the role of human resources, otherwise implying the total failure of the entire investment (Christensen, 1997; Umble, Haft and Umble, 2003; Aloini, Dulmin and Mininno, 2007; Shaul and Tauber, 2013).

The excitement around the new technology, in the form of ERP, but especially ICT (information and communication technologies), in respect of which the term 'general purpose technologies' (GPTs) was coined (Bresnahan and Trajtenberg, 1995) to denote their enormous adaptability and ubiquity, peaked at the turn of the twentieth and twenty-first centuries and then began to decline with the 'dot-com' bubble. The decline of the exuberance for the supposed economic value of activities related to these technological solutions did not, however, stop the spread of ICT, especially in the service sector, although its rate was lower than expected and more varied in space and heterogeneous in time. The reasons were to be found in underestimating the social, political and institutional factors (for example, social injustice, educational policies and different degrees of trade barriers and obstacles to the flow of capital) that created *resistance* to the smooth adoption of ICT, similarly to what occurred in prior regime changes (Perez, 2002; Freeman, 2007). Among the obstacles to change, a significant role was played by the standardisation of the interfaces of various components of ICT and by more appropriate cultural aspects.

With regard to the first point (standardisation), single ICT innovations such as an artefact or device or even a software improvement seldom 'stand alone' (like other technological or organisational innovations) and consequently have to be integrated with existing and other newly emerging technologies; it follows that compatibility standardisation plays a central role in how technological opportunities are exploited: namely, the rate and direction of this exploitation. Market competition *per se* does not lead to a convergence of standards, even taking into account that the key determinants of costs (and the underlying economies of scale, of scope and of industrial coordination)[14] guide the firm's decisions and those of the demand (governed to a great extent by 'interdependency', since the demand of one user depends upon the choices made by other users).[15]

Schumpeterian competition *per se* in fact pushes in the direction of diversifying innovations, unless market processes are guided by either industrial policy, or (inter)governmental organisations that induce compatibility standards by virtue of greater expected social welfare, or again governed by coalitions of firms that 'sponsor' standards in view of greater firm opportunities and market growth. In these contexts, long-term improvements in the quality of standards occur at the cost of short-term losses to users of what will become obsolete standards, as and when superior and incompatible standards emerge.

In terms of the cultural aspects, even though the continuous overloaded flows of (bits of) *infotainment* (sounds, images, data) are far from being a universally (centralised) asserted culture, and closer to a globally produced customised product, locally selected by individuals (Castells, 1996, p. 341), these continuous overloaded flows give the impression of democratic *participation* in creative activities and inter-personal relationships. On the other side of the coin, the risk cannot be ignored that modern ICT gives rise to a real 'appropriation of technological subjectivity' if the cognitive, communications and relational competencies of individuals are not adequately developed at the level of the new and sophisticated communication mechanisms, so as to make sense, construct and communicate understanding in a world of great dissonances and ambiguities, which ICT on one hand contributes to creating and on the other can help resolve.

However, no one can fail to see that – precisely starting from the fact that we are entering into the second machine age, where thinking machines nourished by artificial intelligence are capable of dealing with pattern recognition,[16] complex communication[17] and other domains traditionally considered human fields,[18] and where most people on the planet are connected via a common digital network (Brynjolfsson and McAfee, 2014) – the firm decision-maker may again be tempted by the technical-centric path. Efficiency is at the centre of concern, which in the background sustains the concept of information as equivalent to a signal (a *bit* or their combination) and ends up attributing excessive importance to the information process itself[19] rather than to the human-centric path that rests on the idea that information has not only a syntactic but also a semantic dimension. The focus is on the meaning conveyed by the message and on the fact that the semantic dimension is activated by an interpreter – endowed with a cognitive system (i.e. resources to interpret signals, holding beliefs and acquiring knowledge) – and by a process of interpretation. The meaning can evolve and has a decisive role in the construction and production of knowledge (Dretske, 1981) and, in the end, knowledge – because of the interaction that occurs between language and human action in terms of the subject's 'intentionality' and 'involvement' – orients the action (Searle, 1969) with a focus on effectiveness rather than efficiency.

Support for the techno-centred path, and the vertical configuration of the organisation, could be provided by the ambiguous role that ICT plays if these technologies were to be 'bent' in the direction of communication (CT) rather than information (IT), which could be the result of a cost and performance effect, but also of the *Weltanschauung* of top management with respect to defining their prerogatives. Using data on manufacturing firms in the USA and Europe, Bloom and Garicano (2013) show that information technologies (in this case, ERP and CAD/CAM) are associated with greater autonomy and a wider span of control, while technologies that improve communication (such as data intranets) decrease autonomy for workers and plant managers. The technological evolution in this field, enabled by the wishes and choices of firms and the varying adoption of ICT technologies and content, may propel firms towards one organisational structure rather than another. What the theory of complementarities highlights (below) is that the emphasis on CT is more compatible with the Taylor–Fordist organisational design system, while IC is more compatible with the Ohnist system.

We began this section by stating that military requirements for guns were undeniably a good driver of technological advancements, thereafter passing the baton to the automotive industry. However, we would not want to create the impression that all the good technological things available today are the result of animal spirits and venture capitals that stimulate the private sector of the economy. The need to win wars (during the Second World War and the Cold War era) has always provided a strong impetus for technological innovation, pushing the entrepreneurial state (mainly the USA, but not only) through its agencies, its orders (for manufactured goods but also problem solving), and its regulatory functions in mobilising innovation in many sectors, from semiconductors to computers, from the internet to GPS, from jet planes to civilian nuclear energy, from lasers to bio-and nanotechnologies, in order 'to bridge the gap between blue-sky academic work, with long time horizons, and the more incremental technological development occurring with the military' (Mazzucato, 2013, p. 75) to strengthen technological capabilities for national security.

Complementarity, substitution and performance 'chemistry'

From a historical perspective, empirical evidence shows that the great majority of firms use a mixed collection of elements of old and new technologies, and old and new organisational characteristics, adopted to different degrees and belonging to different steps of sequential paths along which the elements have been adopted. It is, however, very likely that the huge reduction of prices in ICT-based equipment in the last two decades has contributed in the first instance to the relatively greater investments in new technologies than in organisation, rendering the lacking organisational innovations a barrier to additional investments in ICT technologies (Bugamelli and Pagano, 2004) or holding back technological investments while awaiting the development or the adoption of complementary innovations (Rosenberg, 1976).

The empirically observable performance of a working paradigm is not only ascribable to theoretical efficiency or to the intensity of incremental adoption of innovations along the trajectory, but also to social practices in the ongoing use and change of technologies or workplace organisational designs (Bijker, Hughes and Pinch, 1987); more precisely, how people – as they interact with a technology or organisational prescription, or both – enact the structure that shapes their emergent and situated use of these tools. Orlikoswki (2000, p. 408), focusing on technology, suggests a practical lens to view its use as a process of enactment that enables deeper understanding of the constitutive role of social practices.

She points to a useful distinction between *technology as artefact* (the bundle of material and symbolic properties packaged in some socially recognisable form, e.g. hardware, software, techniques) and the *use of technology* (what people actually do with the technological artefact in their recurring, situated practices). From this emerges the fact that technological knowledge is, at a given time, what the practice has made it, in that the users appropriate the technology 'ignoring certain properties or inventing new ones that may go beyond or even contradict designers' expectations and inscriptions' (Orlikoswki, 2000, p. 407). This occurs because they approach a new technology based on their previous experience with other technologies and their participation in workplace communities.[20] More precisely, the process of using the technology involves users interacting with 'facilities' (such as the properties of the technological artefact), 'norms' (such as protocols for using the technology) and 'interpretive schemes' (such as the skills, knowledge and assumptions of the technology that the user has). Following Marengo (1996), one can add that to manage and become familiar with a new tool, a worker has to collect all relevant information on its technical, functional and management aspects; this activity is costly not only from an economic perspective, as it takes time away from productive activity in a strict sense, but also from a cognitive perspective, since the information must be processed and interpreted. This activity can be restricted by considerations of expediency, convenience and economic and cognitive limitations, thereby generating a *knowledge gap* between what individuals know and the technological information available to them, as well as a *problem-solving gap* between the complexity of this information and the ability to manage it effectively and efficiently and reach a solution.[21]

These kinds of arguments, used to support the plausibility of the hypothesis of bounded rationality against the neoclassical assumption of unbounded rationality, enable understanding of the reason why two groups enact diverse technologies-in-practice using the same tool. It is precisely because different users choose to enact the same technological artefact in different ways, in so doing potentially limiting the ability of the technology to deliver the organisational benefits that were expected from the system. It follows that the presumption that technology and humans are essentially different and separate realities is a useful expedient only to isolate analytically the intrinsic characteristics of the subject under analysis. However, for an empirical assessment, the presumption of separateness may be misleading in that it prevents understanding of the temporally emergent socio-material realities that shape contemporary organisations (Orlikoswki, 2010). This risk is appreciable when moving from a speculative to an empirical dimension, from a theoretical achievement to its implementation, and particularly to the diffusion and adoption of a given innovation.

In our view, Orlikowski's argument with reference to technology also holds for theoretical organisational design and human resources practices.

A sphere where the significance of these considerations can be measured is that of complementarity between different technological devices, or between different organisational practices, belonging to the same paradigm. The same relevance also, and above all, emerges in complementarity between technology and organisation. With reference to the historically manifested situation, two technological and organisational paradigms were combined and intertwined, giving rise to the four different outcomes (Figure 13.1).

Quadrant A is the combination of the organisational capital (OK) in the Taylor–Fordist mould and the technological capital (TK) of the electromechanical paradigm that historically dominated the way in which industrial firms operated until the mid-1990s, with high-volume mass production of standardised products, and cumulative gains in productivity by means of economies of scale.[22]

Quadrants B and C represent the combinations pursued by firms in the second half of the 1990s, favouring the change of only one of the constituent factors: the replacement of the technological paradigm with the electro-electronics paradigm (in the case of Western companies), and the organisational paradigm of lean organisation with the Taylor–Fordist (in the case of Japanese companies). In the first case, the driving factor was the replacement of employment with technological capital in the unmanned factory perspective; in the second case, it was the variability of products and their quality in the customer centrality perspective.

The past three decades have witnessed the significant efforts of many Japanese companies to incorporate into their business processes – even if frugally – ERP/ICT technologies, thus moving from quadrant C to quadrant D; several

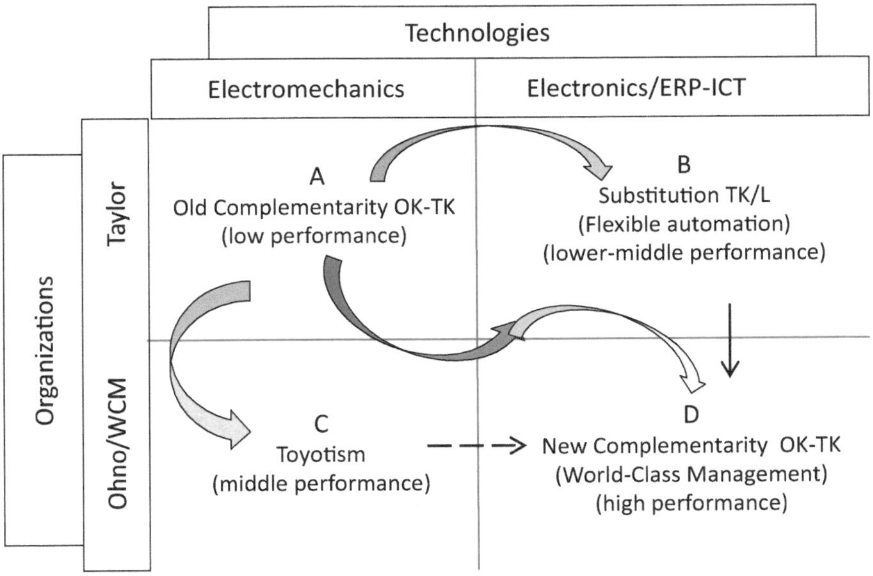

Figure 13.1 The combination of organisational and technological paradigms

Source: Author's computations

Western companies (particularly in the USA) moved differently, increasingly re-engineering the organisation along processes and simultaneously adopting work practices consistent with the lean principles (thus moving from C to D).

Quadrant D is the new winning combination (so-called Word-Class Manufacturing), capable of ensuring top performance by combining flexible technology and flexible internal organisation, and able to satisfy (efficiently and effectively) global markets, characterised by high volatility and substantial uncertainty. The nature of the new technologies allows the involvement of the service sector for the first time in history, traditionally regarded as 'residual' with respect to innovation dynamics and thus changing the WCM acronym into World-Class Management. [23]

A formalisation of the possible combinations of technology and organisation through the mathematical concepts of convexity and concavity for the study of optimality conditions requires the assumption of hypotheses that are hardly plausible, such as the infinite divisibility of choices and the possibility that a choice may be exercised on a single variable (from which it emerges that the effect on performance of a marginal increase of the selected variables decreases to become negative). Not only the non-divisibility (e.g., of plants, but also of certain organisational practices) but also the economies of scale and learning are incompatible with the concavity of the objective function.

An analysis of the transitions between states may prove to be a useful tool, but the situations described in the previous sections are of a 'non-ergodic' nature – for example, path dependency (and therefore turning to non-ergodic Markov chains) – while also having characteristics that are incompatible with the Markovian 'memoryless' property, since they relate to events that occur in the form of stochastic sequential processes (David, 2001). Consider, for example, the information imperfections, the knowledge gap and problem-solving gap, the regulatory institutional regime and structural inertia put forward in our analysis. Consequently, we should empirically specify non-Markovian processes, specifically discrete-time stochastic processes, to give account of dynamic economic processes where history does not always matter in the same way. However, the quantity and quality of information needed to be able to undertake such an econometric test render it prohibitive for now.

For illustrative purposes, we limit ourselves here to using a graphic representation of the problem similar to that used by Roberts (2004, Chapter 2) based on the concept of 'locally best' positioning in a mountainous area that is formed by several ridges interspersed with plateaus (see Figure 13.2).

The representation refers to the plurality of positions of companies as a reflection of their efficiency. Assuming, for simplicity, that TFP is the performance measure of interest, and that this is in some way a function of the different combinations of technology and organisation, and that all these factors are heterogeneous due to their intrinsic characteristics, the topographic image is a series of optimal 'local' positions that are higher or lower than others, each of which reflects a certain 'consistency' of the various ingredients used. Simply put, in our case, optimality represents the most efficient combinations of local

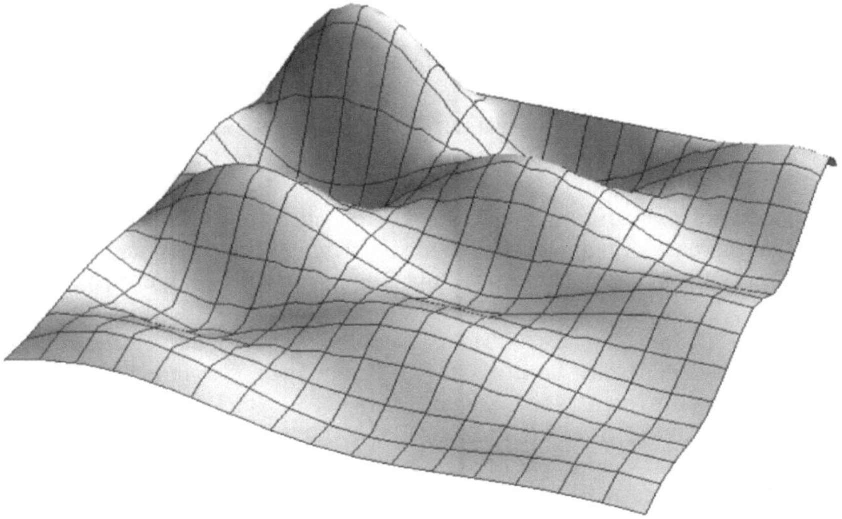

Figure 13.2 Non-concavity and multiplicity of positioning of 'local' congruence

Source: Author's computations

positions with respect to technology and organisation: each different combination gives rise to lower performance, and it is likely that combinations around the optimal local position – being less efficient – are transient in nature, and subject to small movements towards the most efficient local position. Local positions are the result of several variables, such as chances and choices, constraints, prohibitive adjustment costs in the combination and intensity of investments in the two factors, different degrees of coherence between the characteristics of the factors themselves (old and new technologies, old and new organisational practices), and different degrees of connection between the complementary variables (tightly or loosely coupled). Therefore, it is as if the firm were in a state of lock-in, in a trapping region from which it can exit only with a radical and coordinated change of both factors, or with the intervention of external forces.

If we introduce a third element, time (and therefore the occurrence of improvements but also the rupture in the paradigms of the intrinsic characteristics of each of the factors that combine), we may observe a change in the entire topography. This occurs due to the different dynamics in the variables that determine the positions and where classic variables involved in major changes interact, such as inertia, resistance, time and the difficulty of moving from a 'local' learning domain to another far away, and so forth. The firms themselves may thus eventually find different positions in the distribution, resulting in a completely different topographic profile.

Empirical evidence supporting the above-mentioned categories is abundant, even if the analyses and econometric estimates were undertaken without unravelling or specifying the qualitative scope of the stochastic sequential processes underlying the explained outcomes. To mention but a few:

1 On complementarities among different technological devices – in other words, the company-wide integration of all computer systems – we refer to Sethi and Sethi (1990) and Kovács and Haidegger (1992) for CIM, and to Dery et al. (2006), Aloini, Dulmin and Mininno (2007) and Shaul and Tauber (2013) for ERP.
2 On complementarity within resource management practices as well as organisational design, see, for example, Ichniowski, Shaw and Prennushi (1997), Black and Lynch (2004) and Boning, Ichniowski and Shaw (2007) for the USA; Patterson et al. (1997) and Guest et al. (2003) for the UK; Bauer (2003) and Zwick (2004) for Germany; Greenan and Guellec (1998), and Janod and Saint-Martin (2004) on French data; Caroli and Van Reenen (2001) on both French and UK data; Cristini et al. (2003), Piva, Santarelli and Vivarelli (2005), Mazzanti, Pina and Tortia (2006), Colombo, Delmastro and Rabbiosi (2007) and Leoni (2012) for Italy; Bloom and Van Reenen (2010) for several industrialised and non-industrialised countries; and Rizov and Croucher (2008) for European firms.
3 On the simultaneous and sequential complementarity between technology and work organisation, see Greenan (1996a, 1996b), Hitt and Brynjolfsson (1997), Black and Lynch (2001), Bresnahan, Brynjolfsson and Hitt (2002), Brynjolfsson, Hitt and Yang (2002), Brynjolfsson and Hitt (2003), Colombo and Delmastro (2002), Bartel, Ichniowski and Shaw (2007), Cristini, Gaj and Leoni (2008), Bloom, Sadun and Van Reenen (2012) and Battisti, Colombo and Rabbiosi (2014).
4 On a sequential paths analysis along which work practices belonging to the organisational paradigm are adopted, see Freeman, Kleiner and Ostroff (2000) and Lynch (2007). It is very likely that similar paths of adoption for technological devices exist: unfortunately, to the best of our knowledge, no research paper has yet been published on this issue.
5 On the Orlikowski effect, see Cainarca, Massa and Testa (2005) and Dery, Hall and Wailes (2006).

Leoni (2013) undertook a survey of part of the above-listed literature through a critical narrative review, arriving at a provisional positive conclusion indicating that each paradigm and above all each combination of technological and organisational paradigms – once affirmed as superior with respect to the predecessors – developed along not necessarily linear trajectories due to the effect of the different mechanisms operating within firms and the varying weights thereof, giving rise to divergent spiral paths of firm growth. A relevant tool to interpret these outcomes is the complementary theory on groups of activities formalised by Milgrom and Roberts (1990) into a non-differentiable, non-convex, profit-maximisation model of a monopolistic (or a monopolistically competitive) firm. The defining characteristic of a given group of complements is that, if the levels of any subset of activities are increased, then the marginal return to increases in any or all of the remaining activities increases. For example, a number of flexibility aspects are represented in the model by way of including such variables as the number of product improvements per product per period, design cost per product improvement, setup costs on newly changed products, number of setups per period, and delivery time. Milgrom and Roberts use purely algebraic (lattice-theoretic) methods to argue that performance over time generates many of the observed patterns (or bundles of characteristics) that mark modern manufacturing. However, we argue that a new organisational or technological performance practice or a new performance bundle of practices is the result not only of different ingredients but also of the different weights of each ingredient. Hence, the employer has two levers to pursue in the search for efficiency and performance: the ingredients and their intensity of application in potentially innumerable combinations. For example, if one considers the impact on performance of a bundle composed of three work practices, measured with respective coefficients (three main effects and four interactive effects), in the presence of continuous variables, the marginal return depends on the value of each work practice: namely, the intensity of the adoption, which is firm specific. It follows that one obtains different results when reducing or increasing the mean value of one or more practices, or else when enlarging (to four practices) or restricting (to two practices) the bundle.

This idea opens up a completely new perspective in the world of organisational and technological conceptualisations with respect to those relating to simple complementarity, but also with respect to substitution governed by relative prices, reaching a powerful techno-organisational configuration as a result of an 'internal chemistry of the firm' (Grandori and Furnari, 2008), and factors of a dynamic nature such as 'social capabilities' (Abramowitz, 1989), which primarily include learning and knowledge creation in the human-centred version of technology and organisation. These are primary internal sources of innovation that are not easily transferable and require – to become powerful – appropriate workplace design, specific new work practices and organisational well-being (usually, good and trusting industrial relations), which research has recently empirically identified and documented as improving firm performance, worker competencies and innovations.

Some open empirical questions

A great problem with respect to firm performance and growth is the lack of understanding of the complementarity first within the technological and organisational paradigms and secondly among the two paradigms that must be in place at the firm level. It is not easy to answer the question of whether one combination is tangibly more efficient and more profitable than others, tested by robust and incontrovertible estimates, since researchers have to battle with a set of ambiguities, aporias and methodological doubts that still exist in empirical literature and which are worth reviewing briefly.

Subjective versus objective measures

The evaluation of organisational design, activated work practices and technology-in-use, as well as some performance measures (in the case of plants), originate from interviews with business managers or workplace supervisors and as such reflect subjective judgements that may conflict with objective evaluations.

There are essentially two reasons to use subjective measures: on the one hand, the economic character of the information collected through questionnaires, strictly combined with information on organisational design, work practices and technology-in-use; on the other, the impossibility of otherwise observing practices or performance relating to the single site of a multi-sited firm. In many firms, work practices, organisational design and technology differ considerably across workplaces or sites, thus suggesting that the analysis of the elements under study should always be as homogeneous as possible.

Both cases require facing the problem of a potential measurement error in the variables relating to performance. On this issue, it would however be useful to take into account the scepticism of mainstream economic theory in mistrusting the subjectivist approach because of the absence of a set metrics, be it a quantitative scale or even any universal point of origin. Of particular importance in surveys is modulating questions with respect to not only the presence or the absence of a given element, but also the real observed behaviour of individuals, since performance does not concern firm policy towards investments in given elements, but what has actually been implemented and how and what workers do (Green, 2006, p. 10).

Single rater versus multiple raters: is measurement error a significant issue?

The question of the potential measurement error in subjective evaluations is coupled with that of the reliability of a single respondent to be able to assess – as the investigation unit increases – the actual practices in place in the various departments and offices. The alternative would be the use of several evaluators (raters), one for each organisational sub-unit. However, in microeconometrics, reliability is also undermined by other sources, such as the incorrect coding of correct responses and the use of a correctly measured variable as a proxy for another theoretically valid but unobserved variable. All these doubts disappear with aggregate data because it is usually assumed that aggregation results in counterbalancing the measurement errors of the opposite sign, while measurement errors persist in individual-level data. If this were true, then the independent variables that enter the relation between work organisation, technology and performance would be characterised by random errors, preventing the identification of the parameters of interest.

Under these conditions, the parameters of a given relation estimated with the OLS method are distorted (Cameron and Trivedi, 2005, Chapter 26) and thus requires making use of the IV method (instrumental variables), with the difficult problem of finding the appropriate instruments: namely, passing all the validity tests of the instruments themselves and the orthogonality of the explanatory variables. In the case of failure – given that the coefficients are consequently not identifiable – the researcher should first limit the target-testing hypothesis to whether the effect size of the coefficients of interest is different from zero, and secondly, identify the consistent bounds by reverse regressions, searching for lower and upper bounds on the values of the true slope coefficients in order to provide the magnitude of the effect.

However, researchers usually simply bypass the argument by assuming (implicitly or explicitly) that as the investigated unit size increases, the process of filling out the questionnaire involves more than one respondent. Survey designers should be encouraged to improve their efforts in this direction, explicitly requesting that each section of the questionnaire be filled out – under the supervision of a senior manager – by key informants and thus pursuing, *ex-ante*, the greater precision and objectivity of the data gathered.

The question of minimum firm size

Assuming a link between bundles of techno-organisational ingredients and improved economic performance, one can speculate whether this also applies to small firms, usually left out of the sample survey based on the argument that organisation in small firms takes on very informal connotations and as such is difficult to identify and quantify. Should this be the case, one could argue that firm size is therefore a 'contingent' factor (a typical argument of contingency theories). Conversely, one could counter-argue that the effectiveness of a series of bundles could depend on the fact that 'other' managerial practices must be active, which in small organisations may not be implementable. If so, then the discourse should not be so much about contingent factors, as about the impossibility of extending the bundles 'practised'.

Different characterisations of the constructs underlying survey questionnaires

One aspect to be carefully considered in using survey databases is the different constructs that underlie questionnaires designed to identify organisational unit policies on organisational design, technology and human resources with respect to questionnaires aimed at identifying what actually happens (in practice) in a given organisational unit. This may be interpreted as a semantic question, but it is not. The first characterisation tends to depict the project of change, which may only be partially implemented; this could be relevant for studies on adoptions of new practices, where it would be very useful to identify the degree of implementation of the project and any resistance to change. The second characterisation has the advantage of being appropriate for the techno-organisational and performance relation, since it tends to measure the real behaviours, organisational traits and technology-in-practice that most directly affect outcomes. Moreover, this is likely to incorporate less distortion in relation to the respondent's perception, since the questions tend towards measuring the phenomena actually practised.

Bundling single practices to represent a multi-dimensional concept

It is not uncommon in numerous surveys to see single respondents being asked to provide a single numerical rating that describes a given practice or a given technological device used. It is unlikely that broad and profound concepts cannot be reliably measured with a single question (or single item), asking whether or not a given practice is implemented, or a given technological tool is used, while a sequence of specific questions is more suitable to portray several dimensions of a given practice. Naturally, the end user of a survey is constrained by the survey designer's choices upstream of the process.

As an example, some questionnaires ask respondents whether or not there is a 'joint consultative committee' concerned with consultation in their organisational unit. Other questionnaires go further, asking, for example, how often meetings are held (indicating a rising number, for a given period), what proportion of meetings were attended by senior management (again, indicating a rising percentage, sometimes in size-bands) and what issues had been discussed (again, listing a varying number of issues). Unfortunately, however, the metrics used change from questionnaire to questionnaire, with the risk of providing a different empirical picture even if apparently under the same or a similar construct. There are two main ways of combining individual practices to represent a multi-dimensional phenomenon. The first is an additive index that summarises several items, generally expressed in terms of dichotomy dummies: the outcome forms a scalar variable that depicts a given single practice for each single organisational unit; alternatively, a factor analysis can also be used. The latter, which is very popular, may consist of exploratory or confirmatory factor analyses, forming orthogonal and one-dimensional factors. This method is mainly used to transform single practices into bundles of practices. A bundle refers to a systematic interrelationship (that is, mutually reinforcing the effects of multiple elements) among the variables under investigation, and to the extent to which it is confirmed by factor analysis, is equivalent to 'internal' complementarity among the various ingredients (or variables) that form the bundle.

Adoption of changes: altogether simultaneously or a sequence of adoptions?

Have new technological and/or organisational ingredients that form a bundle, identified at the time of a survey, been adopted by the firm simultaneously, or does each simply constitute a step along a sequential process of adoption? In the latter case, is the sequential process the same for all the adopting firms, or is there a specific sequential process for each form? These are still open and relevant questions. On the one hand, the existence of different initial conditions, or different constraints or even the different worldviews of managers, could induce each firm to start the process of change by adopting different ingredients with different intensity with respect to other firms, so that the bundles identified at a point in time (precisely, at the time of the survey) reflect the heterogeneity of adoptions among firms in terms of both number and intensity of ingredients adopted. On the other hand, one might imagine that the path along which adoption starts and is completed is unique, but each firm, for a number of reasons, starts the adoption process at different historical times. The cross-sectional picture that emerges would be observationally equivalent to the previous picture but would in fact reflect a different adoption process. Unfortunately, the temporal dimension of studies on workplace changes typically suffers from poor data, since no information on the time of adoption of each ingredient is usually available.

All this complicates the framework of analysis: let us imagine that firm productivity growth requires not only investments in CIM/ERP/ICT but also investments in complementary organisational changes, and that these changes not only follow sequential-type adoption, but also have time-lagged returns. It follows that the comparison between two firms, at a given point in time, may reveal that – for the same investment in new technological artefacts – one firm shows an acceleration of its TFP and another a deceleration due to the simple fact that the former could have made investments in complementary organisational capital in some previous period, or because the latter has violated the sequential adoption of new practices, or its organisational learning mechanisms are less efficient and effective.

The temporal and staggered lags of effects

We expect that investments in new general-purpose technology (CIM/ERP/ICT) are a relatively low cost and an easy change to make, whereas other changes, specifically those relating to organisational changes and new work practices, are both costlier and slower to activate.[24] A further argument holds that some time needs to elapse for new workplace systems to show their entire effect on productivity: workers need to acquire the necessary competencies, become familiar with the new work methods, and get used to the new role, responsibilities and decision making before performing in the new organisational environment.[25] Thus, it is possible that complementarity between contemporaneous ICT and organisational changes does not emerge or may even be negative in some cases, signalling, for example, that the process of adjustment has not yet been completed or that the adjustment costs outweigh the gains. Moreover, adjustment costs may depend on the extent of reorganisation: a situation where the workplace is undergoing extensive restructuring (many dimensions are being changed) differs considerably from a situation where only a few changes are introduced, although the sign of the difference is not clear. For example, one expects that where many changes are being undertaken, potential complementarity gains are higher, although workers in this case may need more time to learn and adapt to the new environment, or may even resist the change and thereby reduce the benefits of restructuring.

Final considerations

In the introduction to this chapter, we highlighted the fact that heterogeneity in terms of efficiency, as measured by total factor productivity, is a statistically significant and widespread phenomenon. The traditional econometric studies we recalled previously, while offering a significant contribution, are unable to provide an exhaustive explanation of the phenomenon. The main reasons are the focus on routines and capabilities on one side, and the institutions and governance structures on the other. Very little attention has instead been paid to the intrinsic characteristics of technology and organisation, and the conditions necessary to couple them efficiently, such as, for example:

1 the fact that these factors materialise through a set of constitutive principles that are paradigmatic in nature;
2 that the organisational and technological paradigms, which were historically substantiated in the second half of the 1800s and early 1900s (respectively, the technological electro-mechanical paradigm and the Taylor–Fordist organisational paradigm), were reciprocally refined over time, giving rise to a complementarity relation;
3 that these paradigms met with – in part because of internal pressures, in part for the market reasons previously analysed – a profound structural crises following the emergence of a new set of constitutive principles, which from time to time gave rise to a new paradigm;
4 that the structural breaks occurred in an asynchronised way, inducing non-strictly homogeneous combinations in technological–organisational factors, rendering the returns from innovative investments in the context of the respective factors less appealing than simplistic promises; in other words, as though firms found themselves – as a result of selective, self-enforcing and reinforcing processes – in a lock-in situation, in a trapping region;
5 that less appealing returns are very often due to the fact that the innovations and the related investments are conceived as artefacts placed within firms, rather than being understood as not only embedded, but also to a large extent as co-constructed within firms, as a consequence of personal and collective ways of using new technological tools and as a consequence of internal capabilities built through stochastic sequential processes.

The hope is that, in the future, research will take into account the ambiguities, aporias and methodological doubts that still exist in the above-cited empirical literature, and will be able to specify stochastic sequential processes through which the techno-organisational stratification that reflects in performance is consolidated.

Notes

1 Dosi et al. (2012) record a very similar situation for Italy.
2 For example, Smith (2005) develops a model based on two hypotheses: first, the case where the prices of two innovations are expected to decline at different rates and the firm chooses to adopt the innovation whose price decreases at a slower rate, waiting for the second complementary adoption when its market price will be lower; second, where there is uncertainty about the dynamic path of either the benefits from, or the costs of,

adopting the two innovations. Instead, Jovanovic and Stolyarov (1997, 2000) make use of alternative hypotheses (the non-convex adjustment costs or the learning period requirement for one input), reaching the conclusion that the firm is optimal when carrying out an asynchronous, sequential complementarity function.

3 Without claiming to be unquestionably accurate, we here assume the interpretation of Taylor's (1911) proposition that 'In the past the man has been first [with his individual organisational (e.g., the craftsman's workshop) and technological artefacts (e.g., the individual tools)], in the future [after Taylor] the system will be first', as organisational design (forged for the first time by Taylor himself) as well as the integration of technological devices (successfully carried out by Ford in 1932).

4 Homeostatic control (typical of multi-glandular organisms) is the result of the activation of regulation and conformation mechanisms that enable a stable internal balance (homeostasis) to be maintained in the face of environmental changes.

5 This implies that TMS – in other words, the economics of time – is common to both Taylorism and Ohnism, even if resolved in a different way, as in the latter case, time is no longer categorically established *ex-ante*.

6 A significant degree of autonomy and responsibility is nestled in this set of competencies, but without being free of higher control: indeed, *Andon*-type technological devices (which through light displays show the progress of regular and irregular production) allow upper-level managers immediate access to all kinds of information they may require (so-called 'management by eyes').

7 Coriat (2000, p. 238) sees this transfer of ideas to the firm as a form of dispossessing workers of their improvement ideas and know-how; this process starts with the codification of personal knowledge to turn it into organisational knowledge, which management then appropriates. However, if this 'transfer' of ideas is contracted and economically recognised, then dispossession hardly applies.

8 The team concept also applies to in-line production where a group of workers are responsible – in the Ohnist sense – for part of the line.

9 According to Arendt (1958), 'labour' never indicates a finished product, but is the result of work activity and the ability to carry out or perform, while 'product' is invariably derived from the word that indicates 'work': namely, to resolve or accomplish.

10 CE is a set of techniques that puts traditionally conceived sequential operations in parallel along the 'design–production–marketing–industrialisation' path. CE contributes to surmounting the traditional idea that product innovation (in the form of variants, options and customisations) is confined to the R&D function, in favour of the idea that innovation is the output of a process that involves multiple business functions. This does not imply a devaluation of the classic functions of acquisition of technological knowledge in the broadest sense and stimuli for creativity and innovation, which constitute the source of that part of innovation that is ascribable to 'impulse' , but at the same time recognises that innovation *also* consists in problem solving that can originate downstream along the production process (in the diagnostic and problem-solving activities of operators of a production island) or from the customer or market, implying greater interaction between production and design.

11 The so-called revenue resulting from product differentiation as theorised by Chamberlain, and in Ohno's version, quality/customer satisfaction.

12 Egidi (2013) provides a good example, although in the form of an analogy: language can be considered equivalent to a paradigm, while semantics and syntax play the role of heuristic rules with respect to what is said and how it is said. However, the quality of outcomes depends on cumulatively augmented abilities and skills. This is also true for technology.

13 A relay is an electrical device such that current flowing through it in one circuit can switch on and off a current in a second circuit.

14 Economies of industrial coordination refer to combinations of variants in the multicomponents forming a system (e.g. a platform or a modular platform) produced by many different firms.

15 A different issue is if users are able to make rational choices in favour of pieces of a system that are compatible with an existing system, without considering the significant differences in capabilities between users, on one hand, and large corporations equipped with an information system department, on the other: the latter are very likely to be more capable of choosing and constructing an integrated system than an individual user.

16 The comparison is with respect to prior computerised algorithms only capable of following rules.

17 The reference is to IBM Watson's supercomputer performance. It is worth recalling that Watson's victories in the TV game *Jeopardy!* were the result of specifically targeted programming (in other words, constituting a type of dedicated technology), and that its use in other fields required substantial reprogramming by its human creators.

18 The reference is to modern robotics, considered by experts as on the cusp of exploding because of its capacity to execute complex task in dangerous, degraded, human-engineered environments.

19 This role was also foreseen and theorised for workers by Wiener (1948), the father of cybernetics.

20 Dretske (1981) argues that people process information based on knowledge/beliefs and thus visions, which are the result of information they have received and processed in the past according to their personal cognitive algorithm. The author also includes information on the effects of experience and learning, and defines information (p. 44) as 'that commodity capable of yielding knowledge', identifying knowledge (p. 86) 'with information-produced (or-sustained) beliefs'.

21 Two classic examples of the problem-solving skills gap are the 'Rubik's cube' and the game of chess: given the initial configuration, the moves allowed to arrive at a solution are known. Nevertheless, being able to identify and apply the optimal sequence of all the moves is a complex task that normally exceeds the average computational capacity of the human mind (Dosi and Marengo, 1994). The rule is to proceed with a limited set of information and a given interpretation of the same, and then adjust the decisions in light of new information that is acquired and interpreted, or new interpretations of the original information.

22 In this context, several variants should be considered and analysed, such as the German diversified quality production model and the Italian flexible specialisation model: for these analyses, see Appelbaum and Batt (1994).

23 The crucial importance of this technological 'complement' with respect to organisation emerges from the fact that companies which attempted to implement ERP technologies without first re-engineering the organisation in the process perspective met with modest, if not disappointing, results. Devadoss and Pan (2007) estimate that 60 per cent of ERP implementations fail, certainly not due to the characteristics of the technologies adopted but rather – according to Peppard and Ward (2005) – due to issues related to process re-engineering. In the initial phase of change, disturbances and delays in production activities are considerable difficulties to overcome and productivity often drops temporarily; the time to implement an entire ERP system or the programmed costs tend in 90 per cent of cases to be exceeded, and returns occur in the medium to long term (3 to 5 years): see Brynjolfsson, Hitt and Yang (2002), Bloom, Sadun and Van Reenen (2012) and Huang et al. (2009).

24 With reference to American manufacturing firms, Brynjolfsson, Hitt and Yang (2002) estimate that the ratio between hardware and software costs and total investment costs (including those relating to consultancy, manager time, reorganisation and training of the labour force) is equal to 1 in 9.

25 See, for example, the analysis in Robey, Ross and Boudreau (2002).

References

Abramovitz, M. (1989). *Thinking About Growth*, Cambridge: Cambridge University Press.

Aloini, D., R. Dulmin and V. Mininno (2007). Risk management in ERP project introduction: review of the literature, *Information and Management*, 44, 547–67.

American Machinist (1977). *Metalworking: Yesterday and Tomorrow*, 100th Anniversary Issue, New York: McGraw-Hill.

Appelbaum, E. and R. Batt (1994). *The New American Workplace*, Ithaca: IRL/Cornell University Press.

Arendt, H. (1958). *The Human Condition*, Chicago: University of Chicago Press.

Argyris, C. and D. Schön (1978). *Organizational Learning: A Theory of Action Perspective*, Reading, MA: Addison-Wesley.

Ayres, R. U. (1990). History of mechanization. In R. U. Ayres, W. Haywood, M. E. Merchant, J. Ranta and H. J. Warnecke, eds., *Computer Integrated Manufacturing*, Volume II: *The Past, the Present, and the Future*, London: Chapman & Hall, pp. 17–39.

Ayres, R.U. and K. H. Ebel (1990). Human factors in CIM. In R. U. Ayres, W. Haywood, M. E. Merchant, J. Ranta and H. J. Warnecke, eds., *Computer Integrated Manufacturing*, Volume II: *The Past, the Present, and the Future*, London: Chapman & Hall, pp. 219–43.

Bartel, A., C. Ichniowski and K. Shaw (2007). How does information technology affect productivity? Plant-level comparisons of product innovation, process improvement, and worker skills, *Quarterly Journal of Economics*, 122, 1721–58.

Battisti, G., M. G. Colombo and L. Rabbiosi (2014). Simultaneous versus sequential complementarity in the adoption of technological and organizational innovation: the case of innovation in the design sphere, *Industrial and Corporate Change*, forthcoming.

Bauer, T. K. (2003). Flexible workplace practices and labor productivity, *IZA Discussion Papers*, no. 700.

Bijker, W., T. Hughes and T. Pinch (1987). *The Social Construction of Technological Systems*, Cambridge, MA: MIT Press.

Black, S. and L. Lynch (2001). How to compete: the impact of workplace practices and information technology on productivity, *Review of Economics and Statistics*, 83, 434–45.

Black, S. and L. Lynch (2004). What's driving the new economy: the benefits of workplace innovation, *Economic Journal*, 114, 97–116.

Bloom, N. and L. Garicano (2013). The distinct effects of information technology and communication technology on firm organization, *CEPR Discussion Papers*, no. 9762.

Bloom, N. and J. Van Reenen (2010). Why do management practices differ across firms and countries?, *Journal of Economic Perspectives*, 24, 203–24.

Bloom, N., R. Sadun and J. Van Reenen (2012). Americans do IT better: American multinationals and the productivity miracle, *American Economic Review*, 102, 167–201.

Boning, B., C. Ichniowski and K. Shaw (2007). Opportunity counts: teams and the effectiveness of production incentives, *Journal of Labor Economics*, 25, 613–50.

Bresnahan, T. E. and M. Trajtenberg (1995). General purpose technologies: engine of growth?, *Journal of Econometrics*, 65, 83–108.

Bresnahan, T., E. Brynjolfsson and L. M. Hitt (2002). Information technology, workplace organization, and the demand for skilled labor: firm-level evidence, *Quarterly Journal of Economics*, 117, 339–76.

Brynjolfsson, E. and L. M. Hitt (2003). Computing productivity: firm-level evidence, *Review of Economics and Statistics*, 85, 793–808.

Brynjolfsson, E. and A. McAfee (2014). *The Second Machine Age: Work, Progress, and Prosperity in a Time of Brilliant Technologies*, New York: W. W. Norton.

Brynjolfsson, E., L. M. Hitt and S. Yang (2002). Intangible assets: computers and organizational capital, *Brooking Papers on Economic Activity*, 1, 137–81.

Bugamelli, M. and P. Pagano (2004). Barriers to investment in ICT, *Applied Economics*, 36, 2275–86.

Cainarca, G. C., S. Massa and S. Testa (2005). Technology-in-practice: new insight into data warehouse adoption. In R. Leoni and G. Usai, eds., *Organizations Today*, New York: Palgrave Macmillan, pp. 179–86.

Cameron, A. C. and P. K. Trivedi (2005). *Microeconometrics: Methods and Applications*, New York: Cambridge University Press.

Caroli, E. and J. Van Reenen (2001). Skill biased organizational change? Evidence from a panel of British and French establishments, *Quarterly Journal of Economics*, 116, 1449–92.

Castells, M. (1996). *The Information Age: Economy, Society and Culture: The Rise of the Network Society*, Oxford: Blackwell.

Christensen, C. M. (1997). *The Innovator's Dilemma: When New Technologies Cause Great Firms to Fail*, Boston: Harvard Business School Press.

Colombo, M. G. and N. Delmastro (2002). The determinants of organizational change and structural inertia: technological and organizational factors, *Journal of Economics and Management Strategy*, 11, 595–635.

Colombo, M. G., M. Delmastro and L. Rabbiosi (2007). 'High performance' work practices, decentralization, and profitability: evidence from panel data, *Industrial and Corporate Change*, 16, 1037–67.

Coriat, B. (2000). The 'abominable Ohno Production System': competences, monitoring, and routines in Japanese production systems. In G. Dosi, R. R. Nelson and S. G. Winter, eds., *The Nature and Dynamics of Organizational Capabilities*, Oxford: Oxford University Press.

Cristini, A., A. Gaj, and R. Leoni (2008). Direct and indirect complementarity between workplace reorganization and new technology, *Rivista di Politica Economica*, 48, 87–117.

Cristini, A., A. Gaj, S. Labory and R. Leoni (2003). Flat hierarchical structure, bundles of new work practices and firm performance, *Rivista Italiana degli Economisti*, 8, 137–65.

David, P. A. (2001). Path dependence, its critics, and the quest for 'historical economics'. In P. Garrouste and S. Ioannides, eds., *Evolution and Path Dependence in Economic Ideas*, Cheltenham: Edward Elgar, pp. 15–40.

Dery, K., D. Grant, B. Harley and C. Wright (2006). Work, organisation and enterprise resource planning systems: an alternative research agenda, *New Technology, Work and Employment*, 21, 199–214.

Dery, K, R. Hall, and N. Wailes (2006). ERPs as 'technologies-in-practice': social construction, materiality and the role of organisational factors, *New Technology, Work and Employment*, 21, 229–41.

Devadoss, P. and S. Pan (2007). Enterprise systems use: towards a structurational analysis of enterprise systems induced organizational transformation, *Communications of the Association for Information Systems*, 19, 352–85.

Dosi, G. (1983). Technological paradigms and technological trajectories. In C. Freeman, ed., *Long Waves in the World Economy*, London: Butterworths, pp. 78–101.

Dosi, G. (1988). Sources, procedures, and microeconomic effects of innovation, *Journal of Economic Literature*, 26, 1120–71.

Dosi, G. and L. Marengo (1994). Some elements of an evolutionary theory of organizational competences. In A. Arbor, ed., *Evolutionary Concepts in Contemporary Economics*, Chicago: Michigan University Press, pp. 157–78.

Dosi, G., M. Grazzi, C. Tomasi and A. Zeli (2012). Turbulence underneath the big calm? The micro-evidence behind Italian productivity dynamics, *Small Business Economics*, 39, 1043–67.

Dretske, F. I. (1981). *Knowledge and the Flow of Information*, Cambridge, MA: MIT Press.

Egidi, M. (2013). The generation and diffusion of new market routines. In F. Arcangeli, P. David and G. Dosi, eds., *Advances in Modeling Innovation Diffusion*, New York: Oxford University Press (in press).

Freeman, C. (2007). The ICT paradigm. In R. Mansel, C. Avgerou, D. Quah and R. Silverstone, eds., *The Oxford Handbook of Information and Communication Technologies*, Oxford: Oxford University Press, pp. 34–54.

Freeman, C. and F. Louçã (2001). *As Time Goes By*, Oxford: Oxford University Press.

Freeman, R., M. Kleiner and C. Ostroff (2000). The anatomy of worker involvement and its effects on firms and workers, *NBER Working Papers*, no. 8050.

Giedion, S. (1969). *Mechanization Takes Command*, 2nd ed., New York: W.W. Norton.

Grandori, A. and S. Furnari (2008). A chemistry of organization: combinatory analysis and design, *Organization Studies*, 29, 459–85.

Green, F. (2006). *Demanding work: the paradox of job quality in the affluent economy*, Princeton, NJ: Princeton University Press.

Greenan, N. (1996a). Innovation Technologique, changements organisationnels e evolution des compétences: une étude empirique sur l'industrie manufacturière, *Economie et Statistique*, 8, 15–33.

Greenan, N. (1996b). Progrès technique et changements organisationnels: leur impact sur les qualifications et l'emploi, *Economie et Statistique*, 8, 35–44.

Greenan, N. and D. Guellec (1998). Firm organisations, technology and performance: an empirical study, *Economics of Innovation and New Technology*, 6, 313–47.

Guest, D., J. Michies, M. Sheehan and N. Conway (2003). Human resource management and corporate performance in the UK, *British Journal of Industrial Relations*, 41, 291–314.

Hitt, L. and E. Brynjolfsson (1997). Information technology and internal firm organization: an explanatory analysis, *Journal of Management Information Systems*, 14, 81–101.

Huang S. Y., S. M. Huang, T. H. Wu and W. K. Lin (2009). Process efficiency of the enterprise resource planning adoption, *Industrial Management & Data Systems*, 109, 1085–1100.

Ichniowski, C., K. Shaw and G. Prennushi (1997). The effects of HRM systems on productivity: a study of steel finishing lines, *American Economic Review*, 87, 291–313.

Janod, V. and A. Saint-Martin (2004). Measuring the impact of work reorganization on firm performance: evidence from French manufacturing, 1995–1999, *Labour Economics*, 11, 785–98.

Jovanovic, B. and D. Stolyarov (1997). Learning complementarities and asynchronous use of technology, *NBER Working Papers*, no. 5870.

Jovanovic, B. and D. Stolyarov D. (2000). Optimal adoption of complementary technologies, *American Economic Review*, 90, 15–29.

Kochan, T., H. Katz and R. McKersie (1986). *The Transformation of American Industrial Relations*, New York: Basic Books.

Koike, K. (1994). Learning and incentive systems in contemporary Japanese industry. In M. Aoki and R. P. Dore, eds., *The Japanese Firm*, Oxford: Oxford University Press, pp. 41–65.

Kopelman, R. E. (1985). Job redesign and productivity: a review of the evidence, *National Productivity Review*, 4, 237–55.

Kovács, G. L. and G. Haidegger (1992). Integration in manufacturing; from FMS and FMC to CIM. In R. U. Ayres, W. Haywood, M. E. Merchant, J. Ranta and H. J. Warnecke, eds., *Computer Integrated Manufacturing*, Volume II: *The Past, the Present, and the Future*, London: Chapman & Hall, pp. 203–18.

Kuhn, T. S. (1962). *The Structure of Scientific Revolutions*, Chicago: Chicago University Press.

Leoni, R. (2012). Workplace design, complementarities among work practices and the formation of key competencies: evidence from Italian employees, *Industrial and Labor Relations Review*, 65, 316–49.

Leoni, R. (2013). Organization of work practices and productivity: an assessment of research on world-class manufacturing. In A. Grandori, ed., *Handbook of Economic Organization: Integrating Economic and Organization Theory*, Cheltenham: Edward Elgar, pp. 312–34.

Lynch, L. M. (2007). The adoption and diffusion of organizational innovation: evidence for the US economy, *NBER Working Papers*, no. 13156.

Marengo, L. (1996). Structure, competence and learning in an adaptive model of the firm. In G. Dosi and F. Malerba, eds., *Organization and Strategy in the Evolution of the Enterprise*, London: Macmillan, pp. 124–54.

Mayo, E. (1949). *The Social Problems of an Industrial Civilization*, London: Routledge & Kegan Paul.

Mazzanti, M., P. Pini and E. Tortia (2006). Organizational innovations, human resources and firm performance: the Emilia-Romagna food sector, *Journal of Socio-Economics*, 35, 123–41.

Mazzucato, M. (2013). *The Entrepreneurial State: Debunking Public vs. Private Sector Myths*, London: Anthem Press.

Milgrom, P. and J. Roberts (1990). The economics of modern manufacturing: technology, strategy, and organization, *American Economic Review*, 80, 511–28.

Nazemi, E., M. J. Tarokh and G. R. Djavanshir (2012). ERP: a literature survey, *International Journal of Advanced Manufacturing Technology*, 61, 999–1018.

Nelson, R. and S. Winter (1982). *An Evolutionary Theory of Economic Change*, Cambridge, MA: Belknap Press.

Nonaka, I. and H. Takeuchi (1995). *The Knowledge-Creating Company*, Oxford: Oxford University Press.

Ohno, T. (1988). *Toyota Production System: Beyond Large-Scale Production*, Chicago: Productivity Press.

Orlikowski, W. (2000). Using technology and constituting structures, *Organization Science*, 11, 404–28.

Orlikowski, W. (2010). The sociomateriality of organisational life: considering technology in management research, *Cambridge Journal of Economics*, 34, 125–41.

Patterson, M., M. A. West, R. Lawthom and S. Nickell (1997). The impact of people management practices on business performance, Institute of Personnel and Development, London (*Issues in People Management*, no. 22).

Pavitt, K. (1984). Sectoral patterns of technical change: towards a taxonomy and a theory, *Research Policy*, 13, 343–73.

Peppard J. and J. Ward (2005). Unlocking sustained business value from IT investments, *California Management Review*, 48, 52–70.

Perez, C. (1983). Structural change and the assimilation of new technologies in the economic and social systems, *Futures*, 15, 357–75.

Perez, C. (2002). *Technological Revolutions and Financial Capital: The Dynamics of Bubbles and Golden Ages*, Cheltenham: Edward Elgar.

Piva, M., E. Santarelli and M. Vivarelli (2005). The skill bias effect of technological and organisational change: evidence and policy implications, *Research Policy*, 34, 141–57.

Rizov, M. and R. Croucher (2008). Human resource management and performance in European firms, *Cambridge Journal of Economics*, 33, 253–72.

Roberts, J. (2004). *The Modern Firm: Organizational Design for Performance and Growth*, New York: Oxford University Press.

Robey, D., J. W. Ross and M. Boudreau (2002). Learning to implement enterprise systems: an exploratory study of the dialectics of change, *Journal of Management Information Systems*, 19, 17–46.

Rosenberg, N. (1976). *Perspectives on Technology*, Cambridge, MA: Cambridge University Press.

Searle, J. R. (1969). *Speech Acts: An Essay in the Philosophy of Language*, Cambridge: Cambridge University Press.

Sethi, A. K. and S. P. Sethi (1990). Flexibility in manufacturing: a survey, *International Journal of Flexible Manufacturing Systems*, 2, 289–328.

Shannon, C. E. (1948). A mathematical theory of communication, *Bell System Technical Journal*, 27, 379–423.

Shaul, L. and D. Tauber (2013). Critical success factors in enterprise resource planning systems: review of the last decade, *ACM Computing Surveys*, 45, 1–39.

Shewhart, W. A. (1931). *Economic Control of Quality of Manufactured Product*, New York: D. Van Nostrand Co.

Simon, H. (1977). *The New Science of Management Decision*, revised ed., New York: Harper & Row.

Smith, M. H. (2005). Uncertainty and the adoption of complementary technologies, *Industrial and Corporate Change*, 14, 639–50.

Sutton, J. (1998). *Technology and Market Structure: Theory and History*, Cambridge, MA: MIT Press.

Syverson, C. (2004). Product substitutability and productivity dispersion, *Review of Economics and Statistics*, 86, 534–50.

Taylor, F. W. (1911). *Principles of Scientific Management*, New York: Harper and Brother.

Trist, E. (1981). The evolution of socio-technical systems as a conceptual framework and as an action research program. In A. H. Van de Ven and W. F. Joyce, eds., *Perspectives on Organization Design and Behaviour*, New York: Wiley Interscience, pp. 19–75.

Umble, E. J., R. R. Haft and M. M. Umble (2003). Enterprise resource planning: implementation procedures and critical success factors, *European Journal of Operational Research*, 146, 241–57.

Wiener, N. (1948). *Cybernetics: Control and Communications in the Animal and the Machine*, New York: John Wiley.

Winter, S. (1984). Schumpeterian competition in alternative technological regimes, *Journal of Economic Behavior and Organization*, 5, 287–320.

Zwick, T. (2004). Employee participation and productivity, *Labour Economics*, 11, 715–40.

Index